The Magic of
★HOUDINI★
★☆★☆★☆★☆

The Magic of
★HOUDINI★

Gyles Brandreth and John Morley

Illustrated by Clare Hatcher

PELHAM BOOKS

First published in Great Britain by Pelham Books Ltd
52 Bedford Square, London WC1B 3EF
1978

ISBN 0 7207 1114 2

Printed in Great Britain by
Hollen Street Press, Slough
and bound by Redwood Burn, Esher.

Contents

Introduction: THE GREAT HOUDINI   7

1 THE MAN OF MAGIC   27
Houdini's parlour tricks specially designed
for home presentation

2 THE CARD KING   57
Simple magic with playing-cards that
anyone can perform

3 THE MASTER MAGICIAN   79
More spectacular conjuring and trickery
from the Man of Magic

4 THE ESCAPOLOGIST EXTRAORDINARY   101
The secrets of the Handcuff King's
great escapes revealed at last

5 THE GREAT ILLUSIONIST   117
How the impossible becomes possible
before your very eyes

PHOTOGRAPHIC ACKNOWLEDGEMENTS

John Salisse: pages 8, 12, 15, 17, 25 and 112; Radio Times Hulton Picture Library: page 21; Raymond Mander and Joe Mitchenson Theatre Collection: frontispiece.

Introduction
THE GREAT HOUDINI

In the world of magic there has never been anyone to rival The Great Houdini. Escapologist extraordinary, master illusionist, accomplished conjuror, even now – more than half a century after his death – his name remains a household word.

Whether he was making a small playing-card vanish or making an elephant disappear, Houdini could achieve the 'impossible'. Whether he was escaping from a strait-jacket, a prison cell or a coffin buried six feet under ground, only Houdini could 'defy death'. He was a 'miracle-worker' whose miracles had nothing to do with the supernatural. If truth be told – and now it can be told – his achievements were due to a mixture of ingenuity, trickery, training and physical courage, and his success was the result of dogged perseverance and superlative publicity.

Houdini was billed as the 'Man of Many Secrets', the first and most fundamental of which seems to have been the date and place of his birth. He was probably born in a ghetto in Budapest, Hungary on 24 March 1874. In later years, he celebrated his birthday on 6 April and claimed Appleton, Wisconsin, as his birthplace. Certainly it was either immediately before or immediately after his birth that his parents left Hungary and emigrated to the United States. His father, Mayer Samuel Weiss, was a rabbi, with a wife called Cecilia who was twenty years his junior. They had six children, five sons and a daughter. Harry Houdini, as Ehrich Weiss, endured an impoverished childhood, which he never forgot but which at the same time he rarely chose to recall in public in later, more affluent years.

The details of Houdini's boyhood aren't easy to establish, but a few facts are known: in 1888 the Weiss family moved from Wisconsin to New York, where they lived in a small apartment at 305 East 69th Street; in 1892 Rabbi Weiss died and the family had to fend for itself. For a while when he was

Houdini, the young magician

in his teens Harry had been apprenticed to a locksmith, but by the time of his father's death he had already embarked on a career (of sorts) as a man of magic (of a kind).

Legend has it that Harry was first bitten by the magic bug when his father took him to see an English magician called Doctor Lyn who toured the States in the 1880s. Doctor Lyn's most spectacular effect involved his 'chloroforming' a patient and then cutting off his arms, legs and head – only to restore them at the end of the illusion! This apparently inspired young Harry to attempt some spectacular effects of his own – in the first of which he would hang upside down and pick up needles with his eyelashes. When he was still a lad this remarkable acrobatic feat is said to have secured him a brief engagement with Jack Hoeffner's Five Cent Circus when it passed through Appleton.

With an enthusiasm and a driving ambition that never deserted him, the young Houdini was also doing his best to master some rather more basic magic, learning to manipulate cards with the deceptive dexterity that only comes with hour upon hour of painstaking practice. When he was seventeen he turned 'professional', and he and his brother Theo set themselves up as an act called the 'Houdini Brothers'. They borrowed the name from the illustrious nineteenth-century French illusionist Robert-Houdin, a magician who had moved into the loftier spheres of politics and had become an international figure, especially after helping to crush an anti-French revolt in Algeria by means of his secret weapon – not known to the Algerian magicians attempting to rival him – electricity. When Robert-Houdin tried, he could easily lift the metal block (with a concealed magnet inside) off the steel platform. When his rivals tried, and more important when his assistant had switched on the magnetic force, they couldn't lift it and were baffled. Nor could the strongest men in North Africa lift it. Therefore, it was explained to the Algerians, a Frenchman must be all-powerful, and the French nation no less so.

Robert-Houdin fascinated the Weiss brothers and by the simple expedient of adding an 'I' to give the name a more exotic sound, they became the Houdini Brothers and set about looking for work. They found it at Huber's Dime Museum on 14th Street, New York. It wasn't a stylish establishment, and they had to give twenty performances a day for a pittance, but it was a start. Card tricks were the basis of their act, but fellow performers taught them some elementary 'rope tie artistry' and 'handcuff manipulation' and before long they had scraped together enough money to buy a trick 'substitution trunk' that had been invented by the English magician Maskelyne in 1865. Having given it an exotic name to go with their own – 'Metamorphosis' – the brothers took it on tour.

It remains a startling trick even today and it is still being performed. The person standing on the lid of the locked trunk instantly changes place with the person *inside* the trunk, and, what's more, the person inside the trunk has been handcuffed, tied up in a sack and then locked in the trunk by one of the audience! The secret is an ingeniously constructed trapdoor in the lid; though not noticeable to the audience, it allows the instant change to happen. In the early 1890s it appears to have been a rather minor sensation that brought no particular luck to the Houdini Brothers. No doubt their presentation lacked style: they couldn't 'sell it' to their audience.

When the Houdini Brothers were appearing at Coney Island they met Beatrice Rahner, the 'petite soubrette of the Floral Sisters song and dance act', to quote from *The Clipper*, a New York weekly of 1894. Bess and Harry fell in love and were married on 22 June 1894.

Harry had four brothers and a sister and was Jewish. Bess had nine sisters and a brother and was Roman Catholic. Nevertheless they tried to please everyone by marrying in a church, a synagogue and finally in the registry office at New York's City

11

Hall. The Great Houdini never did anything by halves.

A few weeks after the wedding Theo went his own way as 'Professor Houdini', an act that was not a success, and Bess joined Harry as the 'Houdinis', with the ever-reliable Metamorphosis now being performed by husband and wife. They weren't much of a success either and Bess blamed herself for their failure. She considered her slim figure unfashionable and was embarrassed to wear the tights that were then obligatory for a magician's assistant.

Their first worthwhile engagement came when Tony Pastor, perhaps through friendship, perhaps through pity, booked them into his 14th Street theatre. He stated in a reference he gave them in 1895 that he 'found the Houdinis satisfactory and interesting', which, remembering the florid phrasing used by theatrical managers of the time, wasn't exactly a strong recommendation.

Even so, it was enough to get them work at the Welsh Brothers Circus where, ironically, the easily mastered Metamorphosis went well and the desperately-rehearsed card tricks and handcuff escapes went for nothing. Harry still lacked showmanship. Photographs show that he was boyishly good-looking at the time, but his height – he was only five feet three inches tall – and the clumsy Brooklynese phrasing he used for his magician's patter, were two very real handicaps. Before long he was reduced to the alternative of being sacked or accepting the grisly task of impersonating the 'Jungle Wild Man'. He and Bess had no money, so there was no choice. The Great Houdini found himself forced to prowl round a dirty cage and, to add conviction to this impersonation, to eat raw meat and the cigar ends thrown at him by the public.

Eventually, Harry and Bess managed to get another touring job and, at New Brunswick in Canada, the local lunatic-asylum

Houdini and his wife, Bess

officials lent Harry a strait-jacket as an escape challenge to add variety to all the handcuffs. After much struggling, for the escape was no trick, he managed to get free and the audience was enthusiastic. Back they went to the Welsh Brothers Circus in 1898, now with the strait-jacket as well as Metamorphosis. When the touring circus reached Chicago, Harry felt encouraged enough to try further escapology. As he had once been apprenticed to a locksmith, and as all day was spent practising handcuff escapes, maybe he could risk being handcuffed and locked in the local prison cell and yet escape?

Detective Lieutenant 'Big Andy' Rohan decided to go along with the idea, although to make sure there were no duplicate keys smuggled into the cell he had Harry stripped of all his clothes. For years Harry had been training his fingers to enable him to escape from handcuffs, and his toes to enable him to escape from manacles. He was prepared.

Escape from the regulation police handcuffs was easy enough, but what about the doors to the cell? As everyone left the cell, a parting good-luck kiss from Bess ensured a small skeleton key passed from her mouth to his. Thus the inner door was opened, but what of the outer door, which his arms could not quite reach? He managed to stretch his leg until his toes touched the lock, he undid the outer door with his toes clutching the smuggled-in key, and he was free. Big Andy Rohan was surprised, but, far more important, the Press had arrived and were flabbergasted.

The publicity resulting from this escape got the Houdinis a booking on the respectable Orpheum Circuit (sixty dollars a week) and its boss Martin Beck advised them to concentrate on prison escapes in the future. Each town they visited on the tour received the same publicity treatment. Monday morning – the escape from the local jail; Monday afternoon – the Press

Escapologist extraordinary

14

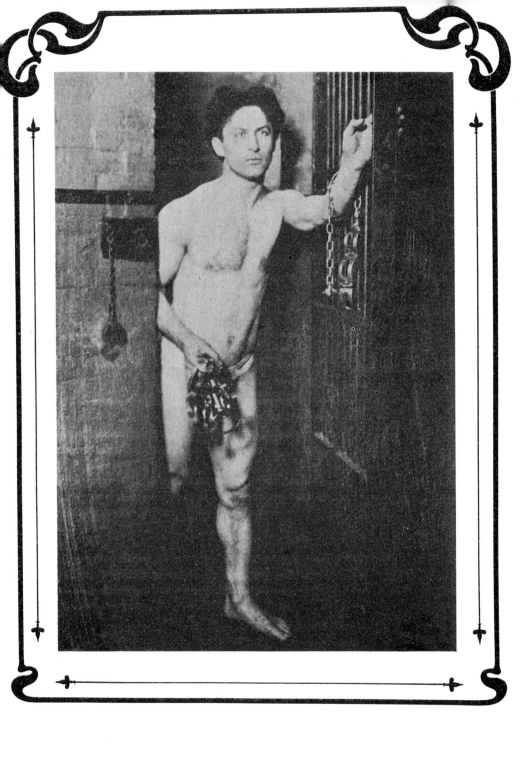

would write it up; Monday evening – the reaping of the harvest: a 'house full' sign outside the theatre, a sign that stayed outside for the rest of the week. At last people were beginning to talk about The Great Houdini.

In 1900, Europe had tremendous prestige in the United States. Harry was doing fairly well, though not sensationally so. But, fanatically ambitious, he managed to organize a one-week booking in London. Aged twenty-six, he sailed to Europe with Bess.

By now he had learnt that his most powerful ally was publicity. He knew the first place for him to visit in London was a police cell at Scotland Yard. He had discovered that – incredibly – the regulation handcuffs of the British police would release themselves if tapped sharply on a hard surface, so escape from them would be simple. Once again, Bess gave him a good-luck kiss as she left the cell. Once again he escaped. Once again the Press were flabbergasted.

Indeed, such was the publicity that Harry's one-week booking at the Alhambra was extended to several months. In 1900 and 1901 he toured most of the United Kingdom and much of Europe and for the rest of his life he remained a firm favourite with British audiences. In 1911 he became first president of the Magicians' Club of London, the forerunner to the Magic Circle, and retained this august office until his death.

But however frequent and extended his tours, his home ties were never forgotten. Because Mama had slaved for him when he was a child, Harry worshipped her all his life. He placed her on a pedestal that even Bess doesn't seem to have been allowed to share. Nothing was too good for Mama. On his first British tour he bought her a dress fit for a queen – an accurate description, for the black bombazine gown had belonged to Queen Victoria.

Houdini and Mama

B

It was a luxury, but things were going well. Theatre management all over Europe were after him. And every Monday morning, whatever town or country, the local police cell was put to use. In Russia, it was the prison van owned by the secret police that made the essential Houdini headlines. The van took prisoners from Moscow to Siberia and was steel-lined with so strong a door that – stripped again, in spite of the below-freezing weather conditions – he had to escape by sawing his way out through the floor. How he did it nobody knows, though many years later he was heard to say it hadn't been a smuggled-in saw but a smuggled-in thousand-rouble note that had ensured his escape on this particular occasion.

Back in the States, the prestige of a European success worked its own magic. He was now a headliner at the grandiloquently named Percy G. Williams Colonial Theater on Broadway and 63rd Street. The year was 1906 and he was doing virtually the same act he had done in New York ten years before. The only difference was the salary – exactly one hundred times greater. In 1896 he had received twelve dollars a week. Now he was earning twelve hundred.

The years went by triumphantly, though not easily. The intense desire to be acclaimed meant ever harder training schedules. Every day he worked with weights and took ice-cold baths. Bess had to pour more and more ice blocks into his bath to ensure absolute safety for his escapes from crates flung into cold harbours and rivers. Sometimes the ice had to be broken before the escapes could proceed. Some of his rivals stole his escape ideas, thinking them easy, not bothering with the heavy training schedule. They drowned themselves. Hard training was essential. He had won his earlier title of the 'Card King' from months of finger exercises, and his later title of the 'Handcuff King' from months of bleeding arms and wrists. He never admitted defeat and he never, throughout his career, left anything to chance. The Great Houdini's motto, although this was

18

kept well out of all the publicity about him, was 'safety first'. He believed in survival.

Inevitably, his public demanded that each thrill had to be capped by a greater thrill the next year. In 1908 he escaped from a packing case flung into the Mississippi by the New Orleans police. Later in the same year he escaped from a massive safe at London's Euston Palace of Varieties – complete with reinforced stage, so massively heavy was the safe. His escape took three minutes. In various theatres, he 'walked through a brick wall', he escaped from a solid-stone tower, from a padlocked leather mail-bag, from a milk can full of water, and, knowing he must improve on even that, he was locked upside down in a tank full of water only to appear – drenched but triumphant – four minutes later.

Freudians have suggested that his career of escapology was an idealized escape from his early poverty, from being treated as an inferior by the rest of the world outside Brooklyn, even an escape from the mother who in his soul he knew controlled his life. There is even the somewhat melodramatic theory that the tank full of water that he was locked into for many of his escapes was, to his subconscious, his mother's womb!

The spectacular illusions that had been added to the act, which by now had blossomed into 'The Magical Revue', needed considerable scenery and props. Sometimes as many as ten railway waggons were required to transport them from town to town. He and Bess played the top theatres and stayed in the top hotels, though even in this luxury he made sure he trained hard every day. He was now accepted as the greatest illusionist and escape artist of all time.

And then, on 17 July 1913, Mama died. When Harry had said goodbye to her before leaving New York for yet another European tour, she had replied: 'Perhaps when you come home I shall not be here.' Much worried, he had reassured her over and over again before the boat finally sailed, but when he reached the theatre at Copenhagen a telegram was waiting.

The tour was cancelled. He returned to New York. He was distraught. His mind dwelt solely on the memory of Mama. Bess tried vainly to persuade him to return to work. His brooding silences lasted for days, even weeks. For the first time ever he was unable to think about the escapes and illusions. Only after three months of daily visits to the grave did he recover enough to accept a booking in Paris. Back in harness, his success continued, and his fame grew. He never stopped working again.

In 1919, realizing the threat to vaudeville that the growing moving-picture industry now represented, he went to Hollywood and made several silent films of his own. In *The Master Mystery* he was the secret agent hero, aptly if not subtly named Quentin Locke. In fifteen-minute instalments, he was threatened by the 'Automaton', a robot that infected its victims with a hysteria called 'Madagascar Madness'. Other series such as *The Grim Game* and *Terror Island* followed. The irony of these films was that though he performed every genuinely dangerous escape himself (including swimming from a crashed canoe on the brink of the Niagara Falls!) the cinema audiences did not realize he had risked everything for them. They didn't appreciate that, unlike most of Hollywood's output that year, these danger-packed stories had no faked camera work and no 'double' for the star. Houdini, as always, worked with superhuman energy and determination, but his movies, with their creaking plots, were only minor successes and some lost money.

After Hollywood, he had to return to the world of vaudeville, but what new sensation could he offer? Achieving the strait-jacket escape as he swung upside down from a skyscraper was no longer enough. The Great War had been so horrific that it made The Great Houdini's dare-devilry pale into insignificance.

On one of his many British tours, Harry had performed an under-water escape at Hull and by request he sent a publicity still of it to a new admirer, Sir Arthur Conan Doyle. Sir Arthur

1921 posters for "Terror Island", another Houdini film

replied that this escape and many of the others were so incredible that they could only possibly be achieved by a man with psychic powers.

Psychic powers! Here was the new ingredient needed for revitalizing his act! And it was rumoured that President Coolidge himself was dabbling in psychic seances at the White House! Harry was no fool. He announced to the world that, yes, he did have psychic powers. Thus began a curious friendship, and one that suited Harry very well. For ever on the look-out for publicity, he realized at once that the distinguished creator of the world-famous Sherlock Holmes would make an ideal friend and patron.

Later, the friendship was to turn sour and Sir Arthur was to say, with probable truth: 'A prevailing feature of Houdini's character was a vanity which was so obvious and childish that it became more amusing than offensive. I can remember, for example, that he introduced his brother to me by saying "This is the brother of The Great Houdini." ' And more to the point, Sir Arthur duly observed that 'Houdini knew there was unlimited publicity to be got from spiritualism.'

Harry certainly did know. Partly to stir up the urgently needed publicity and partly because he soon became cynical about spiritualists, Harry turned against the mediums. It was understandable. Several of them (including Lady Conan Doyle) conjured up a refined voice saying it was his beloved Mama speaking to him from the Beyond. Unfortunately, Mama had spoken almost no English, and that little amount with a strong Hungarian accent. Mama – alive or dead – was the one person in the world Harry worshipped and her memory was sacrosanct. When he discovered that the mediums who professed contact with Mama were frauds, his anger was terrible. The pitch-dark rooms where the seances were held would suddenly be lit by the beam of a searchlight that Harry had smuggled in under his overcoat. The mediums would be discovered standing on chairs, holding absurd 'trumpets' made of cardboard and 'ectoplasm' made of cheesecloth. They were made to look utter idiots. These incidents made for splendid press coverage and tempted the public to visit the local theatre to witness 'The Great Houdini and his unique entertainment: Fraud Mediums Exposed'. This gave Houdini's act topical interest and stopped his audience from feeling he was a dusty has-been from pre-war days. He was the world's top vaudeville star all over again.

He was now fifty, running a magic and mystery show that lasted two and a half hours. The Great Houdini was on stage most of that time. Along with middle age he had at last acquired star quality; for many years the act, not the actor, had been the thing that filled the theatres nightly; but not any more. And the audiences got their money's worth when they went to see him. He started the evening with a coin routine, followed by an oriental illusion called the Yogi's Lamp (though the flame from the lamp could still be seen underneath the exotic cloth, the lamp itself had completely vanished!). Then he would make a rabbit appear in an empty cage, make a girl change into a rose-bush, and chew a packet of needles plus a length of cotton only to draw the needles threaded onto the cotton from his mouth. To end this first part of his show he would introduce Bess as 'the girl I have been travelling with for thirty years' and she would perform the trusty Metamorphosis with him.

Part two had him escaping from increasingly difficult objects: a strait-jacket, a pillory, a coffin, a trunk and finally from the tank that had now developed into the Chinese Water Torture Cell routine.

Part three was the climax of the show. Houdini savagely attacked the local spirit mediums and discredited them by doing on stage precisely what they did at a darkened seance – and he would reveal every trick of their trade while the audience howled with glee. Incredibly, all too often those he ridiculed could not resist coming to see him and their presence in the audience – all spotlights turned onto them – added further spice to the proceedings and further takings at the box-office.

He gave no sign of tiring. In 1926, in a challenge to the fakir Rhaman Bey, he stayed under water for seventy-five minutes – fifteen minutes longer than the fakir – incarcerated in the lead container that was destined to become his coffin.

On 18 October 1926 he was playing the Palace Theatre, Montreal, when an over-enthusiastic student from the local university accepted his light-hearted challenge to hit him hard in the stomach. The Great Houdini was as fit as ever. The student hit him, but before Houdini had time to tense his muscles in readiness for the blow. He was in pain, but the show must go on. At the next theatre on the tour, the Garrick at Detroit, despite the increasing pain, he insisted on being lowered into the water for the Chinese Water Torture Cell routine. No sooner was he inside the tank than he gave the danger signal. He was dragged from the tank and rushed to hospital. The ruptured appendix was removed, but peritonitis set in. He died on 31 October 1926.

At New York's Macpehah Cemetery, he was buried in the grave over which was placed the elaborate monument he had designed himself, as the final resting place of The Great Houdini.

Bess drifted. Following the craze of the day, she opened a tearoom. She even tried to make a come-back as a performer, but the try-out was a failure. Four years later it was her turn to hit the headlines, when she announced that she had received a spiritualistic message from Harry. But people wisely decided that the whole affair was the brain-child of *The Graphic* news-paper. And Theo, Harry's brother, said Bess was 'a misguided woman, easily led, with a lust for publicity'. Perhaps.

So what remains of The Great Houdini now? We can still see his extravagant gravestone, his not very good silent movies and the sensationally designed oriental-style posters for his act that have become collectors' items. We can find a few bits of his oddly over-complicated stage equipment scattered about New York and at the Houdini Magic Hall of Fame at Niagara Falls, close to where he made his movies. We can still marvel at the legend.

He *was* unique. For twenty-five years he continued to intrigue his public from North America to Europe, from Russia to Australia. He was brave; in the early days of flying, he did one escape jumping from one plane to another. He was conceited – he actually suggested that he should be the national hero to lead the 1918 Victory Parade through New York. He was also difficult to live with and difficult to work with. When criticized,

A Cardiff Empire advertisement of 1913

24

CARDIFF
EMPIRE

QUEEN STREET

PROPRIETORS · · · MOSS EMPIRES, LIMITED.
Managing Director · · · Mr FRANK ALLEN
Acting Manager · · · HERBERT J TAYLOR

MONDAY, JAN. 6th, 1913 and TWICE NIGHTLY
AT 6.45 AND 9.0 DURING THE WEEK.

THE WORLD-FAMOUS SELF-LIBERATOR!

HOUDINI

Presenting the Greatest Performance of his Strenuous Career liberating himself
after being Locked in a

WATER TORTURE
CELL

Houdini's own Invention, whilst Standing on his
Head his Ankles Clamped and Locked above in
the Centre of the Massive Cover   A Feat which
borders on to the Supernatural

£200
Houdini offers this sum to
anyone proving that it is
possible to obtain air in
the upside-down position
in which he releases himself from this WATER-
FILLED TORTURE CELL.

CASELLI SISTERS
Vocalists and Dancers

HAPPY TOM
PARKER
COMEDIAN AND DANCER

he showed disapproval by a long unnerving silence and an ice-cold unseeing stare. Yet he was loyal to his assistants and utterly dedicated to his work – often to the detriment of Bess, who was also the victim of his morbid devotion to his mother and her memory.

He was a considerable charmer when entertaining children, and on his tours he was always anxious to visit the local hospital and show the patients a few tricks. He most certainly helped to expose and ridicule the soul-destroying world of the quack spiritualist. All in all, he was a phenomenon, unrivalled in his field. And even after his death, the phenomenon still fascinates: his life inspired an American movie in the 1950s, a British musical in the 1960s, and, in the 1970s, a Dutch opera, a television series and books like this one.

In the pages that follow you will find descriptions of many of Houdini's favourite tricks, escapes and illusions. We have taken the liberty of using the first person singular to give an impression of the way in which The Great Houdini actually presented his material. The tricks in the first three chapters are deliberately elementary (they are all ones any amateur magician could attempt), but you will find that even the 'impossible' escapes and illusions described in the final chapters are of a breath-taking simplicity.

Houdini's secret turns out to be the fact that, after all, there really was no secret. His great illusions were tried and tested magical effects cunningly dressed up. His great escapes involved hiding keys and lock-picking wires, and tensing muscles while chains and ropes were applied. His death-defying feats involved incredible courage, self-discipline, stamina and determination. And yet the curious fascination of the man is that even when all has been revealed, even when we can see how very possible the impossible turns out to be, Ehrich Weiss remains The *Great* Houdini. The legend lingers on.

Part One
THE MAN OF MAGIC

★☆★☆★☆★☆

The Magic Wand

Hi there! So you want to be a man of magic and do some magic at home. Okay, then we start with the magician's source of power, your magic wand. Now, because it is so precious I am wrapping it up in paper for you. This is a nice solid one – I'll bang it on the table so you can hear how solid it is. But, suddenly, I crush the wrapping paper and the wand into a very small ball. So where has the magic wand gone? You think it's in this crushed-up paper but it can't be; the wand is solid. Aha, here it is, in my inside pocket!

The Secret

The wand looks great with white ends and the centre part of it black. When I tap it to show you how solid it is, I tap one of the white ends which are made of solid wood. The black part is just tough black paper, so I can easily screw it up into a small ball. I then take the second wand, the real one, from an inside pocket.

Another Magic Wand

★☆★☆★☆★☆

Here's another wand and this one is solid all through. This one won't let us down and collapse into a paper ball. See, I knock it on the table edge at the middle as well as the end and safely hand it over to you.

Hey, what have you done? This one's collapsed as well as the other one!

The Secret

This one is indeed wooden all the way through, but it isn't solid wood. It's made up of wooden sections which are threaded together by a thick cord and, as you can see now that I am holding it again, I have to push the separate wooden blocks tight together along the cord and hold them tight. If I don't, it collapses again!

The Coin that Falls Through the Hat

I'll carefully put this hat upside down on this empty glass. Then I drop a pile of coins into the hat – and look, one of them has gone right through the hat into the glass below!

The Secret

When I carefully put the hat upside down on the empty glass I took a bit of time doing it. As I balanced the hat on the glass, so with my other hand – as though straightening the hat – I was slipping a coin between the rim of the glass and the hat. Now I make sure I do drop the coins into the hat, as the consequent vibration dislodges the hidden coin and it falls into the glass – clink!

Eggs-traordinary Trick

★☆★☆★★☆

Please, choose a card from the pack. Remember it – and now put it back and shuffle the pack.

You have remembered what it is? Well, I will reveal what it is in a highly unusual way – I'll use a boiled egg. Here, take the egg, and now remove its shell. What is written on the actual egg itself? The letters F D? Was your card by any chance the four of diamonds? So!

The Secret

I fanned out the cards and persuaded you – 'forced' you, as we magicians say – to take a certain card, so I knew it would be the four of diamonds.

But the good part of this trick is the egg, isn't it? I used a small paintbrush and painted on to the egg a special solution made up from one ounce of alum in one pint of vinegar. When it is dry, no sign of writing remains on the egg-shell. Now all I had to do was boil the egg for fifteen minutes and then it and myself were ready for the trick, for when you shell the egg the letters F D will be found marked on the white of the boiled egg.

Handkerchief in a Bag

Here is an ordinary paper bag and here are two handkerchiefs. As you see, the paper bag has nothing in it – please look inside carefully. In fact, I will turn the bag inside out! I have nothing to hide – both the bag and the two handkerchiefs are straight-forward.

I put the handkerchiefs in my trouser pocket, say the magic word 'Presto!' – and the handkerchiefs have gone! To prove this I pull out my pocket lining and show you the pocket is empty. So where are the handkerchiefs? Incredibly, they are now in the empty paper bag and I will take them out . . . if I can . . . yes, here they are!

The Secret

First, I put the handkerchiefs into my trouser pocket – or rather into my trouser leg. For at the top of the pocket (where it will not be noticed) is a cut in the lining and my handkerchiefs were pushed through that cut. I then seemed to have had a struggle taking the handkerchiefs from the bag. That struggle is deliberate as there is one bag inside another and the tops of the two bags are glued together. I had to tear the inside paper bag and take out the handkerchiefs that had been hidden between the two layers of paper bag!

The Oriental Shawl

This shawl I'm holding has a beautiful if involved design on both sides, as you can see. In the middle of the shawl is a tassel and as I hold it by the tassel the rest of the shawl falls in drapes from the tassel. I put my hand under the drapes and somehow manage to produce one, two, three, FOUR huge bouquets of flowers from out of nowhere.

The Secret

I mentioned that the shawl design is involved, and this is deliberate. The design hides four tubes of similar material to the shawl, sewn onto the shawl on the reverse side to the tassel.

Now I put my hand inside the draped shawl and through a ring. This ring is at the end of the artificial flowers that are squeezed into the tubes. As I pull, so the flowers come free from the tubes and at once become about five times the size they were when compressed into the tubes. When all four bunches of flowers are released this simple trick looks nicely spectacular.

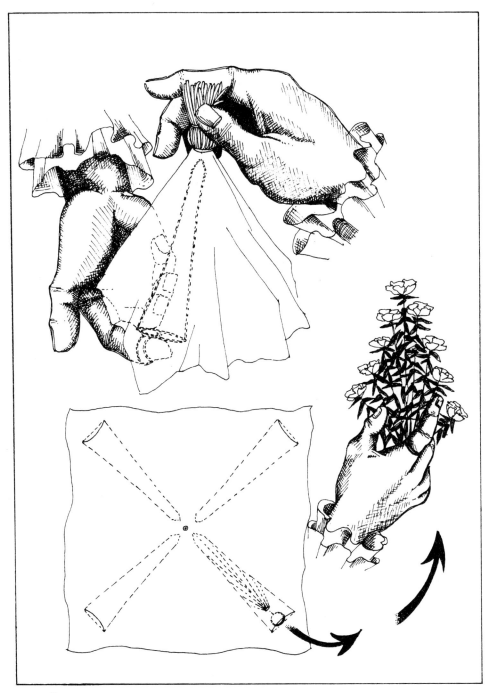

C

Thought Reading

I'll hand you a bunch of envelopes with an elastic band around them, to prove they are fresh from the stationers. And please take this pencil and bit of paper.

Now let's pretend I'm a spiritualist. On the bit of paper I want you to write a message to some dear dead friend. Right. Now I'll take back the envelopes, and will you fold *several times* the paper you've written your message on.

Just a moment – I don't know what I'm thinking about – I should have left one envelope with you so that you can put the message in it! Anyway, here it is now.

Put your message in the envelope, seal it and put the envelope in your pocket. Now we have the usual spiritualist routine of my leaving the room to talk to my spirit guide and then I come back – don't laugh, it's what spiritualists always do!

Okay, so now I've come back into the room and outside I've spoken to my Red Indian spirit guide. *He* says your message is: 'I'll always remember you with affection, Frank'. – *Is* that the message in the sealed envelope in your pocket? I thought so!

The Secret

You wrote the message on a piece of paper that was on top of a pile of envelopes. I then took back the envelopes, only to remember that I should have let you keep the top one so you could put your piece of paper in it.

But the envelope I gave back to you was not the top one, because while you were busy folding your message several times, I had put the top envelope at the bottom of the pile.

I then remembered myself, and handed you back *an* envelope.

When I went outside the room, I opened the top envelope you had used for writing on. Inside, I had previously put some carbon paper and a bit of plain paper – thus I could read the carbon of your message, and then return to tell you what the Red Indian had said to me, or rather, what I had just read on my carbon copy!

Balance the Golf Ball

Even expert jugglers find the feat of balancing one golf ball on top of another almost impossible. . . . But I think I can manage it. . . . I've been practising a lot . . . there, one ball on top of the other!

The Secret

I put a dab of soap on one of the golf balls and press the other against it; it will 'balance' for as long as I want!

35

The Jumping Cigar Band

★☆★☆★☆★☆

All magicians, including myself, think this is one of the cleverest yet most simple of pocket tricks.

I put an ordinary cigar band on the tip of the second finger of my right hand. Okay? Now, here is the cleverness. I can magically make this paper cigar band fly instantly from this finger tip to another!

I place my second finger with the band on it, plus the *next* finger, on the palm of my left hand. The other fingers I curl up in order to hide them. I now quickly take away my right hand and then flip it back on to my left hand's palm again. Look – the cigar band has moved to the *next* finger!

The Secret

What I have in fact just done is to substitute my third finger for my first one. My second finger with the cigar band on it remains.

I removed my hand so quickly that you didn't notice I was changing fingers, and that my second finger still had the one and only band on it. You thought – as everyone else does – that the cigar band was indeed jumping from my second finger to my third, and then back again to my second. As you see, the hand *is* quicker than the eye!

The Tell-Tale Match

Let me show you a really striking trick. I'll take this book of matches and tear off a match and light it. Now I'll hold the match up in front of your eyes so that you can watch it closely.

Now concentrate on it please. Think of the initials of your name, and concentrate still further on the flame at the end of the match . . . now blow it out.

Isn't your name Jane Smith? Because soon . . . look . . . there, you can see 'J.S.' printed on the blackened end of the match!

The Secret

Of course I learnt your name first. Before meeting you I took an ordinary pencil and, using heavy strokes, I printed your initials on the head of the match, keeping the match attached to the book folder.

Magic has to bow down to chemistry – the lead of the pencil has attacked the sulphur of the match! – but I pretended it was magic because I'm a magician, aren't I?

Coloured Loops

★☆★☆★☆★☆

Here I have a piece of string and hanging from it are three loops of paper – one red, one white and one blue – which are about two feet long.

If you and your friend will each hold one end of the string, I'll throw this large handkerchief over the three paper loops and the string.

Okay, tell me which loop you'd like me to choose. The red one? Right, I'll find it under the handkerchief, pull it free of the string, show it you – except that, look, it is still a whole loop! I never had to tear the loop to get it off the piece of string! How have I done this?

The Secret

The secret is underneath the handkerchief, in pockets sewn on to the handkerchief, though inside it. When one of you asked me for the red loop, I took the red loop off the line by mystically reaching underneath the handkerchief, tearing the red loop (thus taking it off the string) and after removing the duplicate from the pocket in the handkerchief, I put the other (torn) loop into the pocket. I then held up the untorn red loop!

★★★

The Floating Paper Ball

Here's some newspaper and I'll crumple a section of it into a ball. And now – believe it or not – I hold the crumpled paper ball in front of me – then I let go of it – and it floats in mid-air!

Not only that, but I can even pass this solid wooden hoop over the floating ball of paper! The hoop is about twelve inches in diameter and as you see it genuinely passes over the floating ball, so there is no trickery!

I see you're watching hard and think there's a trick somewhere. But let me hand over the paper ball and the wooden hoop to you. You're very welcome to examine them.

The Secret

Aerial suspension or, as we call it, 'levitation', is indeed a mystifying business and, of course, you want to know how I managed to levitate the ball of loose paper.

I got a piece of fine silk thread about twenty inches long. One end I looped with a very small loop, just big enough to fit over my finger-tip. At the other end of the thread was another loop, only larger. That one had to fit over my ear!

Before I began this illusion I'd already slipped the thread over my ear – you didn't notice it because it then went round the back of my neck and was therefore hidden. I was then ready.

I picked up the piece of newspaper and when I loosely crumpled it up in mid-air, in actual fact I crumpled it up *around* the thread that now stretched from a finger-tip on my right hand, round behind my neck, and was already looped on

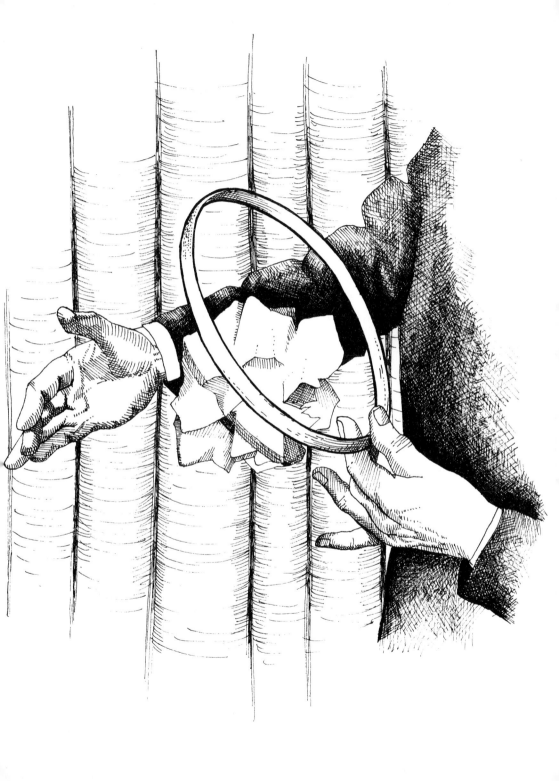

to my left ear.

As I moved my right hand, so the paper was made to rise and fall, seemingly in mid-air. 'Just a minute,' you will say. 'You used that wooden hoop in the illusion. It obviously must be threaded on to the silk thread otherwise you couldn't possibly pass the wooden hoop to and fro across the ball of paper. But how, without my noticing, did you thread the hoop on to the silk thread?'

I'll tell you. At the start, I had picked up the wooden hoop. Now, because I wanted to crumple up the paper with *both* hands, I must put the hoop somewhere. So I casually decided to put it *over my head*, around my neck, and as I did so, I threaded the invisible thread through the wooden hoop. This is really the basis of this illusion; this is what convinces you that there can be no thread anywhere, for I just took the wooden loop from off my head and I could of course easily pass it to and fro over the 'floating ball'!

Magnetic Matchbox Control

★☆★☆★☆★☆

Here is a matchbox full of metal filings, and here is a magnet. I'll open the matchbox and just watch the magnet attract the metal filings!

Now I'll carefully put the metal filings back in the matchbox, so, and hand the box over to you so that you can have a go. . . . That's odd, when you do it the magnet doesn't pick up the metal filings.

42

The Secret

The reason why I *carefully* put the metal filings back in the matchbox was so that I could spend a bit of time doing so – and also doing something else. The moment I had put the filings back in the box, I closed the box and opened the other end of the drawer – and *that* end wasn't full of metal but full of *zinc* filings which will not stick to a magnet!

The Coin in the Magic Orange

★☆★☆★☆★☆

Here's a bowl of oranges and I want you to choose carefully one and hand it to me. This one? Right. I take your magic orange and this ordinary sharp knife and I cut the orange in two. Hey, there's a coin in the orange, look! How did it get in the orange?

The Secret

I'll hold the coin against the blade of the knife to show you it's not as wide as the blade. In other words, you couldn't see the coin behind the blade when I picked the knife up. And I'll get a dab of soap, press it on to the blade and press the coin into the soap.

When I cut this orange, see, the coin comes off and falls into the open orange!

A Hat Full of Rubber Balls

I am holding up a handkerchief for you to look at. As you see, it's empty. I crumple it up, so – and from it I take out this rubber ball! Then I drop the ball in the hat underneath the handkerchief.

Although the handkerchief is now empty – and I'm holding it up to show you that it is, when I crumple it up another ball appears! And I'll drop the second ball into the hat.

Let me do this once again – there, we have three balls in the hat, and I will now hand you the hat to examine. What do you mean, there are *no balls* in the hat? There should be three! That's very mysterious!

The Secret

Each time I hold up the handkerchief, I hold the two top corners and I don't show you the other side of the handkerchief. If I did, you would see that hanging in the middle is *one* rubber ball, attached to the hem by a thread.

There is one ball only, used the three times! The three balls you thought you saw were the same one.

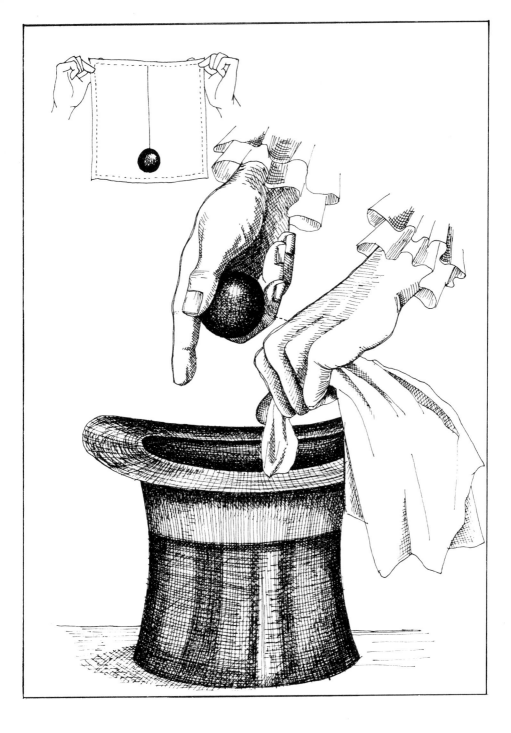

Which Hand Holds the Coin?

I want you to take these two coins, one in each hand, and then – when I've gone out of the room – hold one coin up in front of your eyes, and the other on your knee, and count to twenty.

When I come back into the room, I'll tell you which hand held the coin up to your face and which hand held the coin at your knee.

The Secret

When I returned I could see that one hand was a bit redder, the other a bit whiter, than usual. In the hand held on the knee, your blood drained into it. With your hand held up to your eyes, the blood had drained out of it and that hand was now almost white. Even when you relaxed your hands, the colour difference was still there.

Instant Flowers

Here's a jar with some leaves and a couple of flowers in it. I had hoped the flowers would have grown more, but at least I can water them – watering them might help a bit.

Great Heavens! As I pour water into the jar from this perfectly ordinary jug, they start to grow! But how?

The Secret

The jug of water is straightforward, but I had to prepare the inside of the jar – or if you haven't a jar, anything that isn't made of transparent glass will do, as long as the sides are perfectly straight.

Just inside the jar I fixed some wire in the form of a cross, and where the wire crosses is a small circle or hoop.

I pushed some straight wire through the hoop, and at one end of the wire I tied on the 'growing' flowers and on to the other end of the wire I pushed a large cork.

Yes, you're right. As I poured the water into the jar, so the cork floated and the more water I poured, the higher the level of the cork – and the higher grew the flowers!

47

The Floating Glass

If I use ordinary household things for my magic, such as this bottle of milk and the glass on that table, then there can't be any trickery, can there?

Watch. I pick up the glass in one hand and the bottle of milk in the other and, to show off my demonstration, I hold the glass almost twelve inches below the bottle as I pour the milk out.

You're not going to believe this. I will now let go of the glass and it will float in the air, and quite calmly I continue to pour milk into it!

The Secret

Well, there is no trickery but there is a piece of thin wire (or white cotton, if you're wearing a white shirt and no coat). When you saw the bottle and a glass standing on the table, they were already joined by the wire or thread.

I tie it round the lip of the bottle and – a bit harder, this – I tie it round the glass but also tie a half loop over the top of the glass, its two ends being knotted to the wire now tied round the glass.

To test, I lift up the bottle and the glass will hang about twelve inches below it. The glass must have sloping sides or the wire tied to it will slip up the glass.

The Mystic Orange

Here is an empty hat. You may examine it closely. Right. I put this orange into the hat, make a magic pass over the hat – and bring out an apple! Where did the orange go to? And where has the apple come from?

The Secret

I carefully removed the peel from a large orange, I found a smaller apple, and put the apple *inside* the empty orange peel. Because I had cut the orange skin round its middle, and later held it with that cut at the horizontal, you didn't notice the cut! And I managed to hide the now removed orange skin under the hat band and, to further fool you, I picked up the hat with my fingers over the hidden orange skin.

Four Coins Become Eight

Here's a bit of cardboard, maybe it's a postcard, and I'll hold it in one hand and place four coins on it. And if you will hold up your hand, I'll slide off the four coins into your palm. That's odd – *eight* coins are now in your hand!

The Secret

When I hold the bit of cardboard, I am already holding four coins under it, pressed against the cardboard with my finger. When I slide the top four coins off into your hand, I also release the hidden four – and that makes eight!

Spirits of Aqua

Well, we've had our dinner and I've been talking to you about spiritualism and mediums, so now I'll do a trick that can involve spirits, such as whisky, or plain water which is 'Spirits of Aqua'!

This is an ordinary drinking glass which I have half filled with water. I now put several strips of sticky tape across the top to make sure no human can drink the water. So if the water does disappear, it will have been drunk by some spirit.

Kindly switch off the lights, and let the atmosphere of a seance prevail. As I sit between you in the dark, I must have silence from you. When I say 'Now!', I want you on my right to hold the glass with one hand and *my* hand with the other. And you on my left to do the same.

You will be holding the glass and both my hands, so there will be no way that the liquid can be removed from the glass, except by psychic means. Here's the command – Now!

A few seconds have passed, and if someone will switch on the lights they will see that all the water has vanished. But how?

The Secret

Just before giving the command, I had still got my hands free, so had taken a drinking straw from my inside pocket, and put it in the glass through one of the gaps in the sticky tape under cover of the darkness.

I then said 'Now!' and, though both my hands were held, it was easy for me to lean forward and drink from the straw. After drinking, I took up the straw with my mouth and let it drop to the floor, where it remained unnoticed when the lights were switched on again.

Vanishing Coin

See, here's a small coin in my hand. I'll close my hand and make it into a fist. I open my hand again and, would you believe, the coin has vanished!

The Secret

I smeared a bit of soap on the fingernail of my longest finger before talking to you. I put the coin in my hand, and when I screw my hand into a fist, I make sure the coin presses against the soap.

When I open my hand with a flourish and hold it up for you to see the palm, you can't see my fingernails or the coin which is now stuck on one of them.

51

Trying to Get Loose

★☆★☆★☆★☆

This little trick is interesting, and all I need is this string as I stand between you two.

First, on my left, I'll tie your hands together with this long piece of string, leaving plenty of slack between your hands.

Now, on my right, I'll tie *your* hands together in the same way. But, first, I must pass the 'bight' of your string over the bight of hers, so that you are in fact tied together.

Now try and get apart, without cutting the string or untying the knots. You will see that you can't!

The Secret

You can. If I take the centre of the string holding your wrists and pass it up through one of the loops of string (the one on her left wrist) and bring it down over her left hand, you will find yourselves separated! You don't believe me? Try it.

Balancing the Magic Wand

I pick up the magic wand with my left hand and place it on my right hand. Although I sway my right hand, the wand doesn't fall off it.

Better still, I now put the wand on the table, just touch the end of it with my thumb and can then lift it into the air. How do I manage to lift the wand by just touching it with my thumb? How do I achieve this small-scale levitation?

The Secret

I acquired a girl's long blonde hair, tied it into an endless loop, and put this invisible circle of hair over my right hand. You did not notice me slide the wand between the hair and my hand,

53

but, by careful pressure, I can then balance the wand on almost any part of my hand. Or I can even, as I showed you, seem to elevate the wand!

Getting Rid of the String

As you see, my coat is off but I'm wearing a waistcoat. I've got this continuous loop of string, about three yards long, and it is over my right arm. The loop is 'closed'. The fingers of my right hand are tucked into my waistcoat pocket.

There is no way I can get this loop of string free without taking my right hand from my waistcoat pocket.

The Secret

Oddly enough, this secret is the same as my celebrated Oriental levitation illusion entitled 'The Floating Lady'! For just as the hoop can be made to pass across The Floating Lady, so this loop of string, incredibly, can be got free from me.

My right hand must stay at my waistcoat pocket. With my left hand, I pull the loop through the arm-hole of my waistcoat. I then pull it over my head. I then pull it out through the other arm-hole and over the other arm. I can now reach up under the waistcoat and pull the string down; it will now fall to the floor. I step out of it – and I am free!

Magic Apple

★☆★☆★☆★☆

I have two apples. Here is one of them. See if you can break it in two with your hands. Try a bit harder. You can't manage it? The truth is that it needs an incredible amount of strength to do it, strength given only to The Great Houdini.

The Secret

It needs no strength at all! It needs the treatment I gave to it, and didn't give to *your* apple. I took a needle threaded with strong thread and pushed it in and out of the skin round the apple. Then I pulled on the ends of the thread and this cut the apple beneath the skin.

★★★

Part Two
THE CARD KING
★☆★☆★☆★☆

Please Telephone for Your Card

At the start of my career I was known as 'The Card King', and although this was because I can manipulate cards with great skill, my best card tricks need no manipulation at all! Take this one, for instance.

Here are six cards and I want you to choose one. You've chosen the ten of clubs? Okay. Now, go to that telephone, ring 2827314, ask for Mr Jenkins, and then ask him what card you have chosen. Incredibly, the person you ring up will give you the correct answer!

The Secret

The man at the other end of the phone is in the know, of course. But *how?*

He is indeed Mr Jenkins – or rather, he is Mr Jenkins to me, because you chose the ten of clubs! If you'd chosen the jack of diamonds, he'd have become Mr Graham!

The moment he hears you ask for Mr Jenkins, he looks at his list and sees 'Jenkins means ten of clubs'. Simple – yet you didn't solve the secret did you? And neither does anyone else. Sometimes the simple ones are the best.

Cards

Will you take a card, and sign your name on it with this pencil, and now put it back in the pack. Fine. Now drop the whole pack into this paper bag. Holding the bag in my left hand, I pick up this dagger with my right hand and plunge it into the paper bag.

Now I'll carefully tear away the bag and, look – stuck on the blade of the dagger is your signed card!

The Secret

When I took the signed card back from you, I cut the pack in two, and you put the card *into* the pack, you thought!

But in fact I moved your card to the top of the pack simply by putting the bottom half of the pack on to the top half.

So when I dropped the entire pack into the bag, I was able to hold on to that particular top card while I held on to the folds of the paper bag, and I pressed it against the side of the bag.

Once I had stuck the dagger into the card, I used the dagger to pull the card away from the rest of the pack, deliberately tore the bag – and there was your card!

The Houdini Card

This trick I have named after myself because the card makes an escape from this envelope that I am holding.

Here is the card and I have cut a half-inch hole just above its centre. Please examine the card. Okay, so I put it in this envelope and seal the envelope.

Now I take up this needle and push it through the envelope, through the hole in the card and out of the other side of the envelope. I have thus threaded this bit of ribbon through the envelope and the card. I now want you to hold each end of the ribbon and let the envelope hang on the ribbon.

Now for the Houdini Escape! I take these scissors and cut off one end of the envelope – and take the card out of the envelope. The envelope is still threaded on the ribbon, yet the card is free! Please, examine the envelope and the card, there's no trick to it. Well, almost no trick!

The Secret

The envelope needs preparing before the trick and I'll show you how: I just cut a slit in the bottom of the envelope. I put the card in the envelope and seal the *top* end of the envelope.

But, I also squeeze the sides of the envelope as I hold it. The card will slide down and a little way out of the envelope, but my hand is hiding this and my little finger stops the card from falling on to the floor.

I push the needle through the centre of the envelope, though not through the card, of course, as the card is now below the centre of the envelope. I am holding the envelope in my left

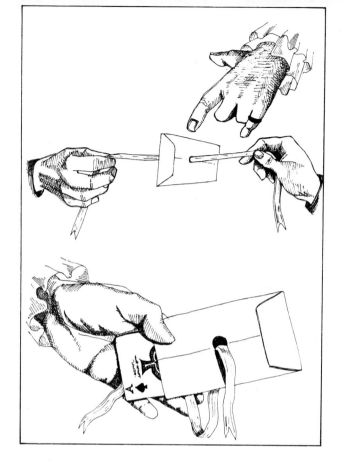

hand, so when I bring my right hand towards my left, I push the card up into the envelope with my right thumb.

This has pushed the card up into the envelope again and the ribbon is running around the edge of the card.

Now, to show both sides of the envelope, I'll turn it upside down on the ribbon and as you can see, the bottom is now the top. I take the scissors and cut the bottom – in truth I am cutting where there is *already* a cut, and thus I've hidden the secret of the trick!

When I take the card out, I whisk it out to make you think there is more of the card in the envelope than there in fact is!

Find the Ace

★☆★☆★☆★☆

I will quickly rest three cards (ace, jack and king) on this small stand made from a piece of wood covered in black velvet. The stand is about fourteen inches long by seven inches high. So there are the three cards resting against the stand with their backs to us.

You saw me put the three cards down, so which is the ace? The centre one? Are you sure? I'll pick it up and show you. No, the one you chose is the king.

Let's try again. I'll take the three cards off the stand and you shuffle them and, if you wish, examine them. Right, I will now quickly put the three cards on the stand again.

Which one is the ace? You're sure it's the left-hand card? Alright, I'll turn it over. No, it's the jack. Oh, you may *say* you were sure it was the ace, but it isn't, is it? It's strange, but you don't seem to be able to find the ace!

The Secret

On the black velvet stand I had already placed three cards, king, jack, and *another* jack. The secret of these three cards is that I had covered their backs with black velvet and although you are only a short distance away, your eyes cannot see this black velvet against the black velvet of the stand as all the velvets have merged.

When I rested the other three cards on the stand, I rested them *on top* of the three cards already resting on the stand, though unnoticed by you. When I took off the centre card, which was the ace, I also took off the card under it, which was not an ace. The ace was hidden by the card I showed you, the one with black velvet on its back.

As none of the three 'velvet backed cards' is an ace, you will *never* find the ace while I'm in charge.

Card Reading

Okay, I want all the lights on for this trick – I've got nothing to hide!

Let me give you and your friends a pack of cards. Will you shuffle them, and will all four of you take a card each?

Now put your card in one of these envelopes and seal it. You're most welcome to examine the cards and the envelopes, because when I'm through with this trick you're bound to say it's something to do with the cards!

Okay, I'll collect up your four envelopes and bring them over here to this top hat. Great. Now, I appreciate that thought transference is considered a joke, but even so, I'll take one of these envelopes out of this hat, press it against my forehead, close my eyes and think hard for a second and . . . this card is the seven of clubs! Yes, I thought it was! I'll take the next envelope out of the hat and press it to my forehead and think deeply . . . er . . . two of hearts? Yes? Good!

And now for the other two envelopes. I did warn you – folk laugh at thought transference but, as you see, it works!

The Secret

Thought transference doesn't work. It's bunkum. And forget

all about my pressing the envelope to my forehead! I've got a pile of *very thin* envelopes, and you can buy thin playing-cards too, which is what I have done in this case.

And why did I ask for the lights to be full on? It's so that you won't notice another light – a torch in this hat, to be precise! I hold the envelope against the torch light as I talk and thus see through the envelope that the card is seven of clubs.

Then I 'do the dressing' which was all that mumbo-jumbo about pressing the envelope to my forehead! Sometimes the dressing is more important than the trick – have you noticed?

A Jumping Card

★☆★☆★☆★☆

Well, I guess you know the expression 'I will make a card jump', and here is how it's done.

I show you the top card of this pack and then place it in the centre of the pack. Now I command it to jump back to its former place on the top of the pack – and it does!

The Secret

I let the top card of the pack be the eight of clubs, and the second card be the seven of clubs. I took these two cards and *showed them as one*. Then I replaced them on top of the pack.

I then took off *the top* card (the eight of clubs) and placed it slowly in the centre of the pack. When it was half-way into the pack I showed the face of it to you and you thought it was the seven of clubs. Of course, I must remember to keep my hand over the index number in the corner, so the card appears to be the seven. I then remove the top card of the pack – and that *is* the seven!

In the Dark

★☆★☆★☆★☆

Take a card and show it to your neighbour, so there's no doubt as to which card you've taken. And now if I may take it back from you? Thanks. I will return it to the pack.

I'm going to put the cards 'in the dark' by placing them on the table and covering them with a handkerchief.

Right, I've done that . . . and the card you chose was the four of hearts! I knew I was right!

The Secret

I asked you to show the card to your neighbour so that you wouldn't notice me *turning over* the bottom card of the pack. Now I hold the pack out to you with that bottom card uppermost and you assume that every card is facing downwards as usual.

When you returned the card, all I have had to do is turn over the pack once more and spread out the cards on a table while I covered them with a big handkerchief. The card I reversed and the card you returned to the pack are the only ones facing upwards, so I can easily see your card through the handkerchief!

Here's Your Card

★☆★☆★☆★☆

Hi! Here's a genuinely new pack of cards. Please open the wrapper and shuffle them. Don't let me see what the card is, but choose one and hold on to it. Tell you what, mark it with a pencil! I'll take the pack now. See, I cut it. So now will you put your card back into the pack? Fine.

Now I've got to find out which is your card . . . I'll fan them out and have a look. It's a bit difficult for me – wait a second – I've got it! Is this your card that I'm holding up? I thought it might be! Here, examine it – I haven't marked it in any way, and your mark is still on it!

The Secret

The pack of cards is genuinely new and so is the card you have chosen, and your careful examination has shown that *I* have not marked it in any way.

While you pencil-marked the card I added one more special card as I collected the pack from you – in fact, when you put your card back into the pack, you put it on top of my special card.

What's so special about it? Nothing that anyone except myself would notice. A small crescent-shaped piece has been cut out of one end.

As I flipped through the cards, the moment I saw my special card, I knew the one before it in the pack was yours!

You Give Me the Pip

I'm holding out a few cards and would like you to select a card, look at it and replace it. Thanks – now I'll take it and place it with the others. Now I'll pick out your chosen card. Six of hearts? I knew it!

The Secret

The secret is, which cards have I allowed you to choose from? Well, I took from the pack the three, five, six, seven, eight and nine of spades, clubs and hearts – *not* diamonds. How do these particular cards help a magician?

On each of these cards, the majority of pips point one way! So beforehand I make sure that all the cards have the majority of pips pointing in the same direction. But when I put the chosen card back with the others, I turn it round.

Now I spread them all out on a table and I can at once see which card has the majority of pips now pointing the wrong way. The secret – and few know this – is the pips!

The Torn Card Trick

Select a card from the pack and give it to me. Thanks. I'll now tear it into pieces. But we must be tidy, so I'll put the torn pieces on this square of paper. Oh, here's one bit of torn card that I can give back to you as a keepsake.

Now I'll fold the square of paper roughly into the shape of an envelope, and using this sticky tape I'll fasten all the corners down so that the 'envelope' is sealed. Having done that, let me hand you the envelope containing the torn pieces.

I wave my wand over the envelope and collect the envelope back from you. I take a penknife and slit open the envelope. Out comes not the torn pieces but the whole card! Oh, *was* the two of diamonds the card you first selected? It was? Then this being the two of diamonds means I must be handing back your chosen card, the one that I had torn to pieces! And look, the card has a corner torn off. Let's see if the one bit of torn card that I gave you as a keepsake fits the corner. It does!

The Secret

The square of paper that became the envelope is in fact *two* squares of paper previously stuck together at their outside edges, and with a card hidden between the two squares of paper.

After slitting open the envelope I took out from between the two squares of paper – yes – the two of diamonds!

So okay, I faked things a bit. The pack of cards I was holding consisted entirely of twos of diamonds!

As for the piece of the torn card, it filled the torn corner of the planted card because when I first tore the pieces up I made sure I was tearing one particular bit in the exact but simple shape that I had torn the corner of the planted card when preparing the trick.

The Uncut Playing-Card

★☆★☆★☆★☆

I put this playing-card into this fairly small business envelope (the kind of envelope with the flap at the narrower end of it). Now I will seal the envelope and cut it in half with this pair of scissors.

I will now take the portions apart and hand you the card – and yet the card is still uncut! But I have just cut the envelope with it inside! I *must* have cut the card!

The Secret

Beforehand, I had made a slit on the underneath side of the envelope, the slit being parallel to the flap, and halfway down the envelope, and just a bit wider than the playing-card.

When I put the card in the envelope you didn't see the slit because it was underneath the envelope. So you saw me slide the card into the envelope, but you didn't see it slide partly *out* of the envelope again as it went out through the slit.

Half the card was *out* of the envelope and when I cut the envelope in half, I cut *between* the card and the envelope. So the card itself was never cut!

A Good Key Card

I'll show you an ordinary pack of playing-cards, and yet I can tell you instantly where the king of spades is.

Please, take the pack and shuffle. I now take it back from you and this card when turned over will, I hope, be the king of spades! It is!

Will you shuffle again? Now return the cards to me – many thanks – and I am sure *this* one must be the king. I'm right, it's the one that I'm taking from the pack! But how do I find the king of spades each time?

The Secret

Many a card trick is done by means of a 'key card', such as this one. The secret lies in the fact that I can always find the key card instantly.

All cards are made from *two* pieces of card glued together. I have taken this king of spades, steamed it and then split it in two. I have put a thin thread in this thin cardboard sandwich, and when re-glued a heavy weight has been put on this trick card for several days.

I now have a card that is just a small amount stiffer and heavier than the others. *I* notice it, but no one else does, for no one else is expecting it! And I have a key card that I can quickly recognize.

A Card Code

★☆★☆★☆★☆

Here's a baffling card trick that mediums use! Yes, it's true, I've been at a seance and I've seen those mediums working this little trick on innocent dupes!

I want you to take three consecutive cards from the pack and place them in a row on the table. Fine. It's quite impossible for me to know the cards, but I'll now look at them, think of them, and transfer my thoughts to a medium sitting at the other end of the room. To make sure there is no trickery, the medium has turned her back on us, as you see, so only thought transference can aid her. She will now name the three cards you chose!

The Secret

Let's look closely at the pack of cards. They've been secretly arranged in a certain order, and when you take away your chosen three cards I will quite casually hold the top half of the pack (from the bottom of which the cards have been selected) with its face towards you – and thus the medium can see the *bottom* card (of this top half) before she turns away.

She knows at once which three cards have been chosen by you! And here's the secret. She knows which cards must follow that bottom one, because she has learnt a 'code sentence'. Here it is: 'Eight kings threatened to save nine fair ladies for one sick knave'.

Now that's an easy sentence to remember, and the interpretation of this code is, quite simply: Eight (eight) kings (king) threatened (three, ten) to (two) save (seven) nine (nine) fair (five) ladies (queen) for (four) one (ace) sick (six) knave (jack).

73

The medium also knows that the pack has been arranged in the order of diamonds, spades, hearts, clubs, and she can therefore tell you exactly what your cards are.

A lot of tricks are done by means of this code and it's ideal for the introduction to the seance that comes later, because I consider the seance to be just as much a trick as the Card Code just explained! Don't you?

Finding the Chosen Card

Here is a brand-new pack of cards. Please, take a card. Right. Don't tell me which card it is, but let me study its back. Mmmm ... Now return it to the pack, and I'll select the card you chose. I'll spread them out on the table so ... is this your card? I thought so!

The Secret

When you took the card from the pack I expressed great interest in it. This was to take your attention away from the rest of the pack that I was secretly *bending!*

You then put your card back and when I spread the cards out, yours was the only card not slightly curved. Easy!

Three-Colour Cards

★☆★☆★☆★☆

Here are three cards: one red, one white and one blue. I'll put the three cards separately into this hat: red, white and blue.

And now out of the hat I will take the red one and the white one, and put them in my pocket. So what colour is the card still in the hat?

Blue, you say? Well I know it's crazy, but it's *white* – see! I'll slide it from my hat on to the table; there it is, the white card.

So where has the blue one gone? It's here in my pocket. I'll put it on the table and there it is – the blue card – along with the red one from my pocket also. Okay, so the white card must be a trick card. Well, turn it over, because I can tell you think it will be blue on the other side. But it isn't, is it? It's white on both sides!

It's all very mysterious.

The Secret

Well, I *have* used a double-sided card, with one side white and one blue, but I used it *early* in the routine and then dispensed with it. I'll show you the trick again:

I show you a red card, a white card and this blue card, which *seems* to be blue but is in fact white on the back. I show the red both sides then drop it in the hat. I show the white both sides then drop it in the hat. I have now lulled your suspicions and I will in fact only show *one* side of the blue card as I throw it casually into the hat.

Now I bring out the red, showing both sides. But when I remove the 'white card' from the hat, I actually take out the trick card with only its white side showing. I now place these two cards into my pocket where the 'white' card is promptly exchanged for a valid blue card – *blue on both sides* – which is in my pocket already!

So the white card found in the hat naturally turns out to be white on both sides, an ordinary white card in fact.

75

Change Places

★☆★☆★☆★☆

This is a good card trick and you'll both like it. Take this ordinary pack of cards, that's it, and now remove the four kings and the four aces from the pack. In fact, if you like, mark them with a pencil. Here's one on the table, I'll get it for you.

Now I'll put the four aces on the table here, and the four kings on the table here, and at the same time you can be examining these two envelopes. They also are quite ordinary. Will you write 'aces' on the one and 'kings' on the other. Thank you.

Now I'll put the four marked aces in the aces envelope and the four marked kings in the kings envelope and here is one envelope for you to hold and the other for *you* to hold.

And now, believe it or not, I'm going to make the marked aces and kings change places!

Open the envelope, and you will see that the aces are now in the kings' envelope – and vice versa.

The Secret

You've been examining the pack of cards and the envelopes. What you should have been examining is the table, or rather the tablecloth. It's a dark colour – so dark you haven't noticed those two oblongs on it!

They happen to be an ace and a king whose backs are the same colour as the tablecloth, so they've become invisible! They're duplicates!

When I collected the four aces from you I put them on top of the duplicate king, and when I collected the four kings I put

76

them on top of the duplicate ace!

I then asked you for your kings' envelope, and picked up one group of cards and showed you the duplicate king and put it and the four aces in the kings' envelope. Then I picked up the other group of cards, showing you the duplicate ace, and put them in the aces' envelope.

When I take out the four aces from the kings' envelope, you won't ask to see the duplicate cards, because you don't know they exist. What the eye doesn't see the heart doesn't grieve for!

77

The Spelling Bee Card Trick

Here is a really clever little trick that I often use in parlours and small circles.

I take thirteen cards and arrange them in such an order as to enable me to spell out the cards in sequence from one (or the ace) right through to the king. I simply hold the thirteen cards in my hand face downwards and I remove one card from the top with each letter I spell out.

O – N – E, one. Having removed one card with each letter, I turn over the fourth card when I pronounce the word 'ONE', and it will indeed be found to be the ace! I place it on the table as I have no further use for it.

I next spell out T – W – O, two, and the fourth card will indeed be found to be two, so I put that on the table also. And so on, right through to the time I spell out K – I – N – G, king.

It's very ingenious, isn't it? The question is, how on earth do I do it?

The Secret

What I must do first is to arrange the cards in the following sequence before spelling them out: 3 – 8 – 7 – 1 –queen– 6 – 4 – 2 – jack – king – 10 – 9 – 5.

You will see that this arrangement face down makes three the top card and five the bottom card. As I spell out the letters and put each card down, I have to remember not to disturb the sequence of cards, and not to replace the removed card, but to put it down on the table and not to use it again.

There is nothing to it – except ingenuity!

Part Three
THE MASTER MAGICIAN

★☆★☆★☆★☆

The Vanishing Bird-Cage

Ladies and gentlemen, I will now produce four doves out of thin air by merely holding a large handkerchief against my chest. And as I hand each dove to my assistant, she in turn puts the doves into the cage standing on that table.

My assistant holds up the table so that I can cover the cage with another large handkerchief. Now I myself take hold of the cage to bring it over from the table to show it to you.

But instead, I throw the cage in the air and it, plus the four doves, vanish! All that I have left is the large handkerchief that covered the cage and as you see (for I am showing you both sides of the handkerchief), there is no bird cage to be seen anywhere. It has disappeared.

The Secret

There are two things you will be wanting to know: how did I make the four doves appear; and after that, how did I make the four doves and their cage *dis*appear.

As I held the large handkerchief close to my chest, I used it to hide the fact that I was putting one finger through a loop of string by my coat lapel. I then pulled the loop. This loop is attached to a 'dove-holder' hidden – along with three others – under my coat. So the dove is now in the handkerchief and pops its head up – as it does, I undo the dove-holder hidden behind the handkerchief and the bird is free. I can then hand it to my assistant.

She places each dove in the cage and puts the lid on the cage again after the fourth dove is safely inside. It so happens that

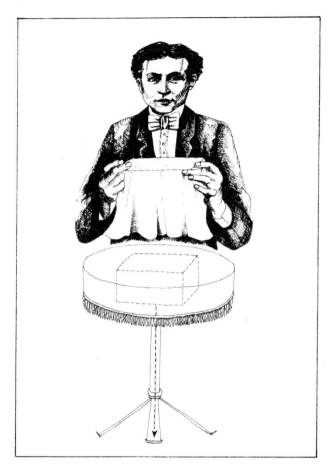

the lid of the cage is covered with the same material as the table top.

I put my large handkerchief over the cage, and to help me to reach the cage, my assistant has casually lifted the table off the ground. She isn't really helping me at all, she is lifting the table off the ground so that a rod, going through the leg of the table and holding up the cage, is now free to drop six inches – that six inches being the height of the cage.

The rod drops, the cage drops, and the cage top's material

merges in with the material of the table top. The cage has 'gone'. But you will not be noticing this, for you will be watching the handkerchief that covers the bird-cage; indeed, as I throw this handkerchief in the air, you will think the bird-cage is up there, because you have seen the outline of the cage through the handkerchief. But the cage isn't in the air, it's in the table, and the outline of the cage is really a wire oblong sewn into the handkerchief.

This ingenious trick I have used successfully for many years as it is impossible to guess how it works unless you know the secret.

The Trick Top Hat

★☆★☆★★☆

No magician can be without a top hat, like this one for instance. As you see, it's a straightforward top hat on the outside, with a black material for lining inside, and the hat is empty.

I make a magic pass over it and it's no longer empty: it has one, two, three, four silk handkerchiefs coming out of it! I could even have taken a rabbit out in the famous traditional way! But how?

The Secret

If you look closely inside, the black lining material is covering the hat's interior *and* a hinged cardboard flap. I move the flap to one side and under there I can easily hide my handkerchiefs or rabbit, can't I? Because the cardboard flap and the rest of the hat's interior are all of the same material, the flap is invisible when you are a few paces from it!

The Floating Table

You may not believe in the hypnosis of humans, let alone in the hypnosis of furniture. And yet, by hypnotizing this table, by forcing the power from my eyes actually *into* this table, I can make the table rise in the air and float!

I will now stand by the table, put my fingers lightly on its surface, concentrate and – see – the table rises. What's more, it floats around as I command it! Now I order it to sink to the floor again and, as you see, it does. I turn my eyes away from it to remove the hypnosis, and I take my bow.

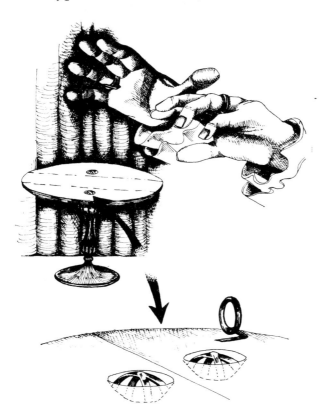

The Secret

You may well have realized that hypnotizing furniture is mumbo-jumbo, and yet the table *did* rise! And as you saw, I didn't hold the table, I merely rested my fingers on it. Glue on my fingers is an impossible theory, so how did I make the table float at my will?

I am wearing a ring on each hand, and attached to each ring on the inside of my hand is a flat hook. Set into the table top are two small unseen clasp-like rings and, as I lightly place my fingers on the table, I slide the unseen flat hooks forward into the unseen rings. As I lift my hands, so I lift the table!

The Mystic Card Box

I'm going to solve this problem by thought-transference. First, let me hand you this small flat box for inspection.

It's a straightforward box, with a hinged lid and the feet are attached at each corner by a screw as with most boxes. The hinges are ornamental but they give the box character . . .

Now you've examined the box, take any card from this pack and place it downwards in the box so I can't see its face. That's it.

Now I'll close the box and work out what the chosen card is by thought-transference . . . I hold the box to my head with both hands . . . I must think deeply . . . the card is the six of hearts? Good. D'you know, some people don't believe in thought-transference. Well, it works for me!

The Secret

Although I let you examine the box, one of the screws that holds the feet is a dummy, and can be quickly unscrewed with a fingernail. I hold the box to my head with *both* hands so that my right hand can easily undo the screw and move the small foot at the corner of the box. It's attached to a small sliding panel exactly in line with the index corner of the card inside the box – and when I slide the little panel away, I can see it is the six of hearts. As I said, thought-transference does work for me!

The Vanishing Bowl of Water

Here is my assistant holding a tray with an empty bowl and a large cloth. Let me pour the water from this jug into the bowl on the tray, cover the bowl with the cloth, and now lift the covered bowl from off the tray.

I toss the bowl covered with the cloth into the air and, although it's full of water, it will vanish into thin air! All I'm left holding is the cloth! It's no use thinking the bowl is somehow still on the tray, because my assistant has turned the tray on its side and so the bowl would have slid off it, on to the floor.

The Secret

I have of course poured the water into the bowl, because you saw me do this. And I put the cloth over the bowl of water because you saw me do this also. What you didn't see, was that

I picked up a plastic disc (exactly the same width as the width of the bowl) and rammed it into the bowl, just above the level of the water. Thus the water is sealed into the bowl.

One last thing. The bowl itself is stuck on to the tray by glue.

My assistant turns the tray on its side as I lift up the cloth, supposedly with the bowl under it.

Watching the trick, you will have decided that the bowl can no longer be on the tray and must therefore be under the cloth I hold, especially as the outline of the bowl shows through the cloth so clearly. But the reason for this is merely a piece of wire shaped like the bowl.

So when I toss the cloth in the air the bowl vanishes from the cloth – of course it does! It's not in the cloth at all but sticking onto the tray that my assistant is cunningly holding sideways to confuse you!

Ghostly Music

★☆★☆★☆★☆

This is a trick used by fraudulent mediums to convince their gullible believers. I am showing it to you because spiritualist effects (though they are evil) interest everyone – especially me!

Please examine this violin. Here is a plain wooden table, on which I will now place the violin. Now I will use some sticky tape to secure it to the table.

If you will come to the other end of the room, sit down and concentrate hard, I will switch off the lights and then leave the room, staying well away from the violin.

Right, I've switched out the lights and as I leave you, please concentrate hard and you will hear ghostly music.

I close the door to the room, wait outside, and like you I can now hear ghostly music from the violin.

I re-enter the room, switch on the light and although you have rushed across to the violin you will see the sticky tape is still intact, no one has picked up the instrument. So how was it played, except by some psychic power?

The Secret

I had made sure the table (and therefore the violin) was fairly near the door; also, that the violin was placed on the table at right angles to the door.

I switched off the light and at once took out of my pocket a long thread with a weight on the end. The thread was placed across the violin, the weight hung down the far side of the table. The other end of the thread was taken out of the room by me.

I closed the door loudly and then softly re-opened it just enough to be able to pull the thread across the violin strings. I then let the weight draw the thread back across the strings, and by repeating this action the 'ghostly' music was produced.

The moment I opened the door I of course pulled the thread and weight clear and pocketed them again, out of sight!

The Magic Box

★☆★☆★☆★☆

Here is a fancy cardboard box, but as you see I've closed the lid and sealed it with sticky paper. And with a razor blade I have cut three sides of a panel to open in the top, and three sides of a panel to open in the front of the box. The fourth side of these panels automatically becomes a hinge.

The panels are almost the size of the top and front respectively. Let us concentrate on the front panel, which I now pull out and downwards, the bottom side working as the hinge.

Now you can see inside. The interior is empty, and lined with some attractively designed paper. I'll close the front panel.

Now I'll open the top panel and take from the box four large handkerchiefs and a toy rabbit! But the box was empty – you're sure it was!

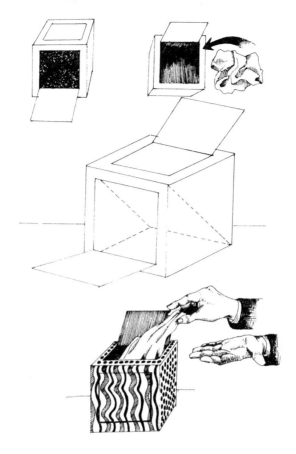

The Secret

Placed in the box at an angle of 45 degrees is a piece of mirror that fits the inside exactly. When I opened the front panel you didn't really see the whole box interior, you just saw half of it.

The other half was an illusion; what you saw was the floor reflected in the mirror and as the floor and the sides were all papered in the attractively designed paper, you thought the reflection of the floor in the mirror was the back wall.

Tucked in behind the mirror were the handkerchiefs and the toy rabbit! Seeing is *not* believing – at least, not when a mirror is involved!

A Patriotic Tube

I'll take this large sheet of paper, show you both sides of it, roll it up into a sort of tube and push three white handkerchiefs through it.

Amazingly – for you saw it was just a sheet of paper – the white handkerchiefs come out of the other end red, white and blue.

To achieve a grand effect, I will now push these three patriotic coloured handkerchiefs through this other separate tube of cardboard and look, they are transformed into the American flag! One minute a handkerchief. Next minute, Old Glory!

The Secret

You will remember that I held up the sheet of paper (which shouldn't be too thin) and showed you both sides.

The front side I showed slowly, the back quickly, because I am holding the paper with my right hand loose, not tightly fisted. I don't want you to notice that my hand hides a fairly small tube of paper stuck on to the edge of the large sheet. I then rolled up the sheet of paper, held it as a roll in my left hand and pushed the three white handkerchiefs into it with my right hand.

All I had to do was remove the coloured silks from the hidden tube of paper at the other end!

With regard to the bigger tube of thicker cardboard which is going to work the second effect for me, I don't hold it too close to you but I do let you peer through it and thus prove to you it is a 'hollow' tube of cardboard.

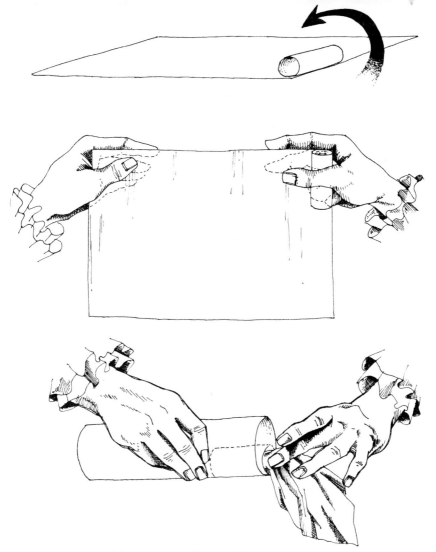

No wonder this second tube is thicker cardboard! The thickness is really due to its being *two* tubes, one inside the other, and carefully pushed into the small space between the two tubes is a whole American flag. If it measures about three feet in length it can come out of a tube half that size, and as you saw, out it came, crumpled but patriotic!

Spirit Writing

★☆★☆★☆★☆

Let me introduce you to another idea often used by spiritualists; it's called Spirit Writing. Here is a slate and you are most welcome to examine it on both sides. And here is a bit of old newspaper. I now have to wrap the slate in the newspaper, or rather I would be able to if it wasn't such an old paper. I'll smooth it out and then I can fold over the sides more neatly. Right, I carefully fold the newspaper under the slate and it's ready.

I put my finger-tips on the newspaper and create a spirit message – any message will do. What about your name? I concentrate spiritually a bit longer. Now I remove the newspaper and there, on the slate, your name has been written spiritually!

The Secret

It isn't just 'a bit of old newspaper'. It is a bit of old newspaper that I have previously written your name on with the edge of a hard piece of soap. But I had to write your name in reverse, using mirror-writing.

Now I saturate the soap letters of your name with chalk dust, and crumple up the newspaper (the letters cannot be seen) in preparation for meeting my audience. When I mention to you that the sheet is crumpled and needs straightening out, I smooth it out *firmly* – and thus press the chalk powder and soap letters on to the blank slate's surface.

I remove the newspaper and reveal your name in 'spiritual' writing!

Evaporating Water

I'll pick up this sheet of newspaper and roll it into a cone. Although it *is* only newspaper, I'm going to pour this large jug of water into it! To make a splash, I'll hold the jug high above the newspaper cone as I pour.

Now I'll put the jug down on the table and come towards you, holding the newspaper in my left hand. With my right hand, I'll take the newspaper – *and unroll it!* Where has the water gone?

The Secret

The jug containing the water is opaque, and so you didn't see that, hooked on to its back (out of sight) was a cone-shaped plastic container.

I was holding up the cone of newspaper in my left hand, and – as though to give the effect a certain style – I held the jug much higher than the newspaper.

As I brought down the jug in a typical flamboyant conjuror's manner, as though just showing the trick off to you, I was in fact bringing down the hooked-on plastic container as well. It was now scooped neatly into the rolled newspaper cone. And now I could easily pour the water 'into the newspaper' because I was really pouring it into the plastic container, inside the newspaper.

Now I reversed my 'conjuror's actions' and held the newspaper cone higher than the jug for a moment – and in that moment the plastic container was hooked back on to the unseen side of the jug once more.

So there was no longer any water or plastic container in the newspaper cone, and I was able to put down the innocent-looking jug and then unroll the newspaper cone, which was of course empty!

The Rising Card

I want you to choose a card from the pack. I'll fan them out for you. Alright, you've taken that card. Please remember it and return it to the pack. Thanks!

I will now tell you what that card is, because when I fix the pack into this small picture frame, the card of your choice will magically rise up!

There. I've placed the pack in the picture frame, I've straightened the frame and I stand back, my services aren't needed any more.

Although I'm nowhere near it, you see that card rising from the pack? It's the four of hearts, isn't it? Was that your card? I thought so!

Oh, you will be wondering about how the card rises in the frame. Obviously you think it must be some clockwork machinery – kindly inspect the frame. . . . You can't find anything unusual in the frame at all? *No mechanism?* Then *how* does the card rise up?

The Secret

When I fanned the cards out I 'forced' the card on you. You chose the card I wanted you to choose, for I had strategically placed it in the fan of cards so you would indeed choose it.

But that is not the main mystery. The main mystery is how does the replica of that card (for that's what the card in the frame is) manage to rise in the frame when I'm nowhere near the frame? And I later allowed you to examine that frame!

During the trick, as I was straightening the frame, I pulled

out two stoppers at the bottom of the frame, making sure you didn't notice. This caused some sand to run out of the frame and now that the inside of the hollow frame is empty of sand, two small weights slowly fall inside the hollow frame. Attached to these weights are wires which are also attached to the chosen card.

Thus, the card elevated itself, although I was nowhere near the frame. When the sand had run out on to the table, I brought the frame over to you. While you were inspecting it, I brushed the sand off the table and onto the floor.

You found no mechanism. And of course there is no way of discovering that the secret is sand in the hollow picture frame!

The Rabbit Cage

Here is a rabbit cage with bars down the front and to prove to you that it really is empty, watch me lift off the roof and put my hand inside the cage. But what use is a rabbit cage without a rabbit? I hold up my handkerchief in front of the cage, I take it away again – and there is bunny in the cage!

The Secret

This is so simple!

Let us look at the floor and walls inside the cage. They are all covered in black velvet – a muzzy material that confuses your eyes because close inspection will show you that the cage is far smaller inside than it is outside!

See, the back wall is false and when I held up my handkerchief close to the cage, I also held it up close to a catch. When I released the catch, down flapped the back wall and it became a second floor – and bunny who has been released walks forward on to this second floor.

A Trick Table

Here's a genuine table of the type we conjurors always use. As you can see, it's on a thin tripod base so there's no trickery there, and it has a thin table-top covered in a bright check pattern to give a bit of colour to the act, so there's no trickery there either. The fringe on the edge of the table I'll flick for you – there, it's hiding nothing.

I'll take my wand out of one pocket and a golf-ball out of the other and put them on the table. Now I'll hold them both up for you to examine. Hey, where's the golf-ball gone? It's vanished! And look, I haven't palmed it, nor is it up my sleeve! So where is it?

The Secret

The golf-ball – or any other item you may want to vanish – was put down on the check tablecloth for a second. It then disappeared. If you look closely at the check design you will see that it isn't there to give a bit of colour to the act at all – it's there because it has divided the table up into squares of about three inches by three inches. One of those squares – just a bit off centre – is in reality a hole and under the hole is a bag, like you see at the corner of a pool table. And of course, that's where the golf-ball vanished to!

This table can be used to vanish many objects and is the conjuror's best friend. For instance, you can attach a bag behind the table, and as you wave one hand to distract the audience so your other hand is sliding objects across this table and down into this bag, thus 'vanishing' them!

The Dog Kennel

Man's best friend is his dog, and here on this conjuror's table I'm going to build a kennel for a dog.

I stand up the front wall of the kennel so, and I collect the sides and back walls from my assistant and just hook them together. And now as I put the roof on, the kennel is completed.

The only trouble is, I haven't got a dog for it, and that's a shame. Why, Great Heavens, the door to the house is opening and out comes Penelope the Peke! I don't know where she came from, because the kennel must have been empty – you saw me building the kennel – but Penelope, take a bow. Or rather a bow wow!

The Secret

Well, I said I didn't know where the dog came from, because the kennel must have been empty – and of course it *was* empty. But the table on which I built the kennel wasn't.

It may look to you like a table with a thin top and a large fringe hanging down all round, but that fringe is hiding the fact that the table is really a box. In that box is the dog, and as I complete the quick building of the kennel so I release a hidden catch and the dog is then able to push up a trapdoor in the top of the table.

The dog is now standing *inside* the house but, like the rest of us, it likes applause, so it pushes open the door to the house, steps out and, because it is a dog, the applause is inevitably louder than for a human!

Part Four
THE ESCAPOLOGIST EXTRAORDINARY

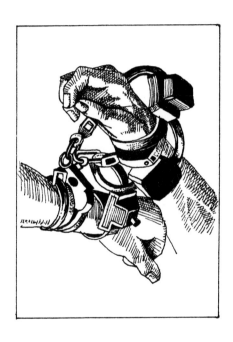

The Bank Safe

It is a great pleasure for me to be here at the Euston Palace of Varieties in King's Cross, London, especially as a well-known firm of safemakers is nearby and has challenged me to escape from their newest and largest safe.

I have examined it thoroughly and so heavy is it that special supports have been built under the stage to prevent the stage collapsing! I am wearing a dressing-gown and a bathing costume, and I must explain that this undertaking is of a dangerous character and might fail. You will realize that a man cannot breathe for long inside a safe.

I will remove my dressing-gown, and before getting into the safe I will be examined by a doctor, and a member of the public shall act as umpire. I would like the doctor to thoroughly search me, and perhaps the umpire will examine the inside of the safe.

And, now that is done, may I thank both you gentlemen, shake you by the hand and as you return to your seats I will enter the safe and be locked in by various other members of the public who will kindly remain on stage. A large screen will be placed in front of the safe and if you hear a series of knocks, you will know that it is a distress signal and that I wish to be released, for I am not sure if I can conquer this particular problem.

The Secret

I know perfectly well I can conquer this particular problem because the safemakers themselves had asked me to examine the safe carefully and I had done so the night before. I had also carefully examined the new springs, which were so strong that I at once decided to replace them with springs of my own.

There had been one complication for me. I had agreed to just wear a swim-suit and there was nowhere to hide the fake key needed for the new and altered locking arrangements that must be opened by me on the *inside*.

You will remember that I shook hands with the kind doctor and the umpire. The doctor was a doctor but it almost goes without saying that the umpire was one of my staff and as I shook hands I collected the fake key. I then climbed in quickly before anyone noticed I had the key.

I realized the audience would expect me to take a long time over this escape, but I hadn't worked at a locksmith's shop when a kid for nothing! So when I had escaped in four minutes flat, I felt it best to sit on the floor behind the screen and read a magazine for about twenty minutes and only then step from behind the screen and collect my applause from an audience that was by now semi-hysterical with worry.

The safe was returned the next day – with the springs replaced.

The Spanish Maiden

You all know of the Spanish Inquisition and recoil from the idea of it with a shudder. Ladies and gentlemen, here is a reproduction of one of its worst instruments of torture – the Spanish Maiden – except that the spikes inside cannot pierce me, but they do prevent me from moving freely.

Both the box proper and the cover (or front) are shaped roughly like the human body and the front is painted to resemble a maiden. When I have stepped into it, I cannot move, and the three padlocks outside that are attached to the three iron bands round the body make escape impossible for me. And yet I *will* escape!

The Secret

You can put twenty padlocks down the side of the Spanish Maiden, for it opens secretly at the *other* side, at the hinges, and it is the padlocked side that becomes the hinge!

Once I'm locked in I have just enough room to hold two of the spikes and lift them up and down several times, thus easing the trick hinges. The pin in each hinge is cut like a ratchet on one side, and two springs are inside the tube of the hinge. They hold the ratchet pin in position, but now that I have eased the hinges I can remove the two springs and open the front of the Maiden, and escape.

Here is the guarantee that the secret cannot be discovered; when the box is open, those pins cannot be removed from the hinges. It is only when I am *inside* that I am able to remove them!

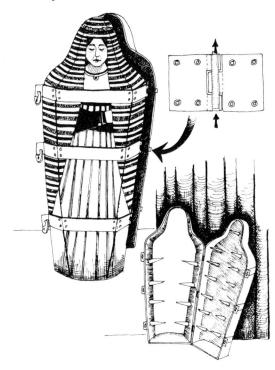

The Mail-Bag Escape

My assistants will now lock me into this leather mail-bag. This will be done by the steel bar being threaded through the top. At each end of this bar several padlocks will be attached, and you may use your own padlocks because nothing can contain The Great Houdini. Yes, you may fix them and lock them yourselves.

My assistants will put a screen in front of me and I will perform the Mail-Bag Escape!

The Secret

The reason why I invite one and all to fasten their own padlocks on the bar that is threaded through the top of the bag, is because the secret of this escape lies elsewhere.

The padlocks are of no concern to me except that once I have been locked in the bag I hold tight (through the bag's leather) to the groups of padlocks at each end of the bar.

I then sharply twist my right hand one way and my left hand the other – and thus unscrew the incredibly strong secret screw in the bar itself. Once it is unscrewed, I break the bar in half, climb out of the bag and screw it together again. The construction of the bar is so perfect, it is virtually impossible to find the joint.

But I never leave anything to chance when you, my public, are examining my escape methods, so, I'll let you into a further Houdini secret: when I put this mail-bag equipment on display, I use a duplicate bar of solid construction. Although the joint is finer than a lady's hair, it's better to be safe than sorry.

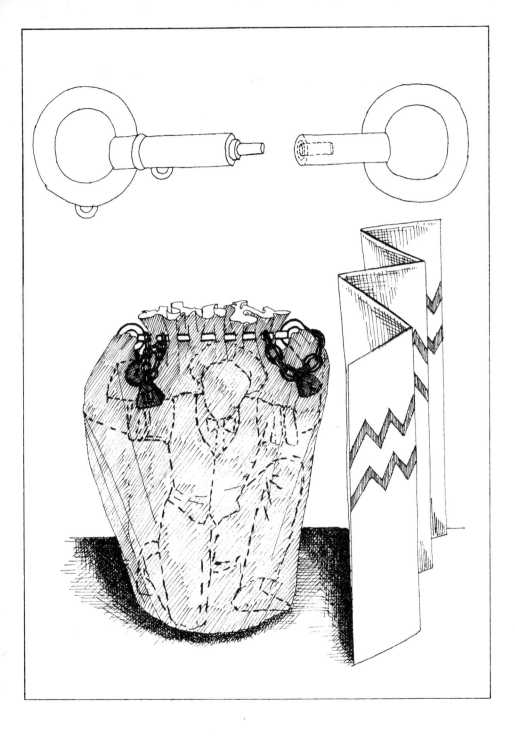

The Milk-Can Challenge

★☆★☆★☆★☆

Here is an escape that has remained popular for many years, probably because none of you can discover its secret!

You will appreciate that I have to wear a bathing costume because once my assistants have filled this milk-can with water I will then get into it. Many of you will have carefully examined this can and inspected all its padlocks and rivets.

Once I have crouched down in the water, which is now overflowing, my assistants screw the lid on the can and members of the public may themselves lock the many padlocks that are used to prevent my forcing open the lid. But do it quickly or I shall drown! I have to escape in record time!

If you will allow my assistants to place the screen in front of the milk-can when I am securely locked into it, I will then endeavour to escape. It's a very small area to manipulate in, and I have to both unscrew the milk-can lid and undo some of the padlocks and free myself from the water – and as soon as possible or it will be death by drowning.

The Secret

The can is indeed a genuine milk-can and the locks are indeed impossible for me to unlock. As with any milk-can, the collar (into which is screwed the lid) is riveted to the rest of the can. This milk-can will stand up to the closest possible scrutiny before I escape from it. The locks cannot be opened, nor can the screw on the lid.

But from inside, and only from inside, it is possible to force out the trick rivets. This then means that all I have to do is to force upwards the top quarter of the milk-can – that is the lid, the collar and the many locks.

Once I am out, I push back the false rivets, which click into place and remain that way until someone else climbs *inside* and pushes them out. But apart from me, who would ever do that?

Walled in Alive

Ladies and gentlemen, so great has been the success of my feat entitled 'Walking through a brick wall' that I am tempted to show it to you again on this, my second visit to your theatre within six months! But I must not submit to temptation and so I offer you this brand-new escape entitled Walled in Alive.

The same masons I met on my last visit are now building four walls of stone – to make a change from brick – and the four walls form an enclosed area, as you see. It is like a room with no ceiling.

I now climb into this area and, in spite of the fact that stone is stronger than brick, I will soon escape and be amongst you again. You will appreciate that I cannot remove a stone from the wall, nor push one *out* from the wall, or the entire edifice will collapse on top of me.

If my assistants will place a screen against one of the walls – any wall will do – I will then make my escape. I thank you.

The Secret

I cannot climb over the top, as the audience will see me. I cannot wriggle underneath, as the wall has been set into a concrete base. It is no exaggeration to say that I am 'walled in alive'.

The first escape secret is that my assistants, although pretending to let the audience command which wall the screen shall be placed in front of, have in fact placed the screen against one particular wall – indeed against one particular stone. When the genuine masons were building the wall they were 'helped' by my assistants who during the building handed yet another heavy stone to be put in place. This particular stone is in fact hollow, with secret doors at each end, though for the moment it is weighted down with another stone inside it to fool the masons.

Once the screen is in place and hiding me and the walls, I open the secret door to the fake stone, remove the heavy real stone, wriggle through the hollow stone, fasten the secret door at the outer side and step forward to take my bow.

I am quite happy if the public ask to inspect the four walls, because the false stone's panel can only be opened from the inside.

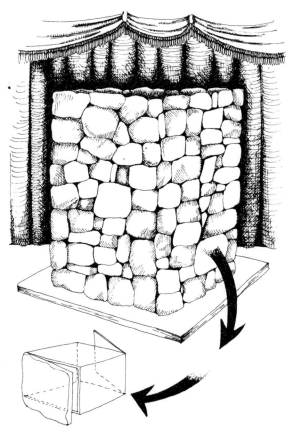

Metamorphosis

This trunk here is the illusion I acquired in 1892. The Victorian magician Maskelyne made it in 1865 in London, and called it a substitution trunk. I call the illusion 'Metamorphosis' and I'll tell you why.

Let my assistant and I show you the trunk is empty. She now puts a sack into the trunk. She locks handcuffs on to my wrists, and helps me into the sack that is in the trunk. She pulls the sack over my head and knots the rope at the opening of the sack, so that I am inside the tied sack. I crouch down inside the trunk and she slams the lid down on top of me, locks it and will then hand you the keys.

As you see, she now stands on the trunk, pulls up a large curtain and with it hides the trunk and herself from your sight, except for her head. She counts one, two, three and lifts the curtain above her head. She lowers it again – but it isn't she that lowers it again, it is me! I have escaped from the tied sack, the patent handcuffs and the locked trunk! And where has my assistant gone?

I will show you, if you will unlock the trunk with the keys you hold. Now undo the knotted rope – as you see she has tied herself up with my knots – and she is stepping from the trunk – and she is handcuffed!

So now please, use these other keys you hold and unlock the handcuffs and set her free. She has changed places with me, so it has been a 'metamorphosis', hasn't it? But how has it happened? And how has it happened so incredibly quickly?

Bess and Harry Houdini present their version of 'Metamorphosis'

The Secret

I'd better explain at once that the sack and the handcuffs are what we magicians call 'dressing'. I'm sorry to disappoint you, but the sack has no bottom to it – it takes one second to slip it on or off one's head, and it doesn't matter how many knots are in the rope at the top.

I blush to tell you that the handcuffs are the simplest pair possible, in fact you can buy them from a toyshop. It is the trunk we must concentrate on.

Let's examine the lid, because how did my assistant and I lock it so quickly? We didn't. Part of the lid is a trapdoor that opens inwards. As she counts up to three and stands on the solid part of the lid, so I've undone the toy handcuffs, pulled the sack off over my head and unlocked the trapdoor in the lid.

As I step out and stand on the lid, so she steps in, clicks the toy handcuffs on, pulls the sack over her head, crouches down into the trunk and fastens the trapdoor. It takes us no time at all – in fact as she fastens the trapdoor so I lower the curtain. Then I ask you where she has gone, and will you please unlock the locks on the seemingly solid lid of the trunk.

It is usual to tie the trunk securely with rope, for, as the trapdoor opens inwards, the rope doesn't bother us at all!

Escape From a Block of Ice

I have performed many illusions from the East for you, so let me now perform one that is inspired by the North Pole. Instead of being locked in an Oriental casket, I am to be imprisoned in a block of ice.

I will be handcuffed and locked into a thick iron cylinder, from which it will be almost impossible to escape. You have been allowed to examine it carefully and will agree. But what will make this escape *utterly* impossible is the huge block of ice, hollowed at the centre, that will be lowered over the iron cylinder. As you see, there is the block of ice hanging above the cylinder and its weight is such that no man could lift it and escape from under it – and yet The Great Houdini will!

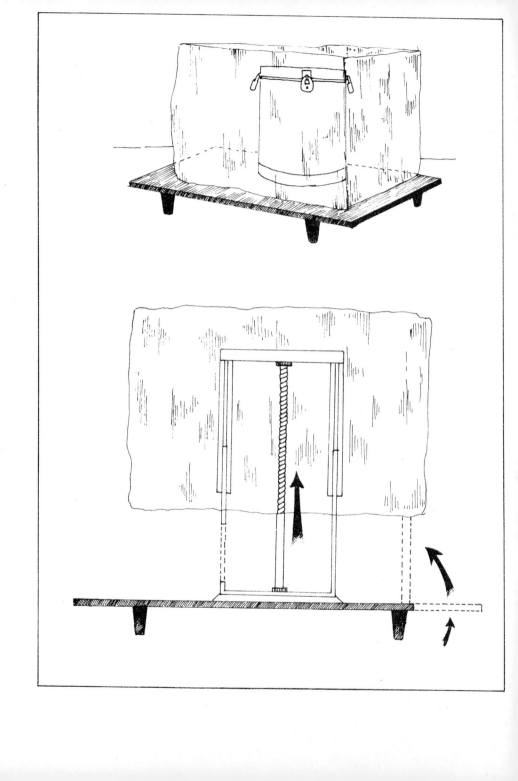

The Secret

The ice is there for a reason. It is to take your attention away from the thick iron cylinder which is in fact three separate thin cylinders, one inside the other. In the side of the second cylinder is a hole large enough for me to escape through – though this hole is hidden by the first and third cylinders.

Only the second cylinder has a bottom to it, the other two are therefore easy to lift up. They have bolts through to prevent anyone else getting this idea of lifting the outer cylinder, but when inside, I can knock out the bolts, lift the first and third cylinders, and escape through the hole in the second one – into what? Into the inside of the block of ice! Of course, you my audience sees none of this, because at the beginning of the illusion my assistants placed a screen around the block of ice.

Before I step into the cylinder, much is made of how cold the ice will be and therefore I can convincingly wear some suitable heavy clothing. This clothing is suitable for another reason; in it is hidden a jack. I must now put the portable jack on the floor of the cylinder and use it to escape from both the cylinder and the ice block.

I have now managed to jack the block of ice up two feet, and escape from the two-foot-high hole in the iron cylinder and crawl out from under the ice block.

But how do I lower the ice again and remove the jack? When the public examine the equipment, they mustn't find a clue of any sort.

Well, the platform on which the cylinders and ice stand has two fake ends. They are removed and used as props under the ice block. Thus the jack can be removed from inside the cylinder and, when clear of the ice, I knock away the two props and replace them at the end of the platform.

I again conceal the jack in my winter clothing, and I invite you to inspect the ice block – and the cylinder, if you can get to it!

The Paper Bag Escape

Ladies and gentlemen, enough of my escaping from steel boxes and wooden crates. This evening I am going to escape from a paper bag. Okay, so I knew you would laugh, but can you escape from a large paper bag *without tearing or destroying the paper?*

No, I won't be able to use a duplicate bag because I'm going to ask you, the members of my audience, to sign your autographs all over it.

I will now be handcuffed, and enter the bag feet first. One of you will please seal down the gummed flap of this six-foot-high paper bag. My assistant will then place a screen in front of me, and I will escape – and the bag you will find to be undamaged, not a tear or a cut anywhere on it. So how have I escaped so neatly?

The Secret

I always like to allow my public to inspect the object I am going to escape from and, though measuring six foot square, this bag is a perfectly straightforward paper bag. Escaping from the handcuffs is easy for me, but how do I escape from the bag, and how is it that there is no cut or tear on it?

The answer is in my shirt. There I have a secret pocket containing a razor. I cut along the gummed flap and escape. I then cut an exact line right across the top of the bag, thus making the bag smaller by about two inches.

I take a tube of quick-drying glue from another secret pocket, glue the new flap down in the identical way the other was glued, and once the glue has dried I am ready to step away – free!

Nobody had thought to measure the length of the six-foot paper bag – it now measures 5 feet 10 inches. But I am quite happy to work in such a space – I am 5 feet 3 inches!

Part Five
THE GREAT ILLUSIONIST
★☆★☆★☆★☆

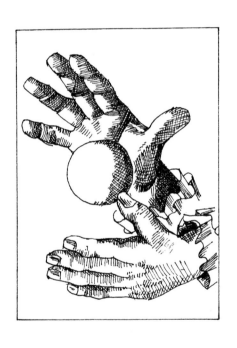

Sawing a Woman in Half

★☆★☆★☆★☆

Ladies and gentlemen, my two assistants are each holding several wooden panels and these men will now piece the panels together on that table, and construct an empty wooden box out of them. There it is, an empty wooden box about five feet long, and with the lid open.

My girl assistant steps into the box, and you will see that at one end of the box there is a hole for her head. She puts her head through the hole, so. At the other end of the box she puts her feet through another hole. She is waving to you with her head and her feet, and my second assistant is closing the lid of the box.

The third assistant brings me a large saw. He and I find the rough centre of the box and we are soon sawing the box in half – and yes, we are sawing the woman in half too!

You noticed that the box was empty. In fact, you saw this very simple box actually being constructed, but, even so, in

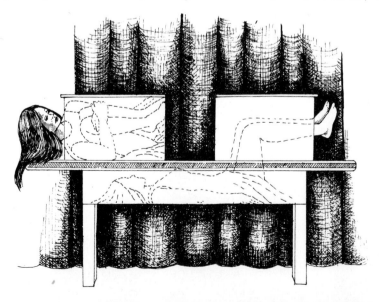

case you think there could be some skulduggery, my two male assistants will now actually pull the two halves of the box apart.

There we are – all the fresh air you could wish between the two halves of the box. The woman in the box is cut in half and see, she waves her head at her feet and they wave back, although they have parted company.

My men assistants will now move the two halves close together again and my girl assistant will soon step out of the box quite intact. She seems none the worse for her adventure, except she now has a split personality!

The Secret

The secret is that there are really *two* secrets. The innocent-looking table you are watching seems to have the usual narrow top but if you look closely at it you will see a thin line painted round it in a bright colour. Your eyes concentrated on that thin line and so did not notice the rest of the table's thickness which, in fact, is the thickness of a girl's body! Which brings me to the other secret. In the table itself is hidden a *second girl* who, once the box is constructed on the table, will lift her legs up through a panel in the bottom of the box and push her feet through the hole at one end of the box. When the two halves of the box are moved apart, her half will not be moved much, just slid about on the table top. And all the while she will thus be able to wiggle her feet.

The other half of the sawn box contains the entire other girl, the one who you saw stepping into the box in the first place, and she has drawn up her legs to squeeze into the smallest area possible. So *her* half can be moved about anywhere, taken any distance away from the other half of the box.

You were mystified as to how her feet were able to wave to the separated top half of her body, weren't you? Now you know – because they *weren't* her feet!

119

The Sword Cabinet

Let me open the door of this cabinet that stands on four legs, and reveal a girl sitting inside. I now close the doors. I push three swords through one side of the cabinet, three swords through the other side of the cabinet, and a further sword down through the top of the cabinet. This is sadism, for the girl must surely be pierced by the swords. In fact, what *has* happened to her?

I open the doors. There are all the swords thrust across the inside of the cabinet. As for the girl, she has vanished! Now I quickly close the doors, remove all the swords, open the doors again – and there she is once more. She has reappeared!

The Secret

Well, what did happen to the girl? She couldn't escape because the cabinet stood on four legs and the cabinet was nowhere near any escape route – it wasn't standing close to any curtains or scenery or a trapdoor in the floor.

The answer is that the girl has remained in the cabinet. The moment I close the doors, she slides two mirrors across in front of her to hide her. They meet at right angles, and so that you will not see that angle, the sword I pushed through the cabinet roof has come down directly in front of it.

The mirrors are now reflecting the side walls of the cabinet, which you think is the *back* wall.

It is easy for me to slide the various swords into the cabinet, in front of the two mirrors, so that when I open the doors you will see all the swords and – you think – the back wall of the cabinet. The moment I have removed the swords, the girl has pushed aside the two mirrors that hide her, and there she is, again in view!

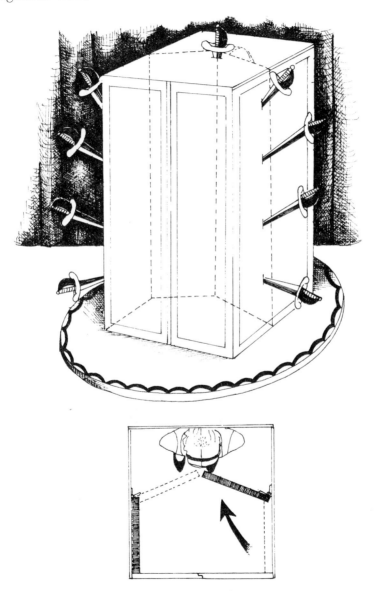

The Instant Vanish

You've all heard of the famous Chinese wizard Chung Ling Soo
– it was he who gave me this incredible Instant Vanish illusion.

My assistant is being placed on that board and also being
strapped to it. She will now be taken away to the tent over
there, which has three curtained sides to it and an open front.

You are now looking at a girl strapped to a board that is
being fitted on to a frame in the curtained tent and, so that
you can clearly see her, the board is tilted towards you. I now
fire a shot from the gun and as the smoke clears away the board
falls to the floor.

You can see that the straps are still there, though now undone.
But where is the girl? She has instantly escaped from the straps,
and also, she has vanished.

The Secret

This is as cunning and confusing as Chung Ling Soo's name,
which is really Billy Robinson. As I fired the gun, you were
distracted. You didn't quite notice the girl drop a *second* board
(which was secretly attached to the underside of *her* board) on
to the ground.

This second, duplicate board had the straps undone, for the
simple reason they had never been fastened in the first place.
This second board is a neat red herring.

At the same time as she allowed the identical board to fall to
the ground, so she twisted her own board round and it is now
almost upside down. It is at an angle. On the back of her board
is a full-scale mirror which is now reflecting the ceiling of the
tent.

The ceiling is made of the same material as the walls and therefore the board that the girl had been strapped on to now *appears* to be merely a frame through which we can see the back wall that is also curtained. But as I say, we are really seeing a reflection of the ceiling of the tent.

The Three Swords Suspension

★☆★☆★☆★☆

Behold, this Arabian wooden base has three scimitars fixed into it, at right angles, their sharp blades pointing upwards towards the sky. An Arabian-looking girl approaches. I ask her if she is willing to be hypnotized and, being told yes, I place her under a hypnotic spell.

Now she is in this trance, I hold her horizontally and place her body on the points of the three scimitars. I move away. Amazingly, she remains balanced on the three swords.

But the illusion is only beginning, for I remove the scimitar that supports the centre of her body. It seems incredible that she can be balanced on only two scimitars – except that now I also remove the scimitar supporting her feet! She indeed must be under a spell, for there is nothing to support her floating body except the remaining scimitar whose point is at her neck!

Let me lift her from her position, stand her up, snap my fingers in front of her eyes. See, she has come out of her trance. Finally, allow me to remove the three scimitars from their wooden base so that you may examine them. They are three genuine Arabian swords. There is no trickery to them, is there? Hypnosis is certainly powerful.

The Secret

Being an intelligent person, you will know that the hypnosis is a bit of Arabian fantasy that my assistant and I work; neither she nor I know anything about hypnosis although my publicity agent will tell you that we do.

You are still holding those three swords and close examination doesn't reveal anything, does it? Now have a look at the wooden base into which the three scimitars were fixed. You are right, there is nothing there either. So how is this incredible illusion done?

No wonder my assistant finds it easy to go rigid when she is 'hypnotized'; she is rigid when she joins us at the start of the illusion, for under her flowing Arabian costume is a tough steel and leather harness strapped round her shoulders. There is a slot in the extremely strong steel.

When the end scimitar – for this is the only one we need concern ourselves with – is fixed securely upright, I lower the girl towards it and make sure the slot in her steel and leather harness slides onto the pointed end of the similarly strong scimitar.

So strong is the steel that only a few inches are needed to slide on to the point of the scimitar; these few inches are sufficient, as long as she remembers to stiffen the rest of her body below the harness. Not a difficult task for a young girl such as she.

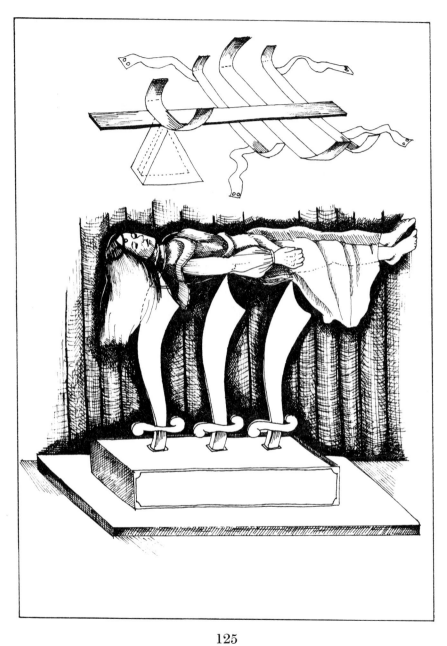

Walking Through a Brick Wall

Ladies and gentlemen, this amazing feat is not my own origination; however I am the one to have introduced it to the American stage. This sensational mystery has already begun, for as you see, the curtains are opening to reveal two men, genuine masons from Davey & Thompson, the builders directly opposite the theatre, building a solid brick wall on the stage.

For this, ladies and gentlemen, is the mystery of how a man can walk through a brick wall – and a genuine brick wall at that. The wall has been built on a solid iron platform to enable it to be moved about the stage, for I have other illusions to follow and we can't have a brick wall centre stage for the whole of the evening!

The gentlemen you see up on the stage are watching the final building of the wall. They are members of the public and, as I can see that you recognize them and know they are local tradespeople, I need not insult you by suggesting they are my accomplices. They are permitted to watch the wall from every angle and indeed they are doing just that.

The iron platform stands on not one, but two thick carpets and three gentlemen will stand on one side of the wall and three the other side on the carpets, thus making the use of any trapdoor on the stage impossible. My assistants now place a screen round one side of the wall, and another at the other side, and I will walk directly through the wall from one side to the other.

I step behind this screen here, call out 'I am going' and after a pause I will shout 'Here I am', the moment I step out from behind the second screen, the one that is on the other side of the brick wall!

126

The Secret

Well, the secret cannot be in the brick wall or in the iron base, for both these have been made by local workpeople. And it can't be in the two carpets, because carpets do not stretch, especially when there are three men standing on them each side of the wall. So how do I get through the wall?

I don't. I get *under* the wall, and carpets *do* stretch. An assistant is under the stage. He releases a trapdoor, and yes, the carpeting (even two layers of it) will give enough (due to the weight of my body) to sag a little into the trapdoor area, enough to let me wriggle under the iron base, and therefore under the brick wall. When I come up the other side, the trapdoor is locked again, and I am ready to call out 'Here I am'. I have walked through a brick wall – at least that's what the newspapers all over town are announcing, I am pleased to say!

The Flight of Venus

Ladies and gentlemen, I have been planning this oriental illusion for many years. It is a useful part of my collection, as it can be performed anywhere, even out of doors. It needs no scenery or curtains.

You are watching these two Arabian gentlemen holding a sheet of plate glass between them, both facing the same way. I now introduce my assistant, and as you see, she reclines (in a brief oriental costume) on the plate glass.

I and another assistant hold up a large cloth in front of the girl and her two Arabian assistants, and please note that although this cloth is screening the girl it does not reach to the

127

floor. So, although I am about to make her vanish, she cannot reach the floor where there might have been a trapdoor through which she could have disappeared.

Now I will remove the cloth. Just as I said, she has vanished! All you see is the sheet of plate glass! But where has she vanished to? Where can she be?

The Secret

If I had said 'All you see is the sheet of plate glass *and the two assistants*' that might have given you a clue. These two assistants look tough customers, standing there firm as a rock. There deliberately hasn't been much time for you to examine them, but the foremost gentleman is in fact a hollow dummy, considerably larger than the girl, and for a good reason.

The moment the sheet is held up in front of her, she moves forward on the plate glass and, parting the folds in the back of the dummy's costume, she slides herself into the dummy, her tight-fitting oriental costume enabling her to enter the figure easily.

Very slowly, the two men exit. This slowness seems to the audience to be due to oriental dignity, but it is of course due to the fact that if she walked any faster, the girl could be in one hell of a mess and might fall over!

Escape in Mid-Air

★☆★☆★☆★☆

Ladies and gentlemen, here is my assistant. She will now step into this cage on this stand and draw the blinds inside the cage.

When the cage has been lifted up to a good height above the stage, she will put out her hand to straighten the front blinds in the cage and that will be the signal for me to fire a pistol. And then, the girl will vanish from the cage in mid-air!

The Secret

Well, you have just seen the illusion, and it *is* mystifying isn't it? Now, there must be a reason for my assistant to draw those blinds inside the cage, mustn't there?

The truth is that once she is in the cage she not only draws the blinds, but also (there being no floor to the cage) she very quickly lifts up a trapdoor into the stand below and climbs down into the stand and closes the trapdoor again. Then the cage is drawn up in the air.

Her 'hand', with which she is to straighten the curtain, is a dummy hand. And when a second rope is pulled the 'cage' collapses in mid-air, to prove that the girl has indeed vanished.

It's odd, but no one has noticed my other assistants wheeling off the uninteresting-looking stand that now has the girl in it. All eyes are on the cage swinging about in mid-air, that's why!

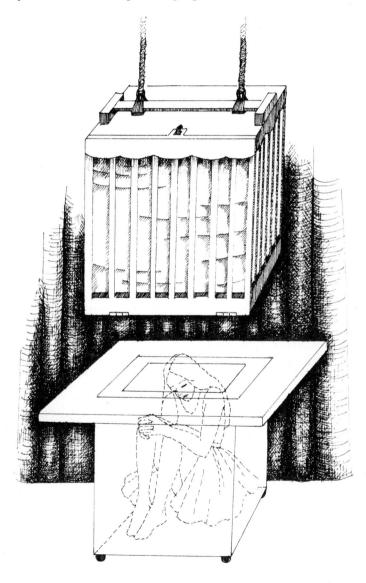

The Vanishing Automobile

Ladies and gentlemen, if the lady can vanish, and the bird-cage can vanish, why don't we try and vanish this automobile? As you see, it is nicely set off with curtains at the side and back, and I am going to get my two assistants to close these two big slatted doors in front of it.

There. The doors are closed but you can still see the automobile through the slats. Now I hold up this gun that was used for starting the Monte Carlo Rally, and I fire it at the automobile. Incredibly, the automobile suddenly disappears!

The Secret

All you can see now is the curtained area, without the automobile, because the auto has vanished. But in fact it only *seems* to have vanished and you only *seem* to see the empty curtained area!

Between the slats of the big doors there are of course equal spaces. When my two assistants pull cords that move large mirrors into those spaces then you are no longer seeing the car but seeing the mirrors. And those mirrors are reflecting the side curtains which are of the same material as the back curtains. So you think you are looking at the back curtains with no automobile, whereas you are seeing the reflection of the side curtains.

As you and everyone else gasp, so the car is being wheeled away to behind the back curtains, out of sight, and once this has happened, my assistants pull back the mirrors to their concealed places and then open the doors – and now the car not only *seems* to have gone, it *has* gone!

A Spirit Cabinet

Ladies and gentlemen, this eight-foot-high cabinet standing on the stage floor is an exact reproduction of one used by many famous spiritualists at their seances. From a cabinet such as this, spirit mediums cause articles to 'materialize'.

In this case, I am representing the medium and as you see I have been searched and tied up with ropes. I am now taken to the cabinet. All this cabinet consists of is four tough posts at each corner with curtains between that can open and close. It is like an old four-poster bed in shape. Outside the cabinet, surrounding it, are several members of the public watching closely.

I am placed inside the cabinet and roped heavily, yet the moment the curtains close manifestations begin! From inside the cabinet, you will hear a flute played, and a clarinet. Huge spirit hands and faces appear between chinks in the curtain and then – most sensational of all – large bunches of flowers are found filling the cabinet when the cabinet curtains are opened.

And once the manifestations are over, here I am still in the cabinet, securely roped. When members of the public search me and the cabinet, they find nothing!

The Secret

The first secret is that I am The Great Houdini and can free myself from trick knots by deep breathing. When the ropes are first tied round me, the deep breathing swells the size of my body so that, when I later relax, the ropes go slack and I can easily escape from them. So, with my hands freed, I am the manipulator of the 'manifestations'.

But if I am the one who manipulates the flute and clarinet and holds out the huge spirit hands and faces, where do all these objects 'materialize' from? There is nowhere to conceal these things in a cabinet that is made of curtains.

The second secret is that though the four stout posts at the corners rest on the floor and support the raised platform on

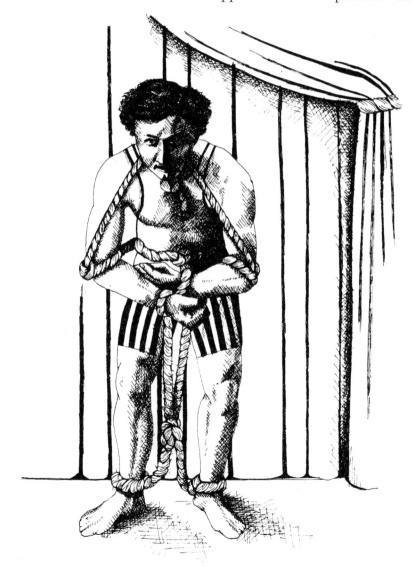

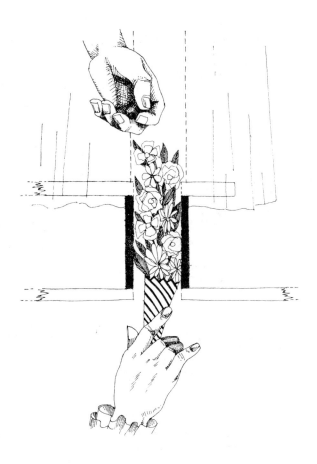

which I am standing, they are *not* in line with their bases.

As soon as the curtains are closed, I free myself from the ropes and I find that the inside core of one of the stout posts has been pulled down and away by my assistant, who is below the stage floor. So, one stout post is now hollow.

The third secret is in the fact that whereas the usual medium plays a trumpet, I can only play the flute and clarinet! This is because they are narrow musical instruments and can be pushed up from underneath the floor of the stage, through the hollow 'stout' post.

I play the flute and clarinet, I collect from the hollow post the rubber spook-mask balloons and blow them up and show them between the curtains, and, finally, many bunches of flowers are pushed up through the stout but hollow post and I place them around the cabinet floor.

I leave the flowers, but the rest I hand back through the hollow post when I have used them. And as I re-tie my ropes around me, a solid block is being pushed up through the floor and into the hollow post.

When I call out that the curtains can be opened, a close inspection still finds me roped and surrounded by dozens of bunches of flowers! Anyone inspecting even the particular post will find it solid. So much for spiritualism!

Crystal-Gazing Mysteries

★☆★☆★☆★☆

Ladies and gentlemen, as you know crystal-gazing has been done recently by magicians dressed in Hindu costume. The reason for this is twofold. The Hindu turban hides the ear-phones, and the Hindu shoes have metal plates on the soles, and the 'magician' stands on similar metal plates screwed into the stage.

These plates are wired to the side of the stage and thus 'crystal-gazing messages' can come to the magician from off-stage, via the metal plates and then up to the earphones hidden by his turban.

To stop this blatant though ingenious trickery, I am wearing an ordinary dinner-jacket. As for collecting the audiences' questions in sealed envelopes, I must reveal also that the velvet bags used for collecting and held by the magicians' assistants, had a double lining. Into one side of the bag were placed your questions in sealed envelopes, and in the other compartment were duplicate envelopes.

The *duplicate* envelopes were put on the burner, and the real messages were then taken off-stage in the now 'empty' velvet bags.

The off-stage assistants could read the messages from the audience and relay the replies of 'Yes' or 'No' either by talking into the earphones under the turban or by holding the messages up through a small trapdoor in the stage that is hidden behind the column that the crystal ball stands on.

But I am The Great Houdini and am proud to present the *new and truthful* Crystal Mystery! It will now begin!

My assistants will now collect messages from you and they will hold them in their hands and *not* put them in trick bags.

As you see, one of my assistants is even now handing several envelopes to me and I put them into this burner standing on this column where they will now be burnt. There, now they have all gone up in smoke. I would be grateful if you would just call out your name, not your question of course, and I will answer the secret questions that were in your sealed envelopes, by means of the crystal.

I will stand alone, with the crystal, in the *centre* of the stage, well clear of the columns and thus I must find the answers from genuinely gazing into the crystal. So please, call out your name!

Mr Dunbar? Forgive me for a moment while I gaze into the crystal. Your question is entering my mind . . . No, everything will be just as you hoped, there is no need for worry. . . . Could you call out your name louder, madam? Miss Tozer? Let me wait for the message . . . Ah. . . . The crystal says yes, you should marry him. . . .

The Secret

If the envelopes containing the messages have all been burnt, how can I answer the messages? The secret is that only some of the envelopes have been burnt.

When I hold them in my hand and drop them into the burner, I drop half of them into a shoot *behind* the burner. This shoot is in the back part of the column and it goes straightaway down to a hole in the floor, below which my assistant is ready to collect them.

Finally, if I stand centre stage and seem to be genuinely crystal-gazing, how can I give out the correct answers to your questions?

The answer is to be found . . . in the footlights. I don't gaze *into* the crystal, I gaze over it, and thus gaze onwards to the footlights. There I see a large magnifying glass and my assistant holds up your questions. The strong lights from the footlights nearby are quite sufficient for me to read your question and I can then give the answer 'Yes, Miss Tozer, you should marry him. . . .'

The Great Houdini dislikes bad crystal-gazing fakery. That does not mean that The Great Houdini dislikes *good* crystal-gazing fakery!

The Giant Ball of Wool

Here is an ordinary ball of wool. I unroll it and from the centre of it I take a ring – so. Now let us see this done on a human scale, let us take the *owner* of the ring herself from a ball of wool!

May I have the curtains opened please. Thank you. There on the trapeze you see a solid ball of heavy wool, about three feet in diameter. Through the ball is threaded the trapeze rod. The end of the wool is attached to that huge reel over there, and my assistant will start to do what I have just done – he will unroll the wool and reveal, not the ring, but the girl!

As the ball of wool is revolving fast, she must indeed be a dizzy blonde! But see, now the wool is nearly unwound, the ball of wool stops revolving and she pushes aside the remaining strands and emerges, jumps down on to the stage and receives her applause! How does she manage to survive being rolled round and round in a massive ball of wool?

The Secret

You have just seen the giant ball of wool revolve on the trapeze like a sphere. What you haven't seen is a second, inner sphere which remains still. Both spheres are attached to the trapeze rod, and both are attached to pivot rods.

The outer sphere is made of thin wire which is covered with the wool, and it revolves when the wool is unwound. But the inner sphere doesn't revolve at all. It is made of a metal framework with a platform at its base, and on this platform the lady sits until she is ready to come out from the ball and take her bow.

The Vanishing Horseman

Ladies and gentlemen, here we are at the circus and you will appreciate that the Big Top with a sawdust floor is not the best place for presenting an illusion!

At this spectacular moment I am riding a horse and wearing a bright blue uniform so that I stand out from the rest. There are several grooms wearing *red* uniforms and they are casually walking their horses round, watching me, the only one mounted on a horse.

When I shout 'Lights out!' all the lights in the circus will go out and then, when they are turned on again, I will have disappeared. There is no scenery, no trapdoor, no way for me to conceal myself – and yet I will now disappear!

The Secret

It's really very simple. You will notice that I am wearing a blue uniform, but it's not so that I can 'stand out from the rest'. My uniform is made of blue paper and the moment the lights go out I tear all the paper from me, jump off the horse and casually walk my horse round the arena like the rest of the grooms.

You see, under the blue paper uniform I have been wearing a red one similar to the grooms and I now *vanish into the crowd!* Before the illusion began you forgot to count how many grooms were walking their horses, didn't you? Well, there is one more now!

The Vanishing Elephant

It's circus time! Last week I was playing my magic show under the big top, this week I am at the Hippodrome, New York City. You will appreciate that the big top circus arena was on solid ground, so there was no way that a trapdoor in the sawdust floor could be used to make anything disappear. And here at the Hippodrome there's a *tank of water* below stage, so there is no trapdoor down there either!

And yet it isn't a dog that I am going to make disappear. Nor a gorilla. Nor yet a horse. Ladies and gentlemen, the incredible will now occur. Here it comes – and I will soon make it disappear – a *genuine African elephant!*

You are watching the big arena at the Hippodrome and in the middle of it is a high square roofless 'tent', three sides of which are brightly designed canvas, with the front side consisting of those magnificent canvas doors. They really are quite something, those canvas doors. So – we have a big bright-coloured tent with no roof, but three walls and a front of high double doors.

My assistant (dressed as a Hindu) guides the elephant into this tent-style area, several more Hindu-style assistants close the great doors at the front and – my, but they're *immediately* opening them again! It can't mean that the elephant has vanished already! The doors are opened wide and wonder of wonders, the elephant *has* already vanished! But how?

The Secret

You will notice I am dwelling a lot on the brightly coloured tent walls. The back wall is really a pair of hinged panels and when the elephant enters the tent area, he walks straight on through

140

those hinged doors because he knows there's a dandy meal waiting for him beyond.

So while the front canvas doors are closed, the elephant has walked straight on through the 'tent' and on out at the back. 'The back', where his meal waits, is a dull insignificant second tent – made insignificant because of all the big high brightly coloured walls of the bigger more splendid tent which does, as they say, dominate.

My Hindu-style attendants have now made a great show of opening the splendid canvas doors at the front – so that you won't look at the back, for that's where the elephant now is, as you know.

They open the doors wide and those big doors now occupy so wide an area that you don't notice the smaller and duller tent beyond at all, in fact you can't even see it. And now my assistants even *remove* the doors of the main tent and start to take them from the arena. They stagger with them, they make out this is a chore, that the trick is long since over and the elephant has most surely long since gone.

But they are in fact now each side of what we are calling the 'dull tent', screening it from your side view and *hiding the elephant* which is being led out and onwards to the actual grand exit of the huge Hippodrome arena.

The elephant has now gone. My assistants can relax all their staggering and just get on with gently taking down the rest of the main tent. So what if someone does now notice a bit of the insignificant dull tent's canvas? Maybe it's some sort of strengthening canvas, they will think. And maybe that same person will notice that the back wall of the tent had been two swinging panels? I reply 'Yes sir, you are right. But you still don't seem to be able to tell me one thing. How did The Great Houdini make that massive elephant *vanish*?'

That wise guy still doesn't know to this day. But you do, 'cos I've just told you. Make 'em watch those glamorous brightly coloured front doors!

142

Levitation

Allow me to present to you perhaps the most eerie illusion of them all, invented by Maskelyne the English magician of Victorian times. Because the illusion is oriental in style, I have an attractive oriental curtain to work in front of.

On a long table or couch (anything will do, you are quite welcome to inspect it), my assistant lies down. Over her I place a beautiful fringed cloth which covers her body, though not her head and feet. I make mystic passes over her, and, incredibly, her body levitates. It actually floats in the air!

You will say there must be a thin rod lifting her up from the couch or table, but you have already inspected the couch and it is not so. Alright, you say there is a horizontal lever to levitate her from behind? Let me now destroy that theory also!

For here is the solid hoop which you have already inspected, it has no break in it, it is genuinely solid. I now pass it over the girl's body while it floats in mid air. The hoop would have hit any lever, so how have I levitated the girl – unless you now feel you do have to believe in magic? For how else can we summon up the power to levitate her?

The Secret

Well, I do need the oriental curtain. It hides the machinery that makes a lever rise up slowly. But if that lever is supporting her in mid air, how do I manage to pass the hoop *right along* her floating body? Why doesn't the hoop hit the lever?

Truth to tell, it does hit it. But as it touches it, I use the part of the hoop touching the lever as a sort of hinge. Keeping the hoop 'hinged' against the lever, I pass the hoop round and

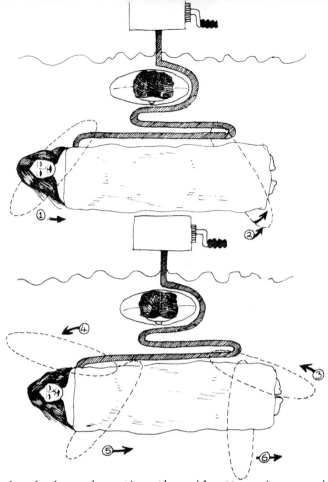

under her body and up the other side. Now the opposite side
of the hoop is made to touch the lever, and if you would care
to try it, you will see to your amazement – for it is amazing –
that the hoop can this time be carried *right across* her floating
body and made free.

The manipulation of the hoop is the cunning part of this
illusion. Yet this manipulation is quickly learnt and quickly
worked! What isn't so easy is the installation of the cumbersome
machinery behind the oriental curtain – but that isn't magic,
that's plain engineering!

PART TWO

The Detour
Of Addiction

2

The Soil

Mythology

For quite some time, I have been fascinated by mythology and myths. Some of these tales constitute a body of the finest spiritual literature and since the human spirit is ageless, their teachings are as relevant today as they were a thousand years ago. Myths are not factual accounts of historical events; they are stories that have been invented to help us understand ourselves and our world. Quite often, myths are attempts to clarify the great mysteries of existence. Perhaps their most important function, however, is to explain who we are, why we are the way we are and how we can deal with the problems we encounter on the journey of life.

Myths form a deep pool of wisdom from which we may draw. Since they deal with topics and concerns that are common to all people, these stories — whether they are called fables, legends or parables — can give us perspective on our problems and point the

13

way to solutions. Thus, good myths can instruct and guide us in our daily lives.

We are incomplete beings, but according to mythology, this has not always been the case. One ancient myth relates that when mankind first came into existence he was a complete being, totally self-contained and self-sufficient. Because he was whole, he was not lonely. He had no needs, no wants, no desires. Because he had no desires, wants or needs, he did not suffer. He lived in a state of bliss.

Seeing that this new being was so complete, the gods became concerned, fearing that if they left him thus, he would become a god also. Since they wanted no more gods, they took action. They split man in half. New man was no longer whole. He was separated, unfinished, incomplete. Now he was a limited being, an individual, an "I." He was alone and lonely. He began to have needs and desires.

He began to suffer. More than anything else, he wanted to be whole again. He longed for it continually. It was as if his deepest being was parched and dry, and he knew that only wholeness could quench his thirst.

Thus did the desire, or thirst, for wholeness come into being. And it became the most fundamental and important drive in humankind. Being an intelligent being, man surmised that since the desire for wholeness had come from separation it could only be satisfied through union. He realized that to live as a separated, incomplete "I" would leave him unfilled, needy, wanting, lonely and suffering.

So, driven by his suffering, he sought relationships with other "I's" and with the gods, knowing at some level that if he could form a union with them — a "we" — his needs would be met, his wants gratified, his loneliness and suffering ended. And so, seeking such unions became mankind's primary goal in life, the very essence of his journey.

The myth that I have just related is not singular. On the contrary, throughout history it has been told, with slight variations, in the creation stories of many cultures. If the myth is accurate, and I believe it is, the thirst for wholeness is the primary motivating force in our lives. It is experienced, according to Carl Jung, as "a secret unrest that gnaws at the roots of our being."[1] It moves us in the direction of others and gives rise to all sorts of relationships, from falling in love to forming groups. Lover and beloved unite, become a "we" and experience wholeness.

Groups supply the unity that the individual wants and needs. Some groups are social, some economic, others religious, still others political. Whatever their nature, the primary function of each is to provide a community that helps individuals in their quest for union by paving the way for relationships with others and with God.

Such relationships are found most easily in an environment that provides conditions in which the necessities of life are available to all and that is founded on the principles of unity, equality, freedom, singleness of purpose and respect for each individual.

Community

A viable community is a living, breathing, growing body that honors each of its members equally and helps them achieve their goals. Communities give their members the power that they, as individuals, do not have. But even as the community provides what each member needs, each member makes provision for the community. The two — member and community — are intimately inter-related and interdependent, as are the human body and its parts. Thus, when one suffers, so does the other; when one becomes ill, its illness affects the other.

Society is the term we use for larger groups of people who associate with one another in order to achieve common goals. Society is much like the human body. Our bodies consist of systems, such as the cardiovascular, respiratory and gastrointestinal. Society, too, contains systems, the major ones usually being economic, religious and political.

Each system in the human body influences the others, and this is just as true for society. If one system in the human body malfunctions, it affects the others in a negative way and the person becomes ill. The same is true of the social body. If the political system is ailing, it affects the economic system and the entire society is harmed.

Systems always interact, be they human or social. If the systems work together as they should, the body will be healthy. If they don't, the body will become ill.

In America, our political system is based on a group of precepts that emphasize the personal rights of each citizen and the proper relationship between government and governed. These principles stress the primacy of the individual, hold that all are born equal and have certain natural rights and maintain that government should always be controlled by the people.

It is interesting to note that ideas such as these represent the "overbeliefs" of our nation's founders, who clearly intended that these notions would play a dominant role in the life of this country.

Good societies today are based on and guided by the principles I have mentioned. Each has as its primary aim the provision of those conditions that protect each person's rights and that enable each to have food, clothing, shelter and the necessities of life. When such conditions are in place, each citizen then has the freedom to seek personal fulfillment. Knowing that such fulfillment is most likely to come about in situations of unity, these societies are "we" institutions, based on "we" principles and ideas.

The United States was founded on such ideas. Even its name speaks of unity. Its Constitution begins with the word "We," and the goals stated in this document give strong evidence that the primary focus of this nation was to help its citizens find fulfillment by setting up a scheme that would make the necessities of life readily available to all, thus freeing them to seek spiritual growth. The founding fathers of this country laid out a beautiful plan, but good plans, like good people, often go wrong.

Frequently societies depart from the fundamental notions on which they were based. Whenever this occurs, a close examination will reveal that this is caused by the failure of one or more of its systems to perform their tasks properly. For example, societies that were based on fine principles have been destroyed from within because their economic or political systems did not adhere to these principles. Many times the systems were acting in violation of the very precepts that formed the foundations of these societies. The lesson of history is that when the systems within societies do not function as they should, the societies sicken and sometimes die.

Reification

Why do systems so often deviate from their intended purpose? According to those who know, it happens because of a certain process which, in time, almost invariably comes about whenever people purposely bond together to meet common needs and goals. Scholars have discovered and described the dynamics of the process, which they call reification.

Simply put, reification occurs when an individual or group comes up with an idea and then creates systems in order to nurture, preserve, carry out and spread the idea to others. Then, with the passage of time, the systems become more interested in themselves than in the ideas they were formed to carry out. They begin to consider themselves more important than the group they're supposed to serve.

In this way, systems that were designed as servants of the people become their masters. Whenever this process occurs, the conditions that are conducive to the achievement of the needs and goals of the group members become limited or even cease to exist. Whenever reification takes place, the needs of people are not filled, their goals not achieved.

Bureaucracies

The end product of reification is the formation of bureaucracies. The major bureaucracies of our time are political, economic and religious. Unlike communities, which are living, breathing, caring bodies, bureaucracies are dead, uncaring "things" that take on an existence of their own, quite apart from the community they were originally designed to serve. Rather than helping community members, these agencies adopt an adversarial relationship with them. They institute myriad complicated, confusing regulations, couched in language they have invented.

This bureaucratic language is completely unintelligible to everyone but the employees of the agency or others who have been specially trained to understand it, as anyone who has ever tried to read an insurance policy or legal document knows.

As if this were not enough, bureaucracies insist that everyone live by their rules or suffer the consequences. Punishment for violating these rules is often harsh and heartless.

To keep people in line, all bureaucracies use threats. Religious bureaucracies tell people they will go to hell, economic ones threaten foreclosure or bad credit ratings and political agencies warn of tax audits. Bureaucracies keep extensive records and know everything about each person in whom they are interested. What's more, they share the information with other agencies to such an extent that individual privacy does not exist.

When people break the rules of any bureaucracy, they are marked for life. If you do not believe this, talk with an ex-convict, or someone who has filed for bankruptcy, or anyone who has been banished by a religion. If you do this, you will soon realize that bureaucracy reigns supreme in this country. And its primary interests are money, power and prestige — not people.

What is important about this from our perspective is that bureaucracy's uncaring, unfeeling, unresponsive, antagonistic attitude can have a disastrous effect on people and on society. How? It's simple. Whenever people feel that their essential needs are not being met and that they are at the mercy of powerful forces beyond their control, they will experience certain feelings, most commonly fear, frustration, impotence, and anger.

These emotions will in turn give rise to different forms of behavior. Some people will resign themselves to circumstances. Others will attempt to change the situation, either peacefully or violently. Still others will move to other societies.

The Detour

In addition to these people, another exceedingly large group tries another way. Unable or unwilling to accept, and despairing of change, they will choose paths that include substances or practices which appear to dull their pain and fill their needs. These paths, however, produce only the illusion of fulfillment, an illusion that is fleeting. Nevertheless, these paths are very powerful, precisely because they can create the illusion that all is well. These illusive and powerful paths are what I call "detours." Initially, each one is very pleasant, but in the end, they all are excruciatingly painful, often deadly.

At the present time, the primary detour in this country is addiction. Dramatically increasing numbers of people are being caught up in this problem. They are becoming addicted to anything or anyone that produces euphoria, for it is the euphoria that deludes them, that gives them the illusion that they have solved their problems, satisfied their deepest needs.

Addictions

There are many addictions, some involving compulsive behaviors, others the use of chemicals. No matter which of these is involved, the underlying dynamics are the same. Unfortunately this has led some people to believe that all addictions are equal and to say that "Addiction is addiction."

My experience has convinced me that such a perspective is not only shallow, inaccurate and misleading — it is very dangerous. I am persuaded that, although the dynamics of all addictions are the same, those that involve the use of mind-altering substances are by far the most perilous and deadly. Nonchemical addictions may poison the mind and emotions, but chemical ones poison the body as well. Make no mistake, addictions that involve the compulsive use of alcohol and other drugs, including tobacco, are the most directly lethal.

Addiction is rampant in America, and it is important to realize that it is not an epidemic. Epidemics are events that run their course and are over. Addiction has not followed this pattern. On the contrary, it has been and remains a continually burgeoning process in this nation. Although it may have ebbed and flowed, it has never gone away. Unlike many epidemic diseases, no cure has been found and in spite of heroic efforts, no uniformly effective methods of prevention have been discovered.

Thus, addiction continues its rampage. Why? The full answer is far beyond the scope of this book. In every single case of addiction that I know, including my own, one fact has always stood out: Something was terribly wrong with the body, mind and spirit of the addict. Could it be that, since addiction is running wild in America, something might be wrong with the body, mind and spirit of this country? I think so.

Lest some of you think I am being overly critical or harsh in the observations that follow, let me assure you I have done my utmost to avoid being so. It would be easy to fall into the trap of cynicism, or slip into negativism or slide into self-righteousness, and to be quite honest, I often find myself doing these very things, so I have made an effort to avoid these snares.

You see, I really love this country. I believe totally in the principles on which it is based and in the God from whom these precepts come. This society is very precious to me. My life is intricately entwined with it, my well-being as an individual is intimately affected by the well-being of this nation-community.

This being so, I have a living interest in the health of this country: If it becomes sick, its sickness affects me directly. Therefore, it is both my right and my responsibility to be aware of, and point out those symptoms that say it is ailing and to suggest some possible remedies.

This country has the resources and capacity to provide every one of its citizens with an abundance of those things that are necessary to sustain and enhance life, but it is not doing so. As a matter of fact, millions of citizens, many of them children, are without even the barest necessities of life, are hungry, sick, barely clothed and homeless.

To me, this indicates that this country is not adhering to its basic principles, for if it were, such intolerable situations would not exist. The very fact that they do exist is evidence that our society is not functioning as it should. In fact, such situations are obvious symptoms that America is not well.

At present, our nation reminds me of a huge, troubled family, blindly tip-toeing around in a world of make-believe, avoiding reality at all costs. Sometimes when I look at what we are doing and why we are doing it, I cannot help but wonder if we have not become completely insane. With regard to its behavior, this country could be described with a phrase from the book *Alcoholics Anonymous* as "an extreme example of self-will run riot."[2]

Not a few people have said that America is an addictive society that reacts to its problems — especially its addictions — in the way an addict would, trying to solve the problems of today with the same old worn-out methods which failed in the past.

Why is our nation sick? Opinions vary widely, sometimes very widely. Certainly, I don't know all the reasons. However, I am convinced that one of the main causes is that reification has taken place. We have become a nation of bureaucracies, and it is painfully clear to me that many, perhaps most, of the political, economic and religious systems that were put into place to carry out the aims and values of our extended community have become more interested in themselves than in the people they are supposed to serve.

We are no longer a nation of shopkeepers and citizen representatives. We are a nation of huge conglomerates and professional politicians. Truly, the servants have become the masters.

How Do You Rate Today's Society?

If you have difficulty believing that the basic systems in our society have, for the most part, become reified, answer the following questions:

1. Of the three main systems in our country (economic, political and religious), do any of them seem more interested in themselves than in their customers, citizens or members?
2. When you have dealings with economic, political or religious agencies, are you confused by their language or methods?
3. Have you been threatened by any one of them?
4. Do you feel these systems are heartless?
5. Do you feel you have any control over them?
6. Are you frightened by some of them?
7. Do you think they care about you as a person?
8. Do you believe they adhere to the basic values and principles of this society?
9. Do you feel they are sometimes trying to hinder rather than to help you?

What are your answers?

In asking these questions I do not include *all* religious, political or economic agencies. There are still some honest, caring businesses, churches, synagogues and temples. Perhaps even some government agencies may continue to serve the people. Also, it is not my intent to give a litany of the shortcomings of our society. I asked the questions simply to stress that enough reification has already taken place that our nation is not functioning as it should and that many of its citizens are being hurt because of it.

How does this relate to addiction? It's simple. When any society becomes dominated by bureaucracy, it causes distress in the citizens. As a consequence, many seek relief through alcohol, drugs and destructive behaviors, and the more pervasive the reification the greater the number of citizens who will become addicted.

One of the most significant effects of the reification process is that it causes society to fragment, separating groups of people from one another. This fragmentation is most often based on economic status. There is a gap between the haves and the have nots in this country, and it is widening. There is no question that this widening economic gap has a tremendous impact on the rate of addiction, for as the gap widens, addiction increases.

The most interesting aspect of this is that addiction is not only increasing among the have-nots, but among the haves as well. This indicates very clearly that addiction is not based on economics, as some would have us believe, but on the isolation that occurs when society breaks down and communities disintegrate, thus frustrating the deepest need of all human beings — union with one another. Addiction is not a disease of poor whites and blacks that is confined to our slums and ghettos; spiritual disconnection, not economics, is the root of addiction.

If there ever was a country that wasn't functioning in a healthy manner, it is ours. And we are exhibiting a multitude of symptoms. To me, the two most significant signs of our country's illness are the rise in drug use and addiction and our response to it. When it comes to drug use and addiction, our culture is as deluded as any addict. All addicts have a drug of choice, and they protect that drug and those who supply it. So does our society, and its drug of choice is alcohol. If there is a sacred drug in our nation, it is alcohol, and the system protects both the drug and those who supply it.

The addict blames his addiction on someone or something else. So does our country. As a matter of fact, if you believe our political leaders, the root of the cocaine problem can be found in several small countries in South America. The addict's major tool of delusion is denial. Not surprisingly, it is also used by our society. And it is when we examine the complexity of its denial, that the depth of its insanity in regards to drug use and addiction is revealed. An entire book could be written concerning our nation's denial, so I will not attempt to investigate it in detail. Rather, I will bring to your attention what I consider to be some of the outstanding symptoms.

Not Seeing The Forest For The Trees

Our society looks at addiction as if it were a modern disease or epidemic, but it is not. On the contrary, addiction has been with us for a long time. Yet the system treats it as if it were an acute problem rather than a chronic one. It fights one or two special drugs at a time, pretending that if it gains control over these, addiction will go away. Right now it is focusing on cocaine. In time, cocaine use will dwindle, but addiction will continue. Already other drugs are beginning to push cocaine out. Crystal methamphetamine is making a move, heroin is regaining popularity, and other more powerful drugs are yet to come.

If our society continues on its present course, it will choose a couple of drugs to fight, and when their popularity and use declines, the system will congratulate itself on beating them, when in truth its efforts have had little, if any, effect. While our society continues to fight each special drug, addiction will laugh for it knows that as long as we focus on a few chosen drugs, we will totally miss the process which gives rise to their use. By obsessively focusing on the drugs, which are the symptoms of addiction, we will miss the causes and conditions that make up the blood, bones and bowels of addiction.

Any addict who thinks his drugs are the sum total of his addiction is seriously deluded, and any society that believes drugs are the only causes of addiction is likewise deluded. Drugs come and go but addiction remains.

Perhaps the most revealing sign of our society's denial is the so-called war on drugs. Although this war is full to overflowing with denial, one aspect illustrates denial more clearly than any other: the war is being waged almost entirely against selected drugs, with the intention of eliminating them entirely.

Our society groups drugs into two categories, which I call "sanctified" and "unsanctified." Sanctified drugs are legal and produce a great deal of income for select members of our economic system. Among these drugs are alcohol, tobacco and prescription medications. Unsanctified drugs are not legal and produce a great deal of income for people who are not select members of our economic system. Among these drugs are cocaine, marijuana and heroin, to name a few.

Now consider the fact that the war is being waged almost entirely against unsanctified drugs. Massive efforts are being made to apprehend and punish those who produce and distribute them. However, no effort is being made to eliminate sanctified drugs or to apprehend and punish those who deal in them. This is denial of the grossest sort, for if we look closely, we will discover that far more people are addicted to sanctified drugs than to unsanctified ones.

In fact, more people are addicted to alcohol alone than to cocaine and all the other illegal drugs combined. In spite of this, we see no raids on the wineries, breweries and distilleries that produce alcoholic beverages, nor are those who produce and distribute them arrested or punished. Smoking kills and cripples thousands each year, yet tobacco crops aren't destroyed nor are those who produce and distribute tobacco products apprehended and punished.

As a matter of fact, it was only after intense pressure from the public that warnings were put on tobacco and alcohol products, and these are woefully inadequate as well as inaccurate. Am I suggesting that we wage war on alcohol and tobacco? No, for even if we did, it would have little or no impact on addiction.

Mind you, I'm not saying that cocaine and other illicit drugs do not exact a terrible toll because they do. I am saying that the war on drugs reveals starkly that our society has a double standard in regard to drugs. It protects, defends and even subsidizes its drugs of choice, the sanctified ones, while it attacks the illicit drugs, pretending that only these are dangerous and deadly, and acting as if they represented the totality of the drug problem. The practice of protecting the sanctified drugs while waging war against unsanctified ones represents an overt denial of the enormous toll taken by sanctified drugs.

The rapid rise in drug use and addiction, plus the evidence that shows that our society's response to both is not a healthy one, are strong indications that our country is sick. But even though our society is unhealthy, it does not and cannot cause addiction. In the very best of conditions many people would become addicted because they are biological or psychological "set-ups" for the illness.

Even as society does not cause addiction, neither can it eliminate it. What it can do is to reduce the magnitude of the problem by taking proper action. The war on drugs is not a solution. Like all violent wars, it is a farce, and no one ever really wins. It is based on delusion, it is failing now, and it will continue to fail.

What's more, it is a political and economic war, dealing only with external symptoms, while addiction has to do with internal causes, with the bodies, minds and spirits of human beings.

In my opinion, the only way to decrease addiction is to reduce the thirst for wholeness that causes people to detour into addiction in the first place. To do this, our country needs to wage a gentle, nonviolent spiritual war, the goal of which would be to assure that all members of society have the necessities of life, to offer healing to those who have been wounded by addiction and to recreate a healthy, unified community in which all who wish to do so can quench their spiritual thirst and find rest for their souls. The only weapon needed in this war would be love.

Is it possible for our society to wage such a war? In order to do it, our economic, political and religious systems would have to undergo a radical transformation and put into practice those principles on which this nation was founded. The problem is that systems, like individuals, have egos, and such a transformation can only come to pass when the ego is deflated.

Ego deflation occurs when a person or a society experiences and admits defeat, realizes the present course of action is futile and gives up. In other words, ego deflation occurs through hitting bottom and surrendering.

Although a number of people feel our society is close to hitting bottom, it hasn't done so yet. Even if it did, I doubt if the systems controlling it would admit defeat, much less surrender. So even though I believe it is possible for this country to wage a war of love, I do not think it is probable.

No less a person than Mother Teresa has said that the United States is the spiritually poorest nation in the world, and I think she is right. I am convinced that unless our economic, political and religious systems give up the lust for wealth, power and prestige and begin to treat people with the fairness, respect and concern they deserve, this spiritual poverty will worsen, and as it does, addiction will increase. In its present state, our country is providing fertile soil in which addiction can take root and flourish.

3

The Longing

Many people believe that anything spiritual deals with dark and mysterious forces that can only be understood by mystics, that spiritual beings are either angels or demons, that spirituality is "far-out," unreal, "twilight zone" stuff that is irrelevant to their daily lives or that it is just a bunch of religious hocus-pocus, full of magic and chanting and totally unintelligible to all but a select few.

Those who believe this are confused and they are wrong. The spiritual is natural, real and practical. It is based totally on common sense, not magic; is not the property of any religious group; is absolutely central to daily living; is the very essence of our being and can be easily understood by anyone.

If the spiritual is so practical, down-to-earth and real, why are so many people so confused about it? One reason is that science and religion have muddied the waters. For the most part, science has dismissed the spiritual because, since it cannot be measured, it does not exist and is therefore meaningless.

Although in recent years new discoveries have caused many scientists to reconsider their position, science in general does not yet assign much importance to the spiritual. Since the scientific view has been in place for so long in our society, most of us have incorporated it into our thinking, even though we may not be aware we have done so.

Science And Religion

Even as science has discounted the spiritual, religion has embraced it. This has led many people to think that it belongs to religion and that they have to look to religion for clarification. This has created problems, for rather than clarifying matters, the various religions have, with their particular theologies, doctrines and dogmas, made it even more obscure. The net result of this mistreatment of the spiritual is that many people are very confused. How could it be otherwise?

I believe science and religion have both made a basic and serious error in dealing with the spiritual: they have tried to comprehend it intellectually. This is simply not possible, yet it seems part of our nature to attempt to grasp things intellectually, to have concrete proof and logical explanations. This need is one of our magnificent attributes, but so is humility, and when our intellect drives us to comprehend the incomprehensible, to name the unnameable and to explain the unexplainable, we must eventually have the humility to admit that we cannot.

In fact, it is the effort to understand with the intellect that makes the spiritual seem dark, unreal, obscure. The spiritual deals with the heart, not the head, with wisdom, not knowledge, with the unseen, not the visible. Just because we cannot intellectually grasp the spiritual does not mean we cannot comprehend it at all, for there is more to our minds than just intellect. The cerebral cortex of our brains is fantastic, but it is not the sum total of our minds.

Time and time again over the years, one fact has become abundantly clear to me: the spiritual cannot be fully understood intellectually. I have tried and failed, so have others. Why? Basically, the intellect is governed by logic, but the spiritual often transcends logic.

For example, the language of the intellect is direct, precise and logical, but spiritual language can be indirect, imprecise and illogical. Spiritual truth is most often transmitted through myths, parables, fables and stories that are full of paradox. A paradox is a statement that seems to be contradictory, illogical and even nonsensical, but is nevertheless true. Through the ages, spiritual teachers have made much use of paradox. Twelve-Step groups are noted for such paradoxes as, "You must surrender to win," or "You have to give it away to keep it." To the intellect, operating on logic, such statements seem senseless, even stupid. However, another part of our minds perceives the truth in them. The truth of a paradox is demonstrated through action, for when people put a paradox into operation in their lives, it turns out to be correct and its logic proves flawless. Ask addicts how they began their recovery, and they will probably tell you they surrendered. Some of them may even be wearing a T-shirt that proclaims, "The war is over. I surrendered. I won."

The Mind

The part of the mind that perceives spiritual truth exists along with the intellectual region. These two regions are seen in different ways and given different labels, such as higher and lower mind, left and right hemispheres or mind and heart. Regardless of the various names that are used, the significant thing is that we humans do have at least two parts to our minds and that these think, perceive and comprehend in different ways.

Whatever they are called, these two areas are intimately related to one another. They are the yin and yang (dark and light, female and male) zones of our mind. These two spheres are not antagonists. On the contrary, when the mind is functioning properly, they embrace and complement one another.

This does not mean they comprehend one another, for they are fundamentally different in many ways. The intellectual mind thinks, the spiritual mind knows; the intellectual sorts out and seeks differences, the spiritual brings together and focuses on similarities; the intellectual attempts to comprehend, the spiritual to observe and relate; the intellectual must have proof and can't abide doubt, the spiritual accepts the unproven and welcomes uncertainty; the intellectual is smart, the spiritual is wise.

It is my conviction that, even though the two realms are partners in the business of perceiving reality, they are not equals, for I believe the spiritual is superior. Without the intellectual (smart thinking) mind, we would be severely flawed, but without the spiritual (wise knowing) mind, we could not survive.

Spirituality And Religion

Although spirituality gives birth to all religions, it is not the same as religion. Yet many believe they are identical, and this belief precipitates all manner of conflict and confusion. The truth of the matter is that spirituality transcends religion. While it encompasses all religions, it is definitely not confined to any one of them.

To clarify the relationship of the two, let us suppose a group of people is sitting around a campfire, roasting marshmallows, lying to each other about how good they taste and looking at the fire.

Since they share a common goal, they make up a small community. Each person in the group would have a different view of the fire, and obviously no one could see all sides of it. In this example, each view of the fire would represent a particular religion, and the perspective of each would be partial and limited. All views taken together would represent spirituality and the perspective would be total and unlimited.

All too often religion causes groups to break up, whereas spirituality bonds them together. To illustrate, let's return to our group of marshmallow roasters. What if one member of the group insists that his own limited perception of the campfire — that is, his particular religion — is the only correct one, refuses to consider the others' points of view and even tells them they will burn in the fire if they don't see things his way?

You know as well as I that an argument would break out and the community would be divided and would eventually break up. The one member's closed-mindedness would have sabotaged the entire group. Unfortunately such tunnel vision is typical of most religions, and it has created division and separation and frustrated the need for unity and wholeness.

But how does the spiritual bond the group together? Suppose that everyone, no matter what their view (religion), respected the views of all the others and asked them to share their perspectives so that everyone would know more about the fire. As a result of such respect and sharing, there would be no argument, each person would know more about the fire and the community would be unified and preserved. Such open-mindedness is characteristic of spiritual groups.

One of the real strengths of 12-Step groups is that all members are not only allowed, but encouraged, to have their own view of the fire and to share it with the others. This is what "God as we understood Him" is all about, and it is one of the major elements that makes these groups spiritual rather than religious. It allows those from different religions and those who have no religion to live together in harmony, unites and preserves the community and smooths the way for pursuit of the common good.

In summary, the views of religion are limited; those of spirituality unlimited. Religion often precipitates separation; spirituality produces union. Spirituality transcends and includes all religions. The two are not the same.

In his conversations with Bill Moyers on public television, Joseph Campbell related a tale that sums up the difference between the religious and the spiritual. While in Japan at an international conference on religion, Campbell overheard an American social philosopher talking to a Japanese Shinto priest. The man told the priest how impressed he was with the Shinto ceremonies and shrines, but he said he was confused about their theology and asked for an explanation. The priest thought deeply, and then he said, "We don't have theology. We dance."[1]

So there it is. The spiritual life is a dance. Sometimes it is fast, sometimes slow. At times, it is joyful, at other times, sorrowful, but always it is a dance. Save for a few notable exceptions, religion doesn't dance. It seems to have forgotten how.

Organized Religion

I think it important to note that the characteristics I have been pointing out belong to what is known today as organized religion.

Organized religion is not, in my opinion, the true religion that was conceived, taught and practiced by the various founders. The founders thought, spoke and lived their religion in its purest form. If we study their lives, we will find in all cases that religion was to them a spiritual way of life that was practiced by individuals and groups who were bound together solely by common beliefs, values, concerns and goals.

In truly religious groups or communities, there was no interest in wealth, power or control; all members were equal, and the primary objective was to relate in love to one another, to neighbors and to God. Most organized religion does not fit this model, for it is held together by rules, has a definite hierarchy and seems to be primarily concerned with wealth, power, control and self-perpetuation. Organized religion is the result of reification. It is not an open community that is controlled by its members. It is a bureaucracy that is controlled by its hierarchy.

These comments are based on my own experience and are meant as observations, not indictments. Religion has some obvious shortcomings, but in spite of these, it provides guidance and help to many people. My sole intent is to make it as plain as possible that religion and spirituality, though related, are not identical because I believe that being confused about them can, and often does, severely hamper, or even preclude, recovery from addiction.

All too frequently those who suffer from addiction get the spiritual and the religious confused, and this confusion forms a tremendous barrier to the process of spiritual growth that is the very essence of recovery. It is my firm conviction, based on experience, that spiritual growth is not possible so long as the addict is bound up by a particular theology, trapped by dogma, or paralyzed by the shame that results from the hideous moral implications that too many religions continue to place on addiction.

In order to recover, addicts must be freed from such constraints, freed from old ideas, freed to believe as they choose to believe. When thus freed, the addict can make a fresh beginning, be reborn and resume the dance of life.

Children

If science discounts the spiritual as unprovable and unreal, and religion obscures its true nature and makes it complicated, how can we make it simple and real again? I believe the best way to learn about it and to perceive its reality is to turn our attention to the most spiritual beings on the face of the earth. I am speaking, of course, about little children. Nowhere is the thirst for wholeness, with its desire for relationships and union, more clearly visible than in these smallest of human beings.

More than anyone else, little children know how to dance, and they do so spontaneously and naturally. They are smart and seem to have been born with certain knowledge.

All little children are open and honest. They are who they are. There is no pretense, no mask, no front. If they like you, they'll say so and if they don't, they'll tell you that, too. Their love is unconditional, and if they love you, there is nothing you can do or say that will stop them from doing so. They may fear you, be angry with you, even dislike you, but they will not stop loving you. Small children are full of awe and wonder. To them, the world is a marvelous place, a giant playground in which to romp and run and learn. And learn they do, for they are curious. They are always asking questions, many of which their parents cannot answer. Daily they practice the art of playing, which is a fundamental spiritual activity — one of the very first to be practiced by any living being. As a result of their playing, children have what is called "fun," and when we think about it, we realize that fun is a spiritual experience. Through playing, children expand and enrich their relationships with others and the world.

Children feel connected to nature, embrace it, savor it and try to capture its essence. For example, have you ever watched children play with a rock? They may sit for hours, holding the rock, stroking it, peering at it, listening to it, dropping it, picking it up, smelling and tasting it, and so on. They become totally involved with the rock, and by the time they have finished playing with it, they know the rock. They will not be able to tell you the weight, dimensions or composition of the rock because such things are unimportant to them. Using their physical senses as tools, they have tapped into the very essence of the rock and have formed a spiritual union with it. To them, it is alive. They know it, have given it a name, and probably consider it a friend.

Little children's ability to form a spiritual union with nonliving things is fascinating. It is as if, through relating to these things in love, they actually breathe life into them.

I remember the teddy bear I got for my oldest daughter. Of course, being an active alcoholic, I purchased it for her on the day she was born. To me, the bear, which we named Ted, was a stuffed toy, made of nonliving material. But to my daughter Ted became a being with a soul, a boon companion to be loved, cuddled and plucked, a confidant with whom she could share her most intimate thoughts and feelings, her very closest friend.

My daughter is now in her early thirties. Many things have changed, but her relationship with Ted remains the same. The last time I visited her, I saw him, in his same honored place, leaning against the pillow on her bed. He was wearing his now-faded green sweater, and it was obvious that time and love had taken their toll. His fur had been plucked out over the years, and the stitches from several "operations" marred his nearly bare body, yet these imperfections gave him character. When my daughter picked him up from the pillow and held him, it was obvious that, in spite of time and wear, Ted was still a being with a soul, a companion to cuddle and love, a confidant and best friend.

Little children do not see rocks and bears and trees and flowers as things, nor do they see the world as a collection of unrelated objects. It is much more. It is all one piece, a living, breathing whole, of which they are a part. All is one. There is no separation. And all of it dances. Unfortunately, this changes when the educational, religious and economic bureaucracies lay hold of children and begin what is euphemistically called the socialization process.

I believe a more correct label for socialization would be spiritual disconnection, for the process divides, separates, isolates and even alienates individuals from one another, their world and their own deepest selves — the child within. But no matter how socialized or old or disillusioned or jaded or cynical or asleep we become, there remains in us a little child who wants to love and cuddle and play — and who knows how to dance. This child is spiritual, and in order to make spirituality simple and real, we must look through the eyes of the child. In order to do this, we must return to the time when we were children.

My Story

My childhood was not a storybook childhood, and neither, I suspect, was yours, for these are found only in storybooks. Some things happened to me as a child that had a negative impact on me and that most certainly played a part in my alcoholism. Perhaps your childhood was not a good one either. Maybe it was even terrible. Yet my experience has taught me that even in the worst possible situations children have good periods, those private, precious times during which they relate, reflect and dream.

Sadly, most of us remember the bad and forget the good. We can recall the wrongs done to us and those who did them in vivid detail, but we are unable to recollect very much that was positive or good. I did this for many years, and it provided me with the raw material for blaming everyone else for my problems. As my recovery has progressed and my acceptance of responsibility has made projection, rationalization and the other modes of dishonesty unnecessary, my attitude has changed, and this has allowed memories of the good times I had as a child to come flooding back.

In attempting to grasp the true nature of spirituality, it is these positive memories that have helped me most, and I have come to believe they can provide similar benefits to others. This being said, let me share some of my good memories with you, and, as I speak of my childhood, you may want to reflect on your own.

I was born in a small textile mill town in North Carolina. Most everything in town was owned by the big cotton mill where the majority of townspeople worked. It seemed to me that the mill owned them too.

The section of town in which I lived was neatly divided by railroad tracks. On one side of the tracks, all the houses were small and nearly identical, and the street that ran in front of them was unpaved. The mill workers lived on this side of the tracks. On the other side were larger houses, most of them having two stories, and the street in front of them was paved. These were the homes of the mill managers, the doctors and the lawyers.

My home was on the workers' side, and one of my earliest goals was to get across the tracks, to live in a big house, to have my own room, to be somebody.

Each of us seems to have at least one person in his or her life who is very special. Perhaps for you, it was a sister, brother or close friend. For me, it was my father. My father was a handsome man, tall and lean, with dark, wavy hair. He was also the kindest, gentlest, sweetest and best man I have ever known. He didn't talk a great deal, and he seldom verbalized his love for me, but he did not have to because the love exuded from him to me.

Just being with him was a spiritual experience. He was a quiet person and so nonassertive that for a long time I believed he was weak. Later in life I discovered he possessed an inner strength that was remarkable.

Dad was not educated because he had to quit school at an early age to help support his family, but although he was not educated, he was deeply wise. I looked forward to the times we spent together. He loved nature, and after church on Sunday, we would sometimes take long walks together in the woods, where he would teach me very important things that I now know were spiritual in nature. For instance, he taught me how to make a flat rock bounce across the top of the water in a pond.

What is spiritual about skipping rocks across water? Just that when I did it, especially that first time, I felt as if I could walk on the water! It felt terrific! It was a meaningful, powerful experience, as anyone who has ever done it knows. These days, I skip rocks across water as often as I can. How long has it been since you have done it?

Dad also taught me how and where to drink water from the creek. "Just after it goes over the rocks," he'd say. "That's where the water is coolest and cleanest." He taught me the common names of trees. "That is a scaley-bark tree," he'd say, and I would look at it and see why it was so named. "See that one? Some call it a chinaberry tree, but around here we call it a 'chainy-ball' tree."

The overall, though unspoken, message I got from my father about nature was, "Isn't this nice, son? Isn't this a beautiful world?" And whenever I was with him, it was. Later in my life, when I had children of my own, whenever my father came to visit, the word would quickly spread to all the kids in the neighborhood that "Big Daddy" (which is what they called him) was at our house.

Soon, all the children and all the dogs would be there, surrounding him. He would walk down the street, followed by a
bunch of kids and dogs. It is my opinion that when children and
animals are drawn to any person, he or she is really something!
My children always said that "Big Daddy" was the "goodest" man
in the whole world and I agree.

The greatest compliment I ever received was given to me by my
father the day before he died. I had been sober a number of years.
We had discussed his impending death, and he had quietly accepted
it with amazing courage. Then he looked at me and said, "Tommy,
I love you. You're one of the finest men I've ever known." The next
day, he died. Quite a man, my father, and I adored him. In fact, one
of my goals in life is to be as much like him as possible.

Everyone who lived on our side of the tracks was one big
family. I don't mean we all had the same name or were blood
related. We were all members of a large extended family, a community that lived, loved and shared with one another. All we
children felt as much at home in one house as in another. We
played together, ate and slept in each other's homes and if we
misbehaved, any parent felt free to discipline us. I knew I belonged
to this community, was certain I was a valued and loved member
of it and felt safe and secure in it.

Today, I feel the same way about the recovery community to
which I belong, and I know that such a community is a fundamental and vital part of any spiritual way of life, providing love,
acceptance, safety and power. I am also persuaded that one of
the chief reasons why addiction is so rapidly growing in this
country is precisely because of the breakdown and disappearance
of community.

I feel blessed to have had the experience of living in my childhood community and doubly blessed now to be a loved and valued
member of a recovery family. I remember my extended childhood
family fondly and well. In sharing with you some of my experiences with them, I'll change only their names.

My Extended Childhood Family

The house on the corner was occupied by Will, his wife, Leah,
and their three children. Leah was a very plump woman with

olive skin. She was a wonderful cook, and she obviously was a very good eater too. Being hugged by Leah was, in itself, a spiritual experience. She had huge breasts, and when she embraced me, her breasts surrounded my head. I loved it when she hugged me! It was just wonderful!

Leah and Will's son, Will, Junior, was one of my most special friends. He was a good-looking little boy, with dark skin and curly ringlets of hair. He hated his hair and wanted it to be straight, like mine. One day I used lard to slick down his hair. Boy, was he happy! But then the curls started popping up all over his head, refusing to stay down, so his joy was short-lived.

Will, Junior, was one of those little boys who seemed to be programmed for self-destruction. He was always getting hurt and you seldom saw him when he was not cut, skinned, broken, bruised or bandaged. If he was within ten yards of your car, you didn't dare slam the door because his hand would be in it. I have never known a child who had his hand squashed in so many car doors!

Will, Junior, also hated to bathe, and if Leah turned her back while bathing him he'd escape. Whenever this happened, she would come out on the front porch and holler for me. "Puddin-head!" she'd yell (most people called me "Puddin-head" because my hair was very light). "He's loose again!"

Then I'd look and see Will, Junior's naked butt flying down the road toward Clay Hill, which was what we called the big pile of red dirt at the end of the block beside the railroad tracks. When it rained and Clay Hill got slick, we kids would slide down on box tops, and every time I did this, I'd get the same feeling as when I skipped rocks across water. That's right. Sliding down Clay Hill was a spiritual experience!

Well, I'd chase Will, Junior (he could fly), catch him, take him home and sometimes hold him while his mother bathed him. I guess it's fond imagination, but when I think back, it sometimes seems as if I spent half my childhood chasing Will, Junior's naked butt down the street.

My family lived next door. There were four of us — me, my father, my sister (a talented musician) and my mother. My mother is a phenomenal woman. At this writing, she is 86 years old, going on 18, is very active and has a thriving baby-sitting business. If memory serves correctly, until recently my mother had never been really sick. She has always been exceedingly intelligent, although not highly educated. She's so smart that I believe she could run AT&T if she had to. She is assertive, gregarious, strong and dominant, and her life has been totally devoted to her children and grandchildren. Mom is also a "Black Belt" Southern Baptist.

I have always been her major focus. As a child, I knew she expected a great deal of me and somehow I never felt she was pleased with my performance. But I knew there was nothing she would not do for me, including breathing for me if she could.

She worked on and off in the cotton mill. She was a "lint head," the label given to the women workers because of the tiny pieces of cotton that got in their hair. We were poor, I guess, but I never knew it because mother made extra money by sewing curtains, draperies and clothing. Strong, proud, resourceful and every inch a lady, my mother.

In the house on the other side of us lived Z and his family. Z was an imposing man with salt and pepper hair, cut short in the style then known as a "GI," and a bushy mustache that matched his hair. He ran the movie theater in town and he was a sweet man. I remember him getting all the kids together on his front lawn on Christmas Eve and putting on a glorious fireworks show for us. While other parents were getting things ready for Santa, Z had all us kids in his yard.

His son, James Q, was another special friend of mine, and Z bought him a pony named Beauty. It wasn't just his pony because in our community what belonged to one was shared by all. Anytime we wanted to ride, we could do so, on condition that when we finished we brushed Beauty and put up the bridle and saddle. Responsibility was a part of our community, and I have learned it is an integral part of every spiritual fellowship.

Entertainment options were limited, but in retrospect this was good, because we spent a lot of time playing, creating games and talking with one another.

Almost every Saturday, I'd go to the movies. Admission was only nine cents, and for this price there was a double feature, usually two Westerns, a couple of serials, like Buck Rogers or Flash Gordon or Fu Manchu, plus several good cartoons. Popcorn was a nickel a box, and since Z ran the theater, we got free refills. The popcorn was always freshly popped and delicious, the movies always exciting. So for fourteen cents, I'd spend the day at the theater.

I loved Westerns and my heroes were cowboys like Hopalong Cassidy, Rocky Lane, the Durango Kid and Wild Bill Elliott, who wore his two guns backwards, causing me to wonder if something was wrong with his wrists. My very favorite cowboy was Lash LaRue. Boy, Lash was something! He was called Lash because he used a bullwhip instead of a gun to overcome the bad guys.

One particular Saturday while watching Lash, I saw him do something totally wonderful, and I'll never forget it. He had run all the desperados out of town and was standing on the roof of the saloon, hands on his hips, looking really macho and cool. Then he popped his whip and whistled, and his horse came running by. Popping the whip again, he jumped off the roof, landed in the saddle and rode majestically off into the sunset, popping his whip as he went.

Watching him, I was completely awestruck and felt goose bumps on my skin. Gosh, I thought, Lash is really something! So moved was I by the scene, I sat through the movie two more times just to see him jump on the horse and ride away again. Still thinking of Lash's wonderful leap, I went home, got a piece of rope and climbed to the roof of the garage. I told James Q to saddle Beauty, and when he had done so, I told him to walk her past the garage, which he did.

When the pony was in the correct position, I popped my rope whip, whistled, and jumped from the roof into the saddle. When I hit the saddle, you could have heard me scream in Myrtle Beach. Boy, did it hurt! Later, when the pain had subsided and I got my breath back, I wondered about Lash LaRue, whether he had had some kind of surgery. I still wonder.

Every day old man Lucas came by our house, pushing his home-made wooden wheelbarrow with the rusty iron wheel, on his way to slop the hogs that were kept in pens down by the creek. For those of you who may not know, to slop hogs means to feed them slop, which was a collection of table scraps and other edible garbage. Sometimes Mr. Lucas would stop in front of my house and call for me. I'd come out and get in the wheelbarrow with the cans of slop, and he'd ride me to the hog pens.

On the way, we'd pass Marla's house. Marla was the first little girl I ever played doctor with, and I'll never forget her. Soon, Mr. Lucas and I would arrive at the hog pens, and while he slopped the hogs, I'd wade in the creek, catch a few crawdads (crayfish), sip the cool water and just be.

Just be-ing like this always made me feel good. Often in this frame of mind I'd walk along the dirt trail that led from the hog pens, feel the sandy soil on my bare feet, the sun and warm air on my skin. My senses seemed completely attuned to the world around me, and without having to understand how or why, I knew I was "at one" with it.

Today, I know that this sense of unity or connectedness, plus the good feeling produced by it, is the stuff of which spirituality is made. And it comes to me now as it did then when I am just be-ing. How long has it been since you just "be-ed"?

When I was a little boy, I spent a good deal of time thinking, and I thought, of course, like a child. Children don't think like adults. Adults reason, analyze, and try to understand what is happening, but children don't. They seem to have no need to do so. They simply observe, accept, experience, and relate to whatever happens.

For instance, sometimes I'd lie on my back in the grass and relax. When resting this way, I could feel the blades of grass brushing against and tickling my ears and hear the sounds made by the tiny beings who lived in it and in the earth below. Often I'd gaze up at the sky and reflect. In reverie, I'd silently exclaim, "Gosh, the sky sure is pretty" and question, "I wonder who made it?" At times a cloud would come into view, and I'd embrace it with my mind, stroke it, enjoy it, and wonder where it came from. And when it vanished, I'd wonder where it had gone. Then, untroubled by not knowing the answers, and refreshed by my experience with the sky and clouds, I'd get up and go about my little boy business.

Today I know that such reflective reveries are basic spiritual activities that feed and enrich the soul. Little children engage in such activities naturally and frequently, but how long has it been since you lay on your back in the grass, relaxed, gazed at the sky and reflected?

When I was a little child, I surveyed my inner thoughts exactly as I did clouds, observing and reflecting on one until it went away, then dealing with the next in the same manner. I believe that all children experience their thoughts in this way, at least while they are very young. Unlike adults, they don't analyze their thoughts, question why they have them, place moral judgments on them, criticize themselves for having them, or become troubled by them. They simply watch their thoughts go by, uncritically observing and accepting each one. Sometimes, in special, magical moments child and thought merge and move as one into the realm of pure meditation.

One of the worst travesties that the adult world perpetrates on children is to teach them that certain thoughts are wrong and unacceptable, that all thoughts should be analyzed, and that daydreaming is a waste of time. Whenever this is done, the child loses the invaluable trait of self-acceptance, is stripped of the gift of uncritical reflection, and is robbed of those treasured times of just be-ing. What is worse, the child begins to feel ashamed for having certain thoughts, to deny and/or repress others, and to feel guilty for "doing nothing."

My favorite place of reflection was up in the chainy-ball tree outside our kitchen window. Often, while roosting in this tree, I could smell the mill village soul food that my mother was preparing in the kitchen. In case you don't know what such food is, it included things like collard greens and pinto beans cooked with fatback, and served with fried chicken and cornbread that was fried in a big black iron pan. Sitting on my limb, I'd think, "Boy, the food smells good! I sure am happy. I have good parents, some nice friends, wonderful food to eat, and fine places to play. Life is good."

At times like this, my thoughts would sometimes spiral in, and I'd think, "Even though life is good, something is missing. I don't know what it is, or where it is, or how to find it, but I know that if I can find it, life will be wonderful." It was as though a part of me were missing, leaving an empty space inside me, a void that needed to be filled, a hole in the middle where the wind blew through, and I longed to have it filled.

The Longing

My experience through the years has persuaded me that all people have experienced the same longing at some level, even though they may have been unaware of what it was. This is because the longing may express itself in many different ways. Sometimes, it appears as boredom, discontent, uneasiness, irritability or restlessness; at other times as a sense of dissatisfaction, emptiness or meaninglessness. Frequently it manifests as a feeling that all is not well.

Many people have spoken or written about this longing and of the restlessness that often accompanies it. As I said earlier, Carl Jung called it "a secret unrest that gnaws at the roots of our being."[2] I believe St. Augustine was referring to this longing when he said, "You have made us for yourself, dear Lord, and our souls are restless till they rest in you."[3] Unlike me, Augustine apparently knew for whom he was longing — the dear Lord. In addition, he seemed to believe that he would be restless until he was united with the Lord.

Dr. William Silkworth, who had such a great influence on the development of Alcoholics Anonymous, was, I believe, referring to this inner longing when he described alcoholics as being "restless, irritable and discontented."[4]

The poet laureate of the shepherds, the psalmist, experienced the longing, which he likened to thirst, and the restlessness, which he referred to as panting, and he expressed the matter beautifully when he wrote:

> As the deer pants for streams of water, so pants my soul for
> you, O God. My soul thirsts for God, for the living God.
>
> Psalm 42:1-2

Saint, psychiatrist and psalmist all agree on the nature and existence of this primal inner force, this energy, this desire, this longing, this thirst for wholeness and have spoken eloquently about it. Yet perhaps the clearest and most concise expression of it can be found in the lyrics of various songs.

To me, a very succinct statement is found in the chorus of the classic country-and-western song, "Detroit City." In this song, after stating the truth about his situation, the singer plaintively wails the following chorus: "I wanna go home. I wanna go home. Lord, how I wanna go home!"⁵ We all do. That's right. We all "wanna go home."

The desire to go home is our deepest desire; it is the very essence of spirituality. Spirituality, quite simply put, is our longing to go home. It is the primal energy that moves us. It is God's longing for Himself. It is, if you will, the thirst for wholeness.

If you have doubts, consider the evidence. Throughout all time, in all places, going home has been a central theme in art, literature, poetry, music, and myth, which are the chief means of conveying spiritual truth. If going home is a universal theme, then there must be a common desire among all people to go home.

Furthermore, if we closely study history we discover not only the existence of this universal desire but also a general belief that such a home exists. It has been called by many names — Paradise, Utopia, Valhalla, Happy Hunting Ground, Nirvana, Heaven, and so on — but despite the different labels, humankind holds to the conviction that a perfect home exists and that they may return to it.

In addition, it seems that human beings have always had paths that were designed to help them return home. These paths have been the central themes in the religious traditions of humankind.

Seen in this light, it is the role of religion to expedite and serve spirituality, and I believe this is its proper role. Each religion has its own specific path, which was laid out by the spiritual leader upon whose teachings it is based. Ranging from the Ten Commandments of Moses, to the Tao of Lao Tzu, to the Eightfold Middle Path of the Buddha, to the Sermon on the Mount of Jesus, the main purpose of each path is to help people live in such a way that they can return home.

Although these various paths diverge in many respects, if one examines them closely, and without prejudice, one will discover that what is really interesting about them is not their differences, but their similarities. Indeed, a common thread runs through them all. So much is this the case that one gets the feeling that each religion is a gate to the same path.

My mother and father were active Southern Baptists. This being the case, we spent a great deal of time in the little white wooden Baptist church in the mill village, and I received my early religious training there. The Baptists believe strongly in home, which they call heaven, and it sounded like a marvelous place, but the path we apparently had to follow to get there really troubled me.

For example, we would sing, "Some glad morning when this life is o'er, I'll fly away. To my home on that celestial shore, I'll fly away." I loved the melody and rhythm of this old gospel song, and I sang it with gusto, but the words troubled me deeply. "Why," I wondered, "do I have to die before I can go to this wonderful place?" I was a child and my life had just begun, and even though I wanted to go to heaven, I sure didn't want to die to get there. I therefore rejected the idea.

Then one Sunday morning something incredible happened. I was sitting beside my mother, next to a stained glass window, through which came a lovely stream of light. My dad was in the choir, as he always was, and they were singing the hymn of invitation, while the minister, who was a wonderful man, exhorted those who had not done so to surrender their lives to Christ.

I don't remember what the minister was saying or what hymn the choir was singing. It was as if the music, the words and the light merged, forming a backdrop for what was about to occur. Then it happened.

All at once it was as though the nicest, warmest shower I'd ever felt was coming down on me, surrounding me like a warm, wonderful cocoon of pure bliss, bathing me with euphoria. I felt as if I were being caressed by big, soft, gentle, amazingly strong arms, and there was a feeling of ecstasy. I was excited, but calm and unafraid. Chill bumps spread over my body, and I began to weep, not for sadness, but for joy.

While all this was happening, I remember thinking, "This is it! This is what has been missing! This is what I've been longing for. Nothing's missing anymore. This must be heaven, and I didn't have to die. I have never felt this good. I hope this feeling never goes away." The experience was incredibly intense, and though I wanted it to last, it vanished as quickly as it had appeared.

Looking back, I understand what happened on that Sunday morning long ago. I had a spiritual, or noetic, experience. The event was powerful, more powerful than anything else that had happened in my life, and of course I wanted it to happen again, but it was not to be. I cannot tell you how many times I went back to that little church, sat in the same pew, listened to the same choir and heard the same preacher, hoping with all my heart that it would happen again, but it never did. I felt somehow cheated, but more important, now that I had experienced a quenching of my spiritual thirst, I was more thirsty than ever. This single spiritual experience, by its very power, had intensified my longing for wholeness.

When I was about 15, I was among a group of singers selected to take part in a music festival held annually at one of our state colleges. One night when a bunch of us were gathered in a hotel room, someone called a taxi driver, talked with him briefly and gave him $7.50. A short while later, the driver returned, bringing with him a bottle of brown fluid labeled Cream of Kentucky. I asked my wisest friend, a boy called Egghead, what to do with the stuff, and he instructed me to drink a glass full of it as fast as I could, drink a glsss of water, and then repeat the procedure.

Standing in front of the bathroom mirror, I followed his directions, watching myself take my first drink of alcohol. The taste was awful, but the effect was wonderful, for as I continued to drink, it felt as if the nicest, warmest shower I'd ever felt was coming down around me, surrounding me, bathing me with euphoria. It was as if big, soft, strong arms caressed me, and there was a feeling of ecstasy. I felt excited, but calm and unafraid, and I thought, "This is it! This is what has been missing, this is what I've been longing for. I feel wonderful."

At that point I made up my mind I'd never be without this stuff again, and that very night, when all my friends had passed out, I called the taxi driver and got a pint of Cream of Kentucky for myself.

In retrospect, I understand what happened that night. Alcohol had produced a spiritual experience, and its effect was exceedingly powerful. For the next 15 years, I sought the same feeling with all my strength and will, but it never happened again, and I almost died in the process.

I now know that the real power involved in my experience in the hotel room was in the effect the alcohol had on me. It made me feel complete and whole, seemed to end my loneliness and to remove my fear. Nothing seemed to be missing and my longing ceased. I felt "at one" with everything and everyone around me.

I have shared my experience with thousands of alcoholics and other addicts over the years and they agree that, at some point in time, alcohol or some other drug or behavior had the same effect on them. For some, like me, it happened the first time, for others, later, but there was always that one point when drugs or behaviors gave them the illusion that they were home.

The real power of alcohol and other drugs is in their capacity to create the illusion of wholeness, causing users to believe they are in the best possible shape, when in fact they aren't.

We all wanna go home, and the major effect of alcohol and other drugs is to modify our perception, causing us to believe that we are home, when, in reality, we are on a detour. Spiritually speaking, addiction is a detour on the way back home.

From the longing come the drinking and using, from the drinking and using comes the illusion of fulfillment, and — if certain psychological and/or biological components are present — from the illusion comes addiction.

You see, all addictions arise from spirituality.

4

The Myths

We live in the last decade of the twentieth century, and in spite of an abundance of information that clearly shows addiction to be one of the top three health problems in this country, most people don't believe it is. Even though a wealth of data is available concerning the nature of addiction, few people understand it. Although the best possible research clearly reveals, beyond the shadow of any doubt, that it is a bonafide illness, most people remain unconvinced. No condition is more shrouded by falsehood and moral innuendo than addiction, and no group of people is less understood or treated with more disdain than addicts.

Scapegoating

Why? After much experience, observation and thought, I have reached the rather disturbing conclusion that many, perhaps most, people don't realize the true nature of addiction simply because they don't want to. They stigmatize the illness and those who have it because it is comfortable to do so. Addicts play an important role in our social family. They are convenient scapegoats and as such, they satisfy the perverse human need to feel superior to someone. Kris Kristofferson stated the matter well in the chorus of one of his songs.

"Cause everybody's gotta have somebody to look down on,
Someone to feel better than at any time they please.
Someone doing something dirty they're supposed to frown on.
If you can't find nobody else, then help yourself to me."[1]

Everyone needs scapegoats, and this need is the basis of all racism, sexism and other prejudices. Even addicts are not immune to this madness! Like others, they gossip, criticize and find fault with each other.

Hell, I know cocaine addicts who feel a cut or two above alcoholics because their drug is so much more expensive, and alcoholics who look down on other alcoholics who drink less than they do! Our society has many scapegoats, some of the most notable being minorities, the poor, the homeless and addicts. Of these, I believe addicts are the ultimate scapegoats because they are such easy targets.

An example of this scapegoating can be seen in the terminology used to refer to alcoholics and addicts. They are called "substance abusers." Every time I hear the term I am disturbed. Why? Because I think the terminology is backward. It implies, if you will, that the person abuses the drug. In fact, it's the other way around. It is the alcoholics and addicts who are harmed by the alcohol and drugs.

As a matter of fact, addicts treat and use their drugs of choice with care and respect, even with reverence. Addicts do not abuse drugs, drugs abuse them and I for one feel the misleading terms now applied to addicts should be changed, for they reveal not only a lack of understanding of addiction but also a tremendous negative bias against those who suffer from the illness.

In order to retain its scapegoats, society creates myths about them. As discussed, myths are stories that are invented to explain things to us. There are good myths and bad myths. Some myths convey truth, provide insight, enhance our understanding and help us to live well. Others, however, are totally and completely false fabrications that can be, and often are, very misleading and harmful. It is myths of this type that have been made up about this society's scapegoats.

These false myths serve to justify society's perception by placing the blame for their condition squarely on the scapegoats themselves. This, of course, frees society not only from any accountability for their condition, but also from any responsibility to do anything about it. And so, in our country, we hear that minorities are shiftless and lazy, the unemployed don't want to work, the poor and homeless are irresponsible and welfare checks are spent on booze, drugs and cigarettes. To prove the falsity of these myths, we need only match them against the facts.

When it comes to addicts, our society has formulated an intricate web of false mythology that usually portrays them as immoral, inferior and weak-willed. Such portraits, of course, make nonaddicts feel superior and absolve society of any responsibility, allowing people to retain their chosen scapegoats.

When these myths are closely examined, they invariably prove to be groundless and false. However, because they are simply accepted as factual and are passed from generation to generation, these malicious tales are embedded in our society. Many to whom they are passed become addicts, and since they have been taught to believe the false mythology, their addiction will generate shame and guilt of a magnitude that is unimaginable to most people. As a result, all of them will deny their addiction and try with all their might to drink, use or behave as nonaddicts do. Since their disease makes this impossible, they will sink ever deeper into the mire of remorse and self-loathing, and unless they discover the truth, they will die.

When I consider the disastrous effects of the mythology surrounding addiction, I shudder at its ugliness and tremble at the evil it can do. What is included in this terrible mythology? What are some of the myths that most people, including many who are addicted, apparently are programmed to believe? There are far too many myths to cover them all, but we can look at a few of the most common ones.

The Stereotypes

The common images of addicts that many people have are stereotypes or caricatures. To them, a drug addict is a no-good bum, a nondescript junkie who shoots illegal dope into a vein in his arm in some back alley. When we examine the facts, we find this image fits only a very small segment of addicts. Most of them have homes, careers and families and never inject any illegal drug into their bodies with a needle.

On the contrary, most of them swallow their drug of choice, which is usually a legal substance, often obtained from a pharmacy by means of a prescription, sometimes acquired unlawfully from a dealer on the street. With the exception of alcohol and tobacco, I believe prescription medications are the major addictive substances in this country. No matter how they are obtained, far more people are addicted to them than to illegal drugs. To me, any picture of addicts that does not include those who line up in a pharmacy to get their painkillers, sleeping pills and tranquilizers is woefully inaccurate, and any version of addiction that does not acknowledge that more are addicted to legal than to illegal drugs is grossly in error.

Alcoholics fare no better, for they have been historically cast in the role of weak-willed guttersnipes who daily imbibe rotgut whiskey or cheap wine. Far too many times they are portrayed as "good ole" boys and girls who drink too much, too long and are deserving of our pity because they just can't help but drink. Like Otis Campbell on the *Andy Griffith Show*, they are to be comforted, pitied, enabled and cared for, but they should never, never be seriously considered our equals.

According to reliable data, most alcoholics are miscast in this role because they do not reach the gutter or go to jail, nor do they drink only rotgut and cheap wine. Like drug addicts, the vast majority of alcoholics have jobs, cars, homes and families. Most often, they are decent men and women who happen to have bodies that can't handle alcohol, and they deserve to be treated as equals — not with pity, but with respect, care and concern.

A number of people believe that addicts are physically weak or inferior. This belief gives rise to such statements as, "A man should be able to hold his liquor," the implication being that if alcohol strongly affects one man, he is not a man. If we look at the facts, this myth falls flat. All we need do is attend a 12-Step meeting and look around. We will see some very fine, strong, healthy people present there.

What is really amazing to me is the physical prowess of the women, especially the older women. These ladies, some in their 70s, run around the meeting, grinning from ear to ear like the proverbial Cheshire cat, hugging and kissing everyone in sight, happy as they can be. The reason I am so amazed by this is simple. These beautiful women have, over the years, drunk enough alcohol and/or taken enough drugs to kill a water buffalo, yet here they are — alive, happy and puckered up!

It is my pleasure to know such a lady, who shall remain nameless. The first thing I see when she comes toward me is her lips. She plants a kiss on me, gives me a big hug and moves off to kiss some more. God, I love this woman! Yet, each time I meet her, I cannot help but think what a miracle it is that she is even alive because she drank and used enough through the years to have killed most people.

Considering the amounts, types and combinations of drugs or behaviors that addicts use, it is obvious they must have tremendous physical constitutions, else they would not survive. Thus, the evidence refutes the myth.

Some think addicts are mentally inferior people who just don't have it in the mind department. I'll never forget my parents and others saying, "If you had any sense, you wouldn't drink like you do." I heard this so often I began to believe it, yet I graduated with honors from a good college, with a double major in philosophy and history. I held a 3.94 grade average and was selected to *Who's Who in American Colleges and Universities*, even though I was drunk most of the time.

If addicts are indeed mentally inferior, why were five out of six Nobel prize winners for literature from America alcoholics? These people had good, fertile, strong, creative minds. Our astronauts are chosen on the basis of intelligence, physical condition and ability, yet at least two of them are admitted alcoholics. Given this evidence, it is easy to realize the belief that addicts are mentally inferior is a fallacy.

Also included in the litany of false myths are those that say addicts are sociopaths who don't care how their actions affect others, that they are bad people, or that they're doing just what they want to do. Let's briefly examine these and move on. If addicts are sociopaths, why do they have so much guilt and shame? In fact, no other group seems to have more of these emotions than addicts. Sociopaths, on the other hand, do not experience these feelings and are oblivious to the feelings of others.

If addicts are bad people, why are so many of them ministers, priests, nuns and Sunday school teachers, and why do they suffer so deeply because of the wrongs they do? My experience suggests to me that, far from being immoral, addicts are moral extremists who set standards of morality for themselves that God could not live up to.

As to addicts doing just what they want to do — which means they have chosen to be addicts — this idea is patently absurd. I have yet to meet an addict who made a conscious choice to be one, and I'm certain I never will.

No addict chooses or intends to be one. This is made abundantly clear in the following excerpts from a poem written by a recovering female addict, Debra:

I never intended to be an alcoholic
or a drug addict.
It wasn't something I dreamed about
or aspired to or wrote about and read
in Miss Young's fourth grade class
"when I grow up I want to be . . ."

I never intended to lie
about the drugs or the amount of booze I drank
or where I was last night or the night before
even if I could remember.
I always intended to come home that night
like all the other nights
but didn't.

I never intended to find myself alone
dying from an overdose

scared and ashamed of who I was or wasn't
or believe it was all for nothing
and that it would not be forgiven
or forgotten.
I never intended to survive that night . . .

Perhaps no myth has perplexed so many for so long as the one that says addicts have no willpower because if they did, they could quit. One reason for the longevity and persistence of this particular myth is that most people apparently don't understand what willpower really is, for if they did, they would soon realize that addicts have an abundance of it. Although willpower is a vague concept, it can be loosely defined as the power or determination to do what you've decided to do or to carry out your intention. Any person who knows anything about addiction can tell many stories that clearly illustrate no group of people is more strongly determined than addicts when it comes to their addiction.

I knew an addict who had injected drugs into his arms so many times that the veins were not usable anymore, so he began using the veins in his hands. When these were collapsed, he used those in his legs, then his feet and, finally, his neck. When I met him, his arms and legs looked like dead masses of scarred flesh, which they were, yet he continued to search for places on his body where he could inject drugs!

To me, this is extreme determination! He may have lacked sanity or intelligence, but this man had plenty of willpower! This man's story is not as unique as it may sound. In fact, if you take the time to listen to the stories of addicts, you will soon discover that strength of will, misdirected though it may be, is a common characteristic of addicts.

Another reason for the endurance of the willpower myth is that many people hold on to the illusion that addiction is a bad habit rather than an illness. Why? Although I cannot fully answer the question, I do know from my own experience that habits and addictive illnesses so closely resemble one another that they are often mistaken, sometimes even by those who should know the difference.

What, then, is the difference between a habit and an illness? To me, a habit can be ended by an act of human will — that is, by making a choice and by carrying it out. I am equally convinced, however, that illness cannot be controlled or ended by a decision. If one has a spreading cancer, one can neither control its growth nor make it go away by choice. No matter how strong one's will, it is simply not powerful enough to overcome the illness without help from people and God.

Habits respond to control by the will, illnesses do not. If addiction were a habit, most addicts could choose to quit entirely, and they would be able to do so. However, the evidence clearly shows that, even though addicts do make such choices many times, they have little or no effect because they cannot carry them out. Like the person with cancer, addicts find themselves unable to control or end their addiction by their own human will, no matter how strong. Unless they receive human and divine aid, they will not recover.

What does all this mean? It means that since addiction can't be controlled or ended by an act of human will, it cannot be a habit because habits respond to human control. Therefore, addiction must be an illness.

The hallmark of addiction is the total inability to stop behavior that is destructive to self and others. The person who has a habit can just say no, but the person who has an addictive illness must say, "Please help me say no."

The New Mythology

In spite of the fact that some of these myths are still believed by many people, they are not so widely accepted as they once were. One reason for this is that millions of people have become addicted, or have had someone close to them become addicted. Thus, ironically, the illness itself has provided the impetus to destroy the myths that obscured it.

In addition, we must acknowledge the role that Alcoholics Anonymous has played in providing accurate information about addiction, enabling millions of addicts and their families to cut through the mythical web of deceit which has surrounded the illness.

As if the old mythical fallacies had not clouded the issue enough, a new mythology has come into being. Unlike the old mythology, which was created by society, the new mythology comes from some who work in the field of addiction, and it is creating problems in the entire recovery community. Whatever their motives, the new mythologists' ideas have brought more heat than light into the world of addictive illness and in some cases have become impediments to the recovery of both addicts and those who are involved with them.

One part of the new mythology has to do with the practice of labeling as separate addictions what might be symptoms of a major addiction. To illustrate, let me share with you an experience I had while working in an addiction treatment center. A young woman about 21 years old had come in to talk with me about the drug addiction for which she had been admitted five days previously. Suddenly, she broke in with the following words: "Oh, Tom, you must understand. I'm not *just* a drug addict. My counselor told me I'm also addicted to sex and food, and we're going to work on all these issues while I'm here."

Perhaps some of you will know how I felt upon hearing this. In only five days, this youngster had been diagnosed as having at least three addictive disorders, all of which were to be addressed in less than 30 days. Through a brief silent prayer, I was able to release my urge to strangle the counselor, and I listened intently as the young woman continued to share with me. As she did so, it became apparent that she had at times gone to extremes with both sex and food, but there was simply not enough evidence to support a diagnosis of addiction to either. As a matter of fact, I felt very strongly that her compulsive behavior regarding food and sex might well be symptoms of her drug addiction, which is very often the case. In my judgment, this woman had been diagnosed as having three addictions when she probably only had one.

If and when drug addicts get compulsive about such things as gambling, food, sex, or religion, it does not necessarily mean that they are addicted to them, for addicts are extremists when it comes to doing anything that produces euphoria. It seems that addicts believe anything which feels good should be done to excess. "If it feels good, overdo it," seems to be the addicts' creed. Therefore, it is common for them to become compulsively involved with anything that makes them feel good, both before and after recovery.

Sex feels good, and if drug addicts really overindulge in it, we can say they have a problem with sex, but we may not be justified in labeling it as sex addiction. Before we can do this, we must allow time for the process of recovery to take effect. As it does, what seemed to be an addiction to sex often turns out to be a symptom of the primary drug addiction. To label it a separate addiction creates an additional myth.

If, however, after a substantial time in recovery, compulsive, uncontrollable sexual behavior persists, we may assume there is a separate addiction and act to treat it. Don't misunderstand what I am saying. It's not that I don't believe separate addictions may exist, because I do. It's just that too many are too quick to label what might be additional symptoms of one disorder as separate entities, and this can be very detrimental to recovery. It is in these cases that we must take heed of the slogans, *Easy Does It*, and *First Things First*, and if we do, we may enhance, rather than impede recovery.

Labels

The most troubling part of the new mythology has to do with applying a new label to an old syndrome that has long been called by another name. Since I believe in the power of story-telling, perhaps the best way to demonstrate this myth is by telling you a story:

Gladys, Clara, Ralph and Fred meet every Wednesday afternoon at their club to play bridge, talk, and drink a little wine. On one particular Wednesday, the conversation turned to the subject of the spare tires that each couple had in their cars. After talking for a while, they decided that the name "spare tire" was just not appropriate, and they tried to come up with a more correct label. Finally, three of the four agreed that the new name should be "co-tire," but because of Clara's insistent disagreement, the term did not last. After much discussion, the other three agreed with Clara, and there was unanimous agreement. From now on, all agreed, what had been called a spare tire would henceforth bear the label, "co-wheel."

When told about the new name, some of their neighbors enthusiastically embraced it. After all, it was new, and that, they felt, made it better. Others, however, did not think it was a good idea at all, and since they felt the old name was good enough, they continued to use it. One of these was Jeff, who ran the only service station in town and sold and fixed everyone's tires.

One day, Gladys drove in to Jeff's place, and after brief greetings were exchanged, she asked him to replace her front left tire with the co-wheel.

"The what?" asked Jeff.

"The co-wheel," replied Gladys.

After some talk, Jeff said, "Oh, you mean the spare tire."

Even though Gladys tried to get Jeff to use the new name, he refused, saying he saw no need to change since the old name had worked so well for so long.

The town was soon divided into two factions arguing over which term to use.

Finally everyone agreed to take the matter to old Joseph, the man acknowledged as the wisest person in town. After listening patiently to both sides, the old man thought deeply for a while, then he said, "Gladys and the others who started this whole thing did not come up with a new idea. In fact, the only thing new was the label. The idea has been around for a long time. Since the new label refers to an old notion and thus has no content of its own, it has no real existence. It is only an empty concept — a myth. You can call spare tires 'whatchamacallits', or 'thingamabobs' or 'co-wheels,' but they are still spare tires. That's what the guys at the service station have always called them, and they've done a real good job changing and fixing them for a long time. Why change the name now?"

The Co-dependent Label

For some time now, there have been those who would change the name of the syndrome manifested both by those who are affected by addiction and by addicts themselves. Why? I don't know. Perhaps they feel the old name is inadequate or inappropriate. A few years ago, they came up with the term "co-alcoholism," but it did not last.

Now they call it co-dependency. Some have enthusiastically embraced it, possibly because it's new. Others, however, have not, and they continue to use the old terminology. Many of these work at the service stations in town — the 12-Step groups. They neither use, acknowledge nor respect the new name because they see no need for it, since the old one has worked so well so long.

Moreover, because of the attempt to give a new name to an old syndrome, there is conflict, unrest and even animosity in the recovery community. And for what? I have a feeling that if we took the matter to old Joseph, he would say, "The only thing new is the label. You can call the syndrome a 'whatchamacallit,' or a 'thingamabob' or 'co-dependency,' but it remains self-centeredness. The people who work at Al-Anon, AA and the other 12-Step service stations have always called it that, and they've been doing a good job changing and fixing it for a long time. Why change the name now?" Why indeed?*

False myths divide and separate people, and as the gap widens, the thirst for wholeness intensifies and addiction increases. Bogus mythology can also prevent the bonding that is so vital to recovery. If we would decrease addictive disease and help those already in its grip to recover, we must destroy such myths, and the best way to do this is to dissolve them with the hot light of truth.

---

*To my friends who are advocates of co-dependency, let me say that a part of me (you'd call it the co-dependent part) would like to avoid disagreement with you, but integrity demands that I call them like I see them. I may be wrong, but I think co-dependency is an empty, unnecessary concept that adds nothing to the body of knowledge concerning addiction. What it has added, unfortunately, is conflict and confusion.

5

The Facts

Anyone who is inclined to do so can be freed from ignorance by learning, from fiction by fact, and from delusion by truth. Therefore, any addict, or any person involved with addiction, who is willing to do so can be loosed from the ignorance surrounding the illness by learning the real facts about it.

These facts are available and have been for a long time. They were not gathered by disinterested scholars, but by men and women whose lives depended on them. For them, the discovery of the real nature of their addiction was, quite literally, a life-or-death matter, and their subsequent recovery gave the most powerful evidence that they did, indeed, find the facts. These men and women were the first one hundred or so members of Alcoholics Anonymous (AA) and their pioneering work not only freed them to live sober lives, but also has resulted in freedom from addiction for millions more.

AA And The Identification Of Symptoms

Although a great deal was known about alcohol addiction and recovery prior to AA, the information existed only in scattered bits and pieces. Men like Charles Parker, Carl Jung, Richard Peabody, William Silkworth and William James had substantial understanding of the problem and some ideas about how to solve it. The Washingtonians had demonstrated the power of a community united in a common purpose and the value of personal testimony. The Oxford Group had come upon the basic principles of spiritual growth and had shown the power involved in sharing. However, in spite of a significant amount of information, it had little impact until it was all brought together and published in 1939 in a book that I consider to be the most important book ever written on addiction, *Alcoholics Anonymous*.

To me, the genius of the early members of AA was not that they created any new ideas on alcoholism and recovery because they didn't. Their genius lay in the fact that they gathered the most important information that existed, added 28 individual stories to validate it, put it in a book, and gave it to the world. As a result, the old mythology received a devastating blow, and some of those who had been trapped began to pick up their beds and walk again.

To this day, the contents of this magnificent book continue to inform, instruct and release the reader from the bondage of alcoholism and other addictions. What's more, the groups that have been formed around its teachings are living, breathing communities in which all members are considered equal and are given the opportunity to quench their spiritual thirst.

An illness may be defined as a group of symptoms appearing in the same form in different people in various times and places, and following a certain progression. For example, if a woman in Toronto has appendicitis, she will have the same symptoms as a woman in Miami who has it, and the illness will progress in the same way in both of them.

This is true of addiction. I have talked with addicts all over this country and in Canada, and the basic symptoms of our problem match. All of us have experienced loss of control, preoccupation with our drug or behavior of choice, compulsive use, continued use in spite of bad consequences and an inability to quit. These symptoms are common to all addictions, whether they involve mood-altering drugs or destructive behavior. I believe the main reason why the 12 Steps work so well on all addictions is because they eliminate these common symptoms.

These basic symptoms are common to all addictions but this does not mean all addictions are identical, for each has one symptom that sets it apart from the others and makes it a distinct entity. I call this the identifying symptom because it identifies each addiction according to the substance and/or behavior that is central to it and defines its recovery goal.

For example, the substance that is central to alcoholism is alcohol, the unique behavior is uncontrolled drinking, and the goal of recovery is abstinence, while the substance in overeating is food, the unique behavior is uncontrolled eating, and the recovery goal is moderation. When we make such observations, we can see that even though all addictions share certain symptoms, each is a separate entity that is similar, but not identical, to the others.

The various identifying symptoms divide the community of addiction into family groups. Each family is bonded together by the unique symptom that all its members have in common. This symptom cements the family together, and since all its members share the same problem, they can move in unity toward a common solution. Addicts who do not possess the identifying symptom of a certain family cannot fit into it, bond with its members or share its goals. If they cannot bond with the group, their chances of recovery are drastically reduced, and the unity of the group is threatened. It is this recognition of the importance of individual bonding and group unity in the process of recovery that is the basis for the longevity and success of AA. Interestingly, other groups, such as Narcotics Anonymous (NA), are adhering to the same principles.

It amazes me how many people misunderstand or criticize AA regarding this. Cardiologists can limit their medical practice to those who have heart disease, for example, and nobody lifts an eyebrow; yet when AA wisely and humbly chooses to limit its practice to alcoholics, people don't understand and often disparage AA. Contrary to those who fault this position, AA does not reserve its membership to "pure" alcoholics who have no other problems. In fact, a person can have ten addictions and still bond with the AA group — provided one of his addictions is to alcohol, because individuals have a much greater chance of recovery when they bond with a group that shares a unique symptom.

If the 12-Step movement begun by AA has demonstrated anything over the years, it is the paramount importance of the bonding that creates the group unity so vital to recovery. It is important, then, to understand that bonding occurs not only because the members of the group have the same problem and agree on how to solve it, but also because they share a common perspective of both illness and recovery and use specific language regarding each.

For example, the members of NA share a certain point of view about drug addiction and recovery and use specific terminology regarding both. It is here that the new mythology causes problems. How? Suppose an addict has been in treatment and has been taught that the root of addiction is co-dependency. After treatment, this addict comes to NA, whose members believe the root of addiction is selfishness. What happens? When the new person begins to talk about co-dependency, using its perspective and language, it is as though an unknown tongue were being spoken. What's more, some members of the group will see this differing opinion as a challenge to the point of view that plays such a large role in group unity. If the individual does not adopt the group's perspective and language, he will eventually leave and will use drugs again. I'm not theorizing. I have seen this happen many times. Moreover, others say the same thing is happening in Al-Anon, AA and other 12-Step groups.

Few groups allow as much diversity of opinion as do 12-Step groups. However, if something is perceived as an attempt to alter the beliefs that are basic not only to their unity but also to their survival, the situation changes radically. These groups then rise up to protect the principles they cherish. It is obvious to me that the new mythology is seen by many members of these groups as an attempt to alter their basic ideas. They are reacting in a predictable manner for they consider it an attack on group integrity. Tragically some addicts suffer and others will die. And for what? New labels?

No matter what the drug or behavior may be, its potential for addiction lies in its power to bring about what seems to be real, positive changes in the mental, emotional and spiritual states of the individual. Alcohol, sex, food, religion and certain behaviors can be addictive because each has the capacity to change perception, produce euphoria and give a sense of connectedness and wholeness. Even though such changes are illusory and temporary, they are nonetheless powerful. Therefore, their addictive potential is quite substantial. Ironically, the very changes that seem to occur through using certain drugs or practicing certain behaviors really do occur in recovery, the difference being they are real, not illusory, and can be permanent, not temporary.

Causes Of Alcoholism

Dr. William D. Silkworth is usually credited with giving AA the basic ideas about alcoholism that have played a central role in the success of the fellowship. Silkworth was, however, familiar with a little-known book on alcoholism with the unfortunate title *The Common Sense Of Drinking*,[1] written by Richard R. Peabody, and many of the ideas he passed on to Bill W. were obviously gleaned from this volume. As a matter of interest, a significant amount of what the book *Alcoholics Anonymous* has to say about alcoholism seems to have come from Peabody's book, some of it almost verbatim, and many of the early members of what was to become AA used the book before the publication of their own text.

Silkworth laid particular stress on the mind and body of the alcoholic, holding that the illness consisted mainly of a mental obsession that drove the alcoholic to drink and a physical allergy to alcohol that assured a loss of control over consumption once drinking started. It is worth noting that modern descriptions of addiction always include compulsive use and loss of control, thus supporting these notions.

Those who recovered first gathered together all the information that was verified by their own experience and published it in what came to be called the "Big Book." The text presented a view of alcoholism on which the first 100-plus members were in total agreement, primarily because it matched their own personal experiences as alcoholics.

The picture they presented was of an illness consisting of three parts: a spiritual malady, a mental obsession, and a physical allergy to alcohol. The validity of this view is supported by most research and is confirmed by the experience of modern alcoholics. In addition, although initially confined to alcoholism, the AA perspective has proved to be just as sound for other drug addictions. In addition, the mental and spiritual aspects are proving to be valid in relation to nondrug addictions.

Since its formulation, the AA perception of the addictive illness has proved to be the simplest and best; therefore, it forms the basis of my remarks concerning the disease. However, let me say that I am not a chosen spokesperson for AA. Whatever I say represents my own opinion.

After covering the symptoms of compulsiveness, loss of control, preoccupation with the drug and the inability to quit in masterful detail in its early chapters, the Big Book provides us with a definition of alcoholism that boils everything down to utter simplicity: "If, when you honestly want to, you find you cannot quit entirely, or if when drinking, you have little control over the amount you take, you are probably alcoholic."[2] The beauty of this definition is that by changing the words "drinking" and "alcoholic," it will describe any addiction under the sun!

According to this definition, addicts are people who have lost control over the drug or behavior with which they are involved and who find it impossible to stop. Addicts are, indeed, powerless, their lives unmanageable!

The Body And Addiction

Earlier I discussed the beginnings of addiction as being in human spirituality and as representing an attempt to fill the void that comes from separation or disconnection. Now I want to explain, in a simple way, the other two parts of this complex malady, the physical and mental, for it is the interaction of the three that gives addiction its killing power.

The human body is a phenomenal organism, consisting of intricately connected, complex systems that work together to sustain life. Truly, it is marvelous! It was the realization of this that caused the psalmist to exclaim, "I will praise thee; for I am fearfully and wonderfully made!"[3] Even though the body is fantastic, it is never perfect. As a matter of fact, most of our bodies are flawed in one way or another. Some people are born blind, crippled or deaf. Others are born with bodies that are unable to handle certain substances, such as sugar, pollen or penicillin. Others who did not have defects at birth develop them later. Some physical imperfections seem to be inherited, others acquired.

A significant number of people, including me, believe the bodies of some addicts are flawed in such a way that they are incapable of handling certain substances. Some believe the defect is inborn, while others think it is acquired. A rather large group of highly intelligent scientists contend that these addicts' inability to metabolize drugs properly is due to a biochemical genetic disorder.

In other words, they believe addiction is caused by an inherited defect in body chemistry. Their view is strongly supported by the fact that millions of addicts lose control of their drug intake from the very first. For instance, many alcoholics, such as myself, drank more than they intended the very first time and lost control whenever they drank. This is not the case with all addicts, for some seem to handle drugs well for a period of time before loss of control occurs.

Does this mean the defect is acquired or does it indicate that, although inborn, it is sometimes latent? I don't know and am content to leave the matter up to the scientists. What is important to me is the fact that many very intelligent men and women agree that whether inherited or acquired, the addict's body simply won't handle drugs like those of other people.

Certainly Dr. Silkworth held this point of view for he was convinced that alcoholics were allergic to alcohol and that their loss of control was a manifestation of this allergy. An allergy, as you may know, is an involuntary physical reaction to a given substance. Some people are very allergic to pollen, and when exposed to it, their eyes water, their sinuses fill up, their noses run and they sneeze. Others have similar reactions when they eat sugar or take penicillin. Allergic reactions are not controlled by those who have them, they just happen, and Silkworth believed this to be the case with alcoholics.

Whenever the alcoholic drank, wrote Silkworth, an involuntary physical reaction to the alcohol developed, which he called the "phenomenon of craving."[4] This phenomenon, Silkworth believed, resulted in a loss of control over alcohol consumption, which is the identifying symptom of alcoholism. He observed that this craving never developed in the average drinker, just in alcoholics, and he claimed that it was this phenomenon that set alcoholics apart and defined their illness. Rich or poor, you were alcoholic if you manifested the phenomenon of craving.

Let's look more closely at this craving. Over the years, I have learned some things about my own body that I believe are relevant to our discussion. My body does not lie to me, nor does it argue with me and what it wants, it gets. I can argue with my mind and often do. Arguing with our minds is what we euphemistically refer to as thinking. When it comes to my body, however, no argument I come up with will deter it from having what it wants.

For instance, sometimes my body tells me it needs some sleep, and I tell it I don't have time to sleep and try to stay awake. Invariably I fall asleep. It's almost as if my body were saying to me, "Tom, I told you I want to sleep and you *will* sleep!"

What the body wants to do, the body does, and argument does no good. Did any of you ever win an argument with a case of diarrhea? Sometimes I eat things that don't agree with my body, and what does my body do? It sends me a message: "Tom, you know that junk you just ate? Well, I don't like it and I'm getting rid of it." At such times, I can try with all my might not to vomit, but I'll throw up anyhow. Is the same not true for you?

But what exactly does all this have to do with the phenomenon of craving? Just this, when addicts use drugs, their bodies say, "Get me more of that stuff, and get it now!" Thus, the body takes over because of an involuntary physical reaction to the drug (the phenomenon of craving), and addicts have no control over the amount of drug they will use. They lose control.

The Mind And Addiction

If the addicts know that whenever they use drugs, it will result in a loss of control and in behavior that is harmful to themselves and others, why do they use drugs? Are they crazy? According to the Big Book, the answer is yes. However, I do not think those who compiled the book meant that alcoholics were mentally ill in the usual sense of the term. The text does not say, directly or indirectly, that alcoholic insanity is among the regular neuroses or psychoses. On the contrary, the observation is made that alcoholics are often able, intelligent, friendly people who seem normal in every respect except for the effect alcohol has on them.[5]

Then the book makes a telling comment about why alcoholics continue to drink. When it comes to alcohol, it reads, alcoholics are "strangely insane."[6] I have become aware that this strange form of insanity is a common attribute of all addicts, not just alcoholics. What does it mean to be "strangely insane?" How can it be described? Perhaps the best way is through an example.

Imagine a group of people sitting in a room, warming themselves around a stove that is very hot. A woman, Nancy, comes into the room. She walks over to the hot stove and before anyone can stop her, she puts her hand on it. Her hand is badly burned, so she is taken to a hospital, where the hand is treated. Three weeks later, the group is again in the room, warming their hands, when Nancy appears in the doorway. Calling for attention, she informs the others that she is going to put her hand on the stove again, but she is sure that it will not burn her this time.

Before anyone can intervene, she has walked to the stove, put her hand on it and been burned again. She is returned to the hospital for treatment. Later, back in the room, one of the people says to the others, "You know, Nancy seems to be an intelligent person in most respects, but when it comes to stoves, she doesn't have a damned lick of sense!" This, then, is the strange insanity, and if we substitute any addict's drug or behavior of choice for the stove, the analogy becomes clear, for all addicts return time and again to "burn" themselves on their particular "stove."

As a further illustration of the destructive depth of such insanity: Four people are sitting in a room. One is normal, the second is schizophrenic, the other two are addicts. When they try to leave the room by the main door, a man standing outside hits them on their heads with a baseball bat. The normal man won't leave by the same door again, for he has learned what will happen if he does. The schizophrenic will go out the same door at least once more, just to see if the experience was real, and when he is hit again, he will not go through the door again because he knows that whichever world he is in, the man with the bat is there. In his own way, he too, has learned from his experience.

The two addicts, however, will hold hands and skip to the door, saying to each other, "The man with the bat is not there this time, and if he is, he won't hit us." Again and again they go out the same door, and again and again they are hit on the head. Then one day, they go to the door and discover that the man with the bat is not there, so they sit down and wait for him. These two are "strangely insane," and their behavior shows that the core of such insanity is the inability to learn from personal experience, plus an impotence to stop doing what is harmful.

At this point, it is important to note that their insanity, unlike some other forms, is not based on a chemical imbalance in the brain that can be controlled or corrected by medication. Quite the contrary, it is based on disconnection from their own internal source of power and intelligence and is, therefore, a deeply spiritual form of insanity that no medication can either slow down or eliminate.

However intelligent addicts may be, when it comes to their drug or behavior of choice, a breakdown in intelligence prevents their learning from experience, and a loss of power prevents them from stopping their destructive behavior.

Whether it is a stove or a bat, their strange insanity will cause them to return to it, and whenever they do, they will be burned or hit.

Dr. Silkworth described this by saying that addicts have a mental obsession that drives them to use, and, in the case of chemical addiction, a physical allergy that causes them to lose control once they begin. Thus the twin ogres, obsession and allergy, work together to perpetuate drug addiction. In nonchemical addictions, it is currently believed that the addictive behavior not only produces euphoria, but brings about biochemical changes that may cause loss of control.

Although some may dispute the evidence, I am sure addiction is an illness. I am equally certain that those who have a vested interest in the image of the addict as worthless, immoral, and anti-social will continue to deny the facts, for these people must have a scapegoat.

The straightforward information given to us by AA has brought light into the dark world of addiction. It is clear to me that we owe a tremendous debt of gratitude to these early alcoholic pioneers, for largely due to their insight and effort addicts of all kinds have an excellent opportunity to recover. I for one am most grateful to them.

In summary, the best available evidence makes it clear that alcoholics and drug addicts initially use because of spiritual need, can't use successfully because of their biological makeup and can't quit using because of a strange mental obsession. This description, however, does not cover those who are addicted to self-destructive behaviors in which no biological defect has been demonstrated. Why are they unable to control or stop these behaviors? I believe the answer to this question lies in the intricate interplay of the mental and spiritual elements that are common to all addictive diseases. This being the case, I will now show how these work together to create and perpetuate all types of addiction. Let's look at the mind-spirit dynamics of the illness.

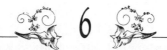

6

The Dynamics

To me, it is a great tragedy that most addicts go to their graves still addicted, even though recovery is achievable. Why? I believe strongly that most addicts don't recover because they simply do not understand what is wrong with them.

Considering all the myths, misinformation, and other forms of madness that surround addiction, it is not surprising that they don't understand their illness. It's not that they don't know they have a problem because they do. Given their suffering and pain, how could they not know? But even though they know there is a problem, they have little or no understanding about its nature or its severity.

Addicts' View

Many addicts treat their addiction as if it were a minor acute illness, like the measles. After each episode, they assume that the malady is over and will not recur. How many times do we hear addicts say they

73

will not do it again, this was the last time or it won't happen this way again? Such statements abound among addicts, and they clearly indicate a lack of comprehension of the problem, as well as its gravity.

Addicts must come to know that addiction is not like the measles. It doesn't just come along, run its course, and go away. It is not temporary and relatively minor. On the contrary, it is chronic, extremely severe, and deadly.

Almost all addicts tend to see their addiction in terms of the behavior associated with it. For example, if you ask a group of addicts what their problem is, drug addicts will say their problem is using drugs, gamblers will say their trouble is gambling, and alcoholics will say they drink too much. Few seem to realize that these behaviors, although they do create serious difficulties, are not the problem, but only the most obvious symptom of it.

Since helping them to realize the nature of their illness is a necessary first step to recovery, they must somehow be freed from the delusion that it consists only of what they are doing. I believe the best way to do this is to ask them why they do drugs, gamble or drink. Their own answers will help them begin to grasp the nature of their disease.

When asked the reason for their behavior, addicts will come up with a wide range of answers, for they have fertile minds. Not surprisingly, many will give some psychological motivation, such as a bad childhood, harsh toilet training, or the like. However, when challenged, they will see that the real reason was the effect that was produced by the gambling, drinking, drugging or other behaviors.

And what was this effect? These things made addicts feel good. That's why they use, drink and behave in certain ways. It makes them feel good! Dr. Silkworth wrote: "Men and women drink essentially because they like the effect produced by alcohol."[1] Some people call this effect being high. The Greek word is euphoria. God, what a beautiful word — euphoria! Every time I hear it, I visualize seagulls flying effortlessly over the beach, just sort of floating, going whichever way the wind may take them. Then I think of those times when I had drunk just the right amount of booze, and I felt as if I were floating above everything and everyone, just going with the flow, like the seagull. What a feeling! It was great! Feeling good!

Is feeling good a problem? No. As a matter of fact, most people would give it a high priority. Everybody wants and likes to feel good. With this in mind, we can see that the effect of drugs, alcohol, and other behaviors — feeling good — being high — experiencing euphoria — is not the problem at all. As a matter of fact, for all addicts, it seems to be a solution!

Ask addicts anywhere and they will tell you about the times when the world seemed to be caving in, and they felt as if they were going to explode into a million pieces. But when they used their drug or behavior of choice, everything came together and they experienced peace. So the behavior, the gambling, drugging, drinking and so on is not the problem. On the contrary, the effect is a very desirable one.

Unfortunately, what seems to be a solution turns out to be a monster problem. It is the nature of all addictive detours to be pleasant and rewarding at the outset, only to change into horrible, destructive paths as time passes.

Feelings

If using a drug or behavior is not the problem, what is? Why must addicts use such things as gambling, religion, sex or chemicals in order to feel good? Why don't they feel good? My own experience plus what has been shared with me by many other addicts indicates there are a number of reasons, some of which have to do with certain negative feelings that have been internalized, and thus have become more than just feelings.

Guilt

Guilt is a powerful negative emotion that comes into being when we realize we have wronged another. All but a few human beings experience guilt. It is a very normal, natural emotion. There are those, however, who never feel guilt. Also, others seem to feel guilty all the time, whether there is any basis for it or not. For these people, guilt is not just an emotion, it is a state of being.

In other words, these are not people who feel guilt, these are guilty people. Through certain internal processes, which I will explain later, guilt has become a part of their character. So much is this the case that many of them can't remember a time when they didn't feel guilty. They have a persistent sense of being wrong. Even when there is no reason for it, they feel as if they're wrong. When they do something well, they feel as if they didn't do it well enough, so even when they succeed, there is a sense of falling short. Addicts fall into this category. Addicts are not people who feel guilt. They are guilty people.

Anger

Anger is an outstanding characteristic of addicts. In my own case, I was mad as hell for most of my first thirty years, but most of the time I either was not aware of it or could not tell you why I was angry. It was as if I had a compartment inside me full of rage. Most of the time it remained closed and locked, but there were times, usually when I was drinking, when it would break loose in uncontrollable fury, with a power and intensity that not only frightened me, but made me terribly ashamed. After all, I had been taught repeatedly as a child that anger was not a nice emotion, that I shouldn't be angry.

So driven by fear and shame, I resolved to control my anger by hiding it inside myself. This produced some disastrous results for I became so full of anger, it began to burst out even when I was not drinking, and I began to have physical symptoms of the emotion I was attempting to suppress, such as headaches and gastrointestinal problems. As if this were not enough, I became angry at myself for not being able to control my anger. As the process continued, I became a boiling cauldron of resentment and remorse. I had stored up the anger inside myself for so long it had become a large part of me. I wasn't a person who felt anger. I was an angry person. All addicts are.

Loneliness

Addicts are loners who cannot stand being alone, so they seek out places where there are people. Yet even when they are in the company of others, they still feel alone and lonely. If asked, most addicts will tell you they have never felt themselves to be a part of any group. Whether it was their family, school class, or club, they always felt somehow different, outsiders who didn't really belong.

When I was a child, I remember wondering if I really belonged in my family. My dad was a tall, handsome man with wavy black hair, my mom was a pretty woman with wavy brown hair and my sister was a lovely girl who also had nice wavy hair. I was not handsome, tall, or lovely, and my hair was neither dark nor wavy. I was painfully skinny, covered with freckles from head to toe, had straight blond hair, and was, in my own eyes, ugly. In spite of assurances from my parents, I could not believe I really belonged.

This was the case not only with my family. I never felt I belonged anywhere. Even when I began to recover, I had great difficulty integrating into the recovery group. I still believed I was different, an outsider who didn't belong, and this belief formed a significant obstacle to sobriety. All addicts tell about having similar beliefs and feelings in their lives. They believe they are different and feel like outsiders who don't belong. Addicts are not people who feel lonely once in a while. They are lonely people. Loneliness is a part of their being.

═ Fear

Deep, abiding fear is another trademark of addiction, and it may be the main reason why addicts do not feel good. Fear, like guilt, anger, and loneliness, is a natural emotion that occurs in all people from time to time. Fear normally arises when a person senses danger or anticipates the loss or lack of something valuable. Fear, like the other emotions, can protect life. However, when it is constantly present, it can threaten life or turn it into a living hell.

Most addicts, whether conscious of it or not, live in constant fear, and it has a tremendous effect on their behavior. In fact, it is through examining their behavior that addicts become aware of the depth and extent of their fear and begin to realize the prominent role it has played in their lives.

Driven by fear, addicts often imagine, and even expect, disasters of many kinds, and this can lead to erratic, irrational behavior.

For example, I vividly remember being afraid that my daughter was going to die because of the way I was living. I can remember waking up in a panic, running to her room, kneeling by her bed and listening to see if she was breathing. Not being satisfied, I would put my hand over her heart to feel if it was beating. Relieved to know she was alive, I would sit on the floor by her bed and weep. Finally, I'd return to bed and fall asleep, only to wake up an hour or two later in panic and repeat the whole process again.

I once read a book in which a psychologist listed 206 types of fear. When I had finished, I realized I had experienced all 206. Upon reflection, however, I became aware that there was one fear he had not listed. This was fear number 207, the fear of impending doom, and it was 207 that was with me constantly. Under its ubiquitous influence, I'd think, "I don't know what's going to happen to me, where it will take place, why or who or what will do it, but something terrible is going to happen to me soon."

All addicts have this fear, and even if they know it's irrational, they cannot reason or make it go away. Fear holds addicts tightly in its grip. In a real way, they belong to their fear. It owns them. Addicts are not people who feel fear. They are fearful people.

Although there are many other reasons why addicts do not feel good and therefore must use substances or behaviors that produce euphoria, the ones I have just covered should be sufficient to illustrate the matter. Addicts don't feel good because they are fearful, angry, lonely, guilty people. It is important to remember that I am not speaking of feelings, but states of being. The various negative emotions that all people feel from time to time have literally become a part of the character of addicts.

Addicts do not just feel these emotions occasionally. These emotions have become part of their being, flaws in their character. Feelings come and go, but character remains, and it is character that generates behavior. If one's character is flawed, one will sometimes behave in ways that are destructive to self and others, and quite often one will become addicted, for flaws in character are a significant factor in addiction.

Common Inner Traits

The community of addicts consists of a variety of people with widely divergent backgrounds. Addicts can be from every race, creed and sex, every educational level and every vocation. Some are addicted to substances, others to behaviors; some practice their addiction daily, others periodically; some use a lot, others a little. Although addicts differ from one another, however, it is vital to understand that these differences are only external.

Unfortunately, almost all addicts will at some time misunderstand this and will use their differentness to deny their addiction. If, however, they can see that addiction has little to do with external differences and look inside themselves, they may discover they have a great deal in common with other addicts, admit their condition and commence to recover.

Although addicts are different on the outside, they are the same on the inside. Indeed, on the inside, an addict is an addict like a rose is a rose. How can this be? How can such dissimilar people be so alike? Part of the answer is that we often confuse character with personality, and they are not the same. Personality is the outer, public self, the one that people see. It's the role we play, the mask we wear, and it may or may not give a true picture of who we really are. Character, on the other hand, is the inner, private self, the complex of inner traits that make up the person. Character is who we really are.

My experience has shown me that addicts invariably share certain specific traits of character that play a large part in the dynamics of their illness. In addition to the character flaws that are created by the internalization of negative feelings, several other traits that addicts have in common contribute to the disease. How, when, and why these came into being, I do not know. What I do know is that they exist in relatively pure form in every addict I have ever met.

=== Perfectionism

Addicts are perfectionists. For them, everything has to be in perfect order, or they become upset. Something as simple as hanging a picture is a major task because it must hang perfectly straight on the wall, both sides equidistant from floor and ceiling. I have often said that you can identify the addicts in any group by seating them opposite a picture that is hanging crooked and instructing them to look at it. The addicts will be obviously uneasy. They will look away from the picture, and you can almost sense the heroic efforts they are making to keep from jumping out of their seats and straightening it.

Though the example is humorous, perfectionism is a destructive trait that causes severe damage to self and others, for those who have it expect perfection not only of themselves but of others also. Perfectionists believe they should be and do the best at everything, and in their own minds, if they are not the best, they are the worst. Since to them to be the best means to be perfect, which is impossible, they begin to feel like failures. Because their own perfectionism ensures their failure, they cannot possibly succeed, and each failure robs them of self-esteem and deepens their feelings of worthlessness.

These feelings, however, are internalized and hidden in the unconscious mind. Thus, the person is not aware of them, and this is precisely why they are so damaging. Addicts are filled with unconscious feelings of unworthiness and believe deep inside that they are failures. These feelings drive them to act in ways that are destructive.

═══ Hypersensitivity

Addicts are hypersensitive. They get their feelings hurt very easily. A slighting remark or criticism that would be sloughed off by the average person can result in roaring, raging resentment in them. A compliment that would be accepted by others is unacceptable to them, and they are even hurt by it. In other words, if you criticize them, you have said too much, and if you compliment them, you have said too little! They are bound and determined to be hurt.

To say they are difficult to deal with would be an understatement, for what can you say to them that they will not take in the wrong way? In addition to this, they have an absolute genius for magnifying things out of proportion. As a matter of fact, any addict can take a minute problem and, given sufficient time, turn it into the greatest dilemma the world has ever known.

Psychologists and psychiatrists, those beloved mind jockeys who are so fond of multisyllabic descriptive terms, have dubbed this propensity to blow things out of proportion "stimulus augmentation." Personally, I think a better term would be "ballooning," but no matter what we call it, it is an unhealthy condition that keeps the process of addiction in motion.

Romanticism

Addicts are romantics. They are dreamers and lovers of soft lights, music, and romance. A good deal of their time is spent in dreaming, fantasizing, and wishful thinking. More often than not, the content of their thoughts, fantasies, and dreams has to do with being someone else, some place else, doing something else. And of course, the person, place, and things are all ideal.

For example, I used to sit and dream about living in the court of King Arthur where, naturally, I would be the premier knight, riding off to slay dragons, with the most beautiful maiden's scarf tucked into my armor.

All people fantasize such things from time to time, but I did it often. The reason? I couldn't stand who I was, where I was or what I was doing. I was disgusted with me and longed to be someone else. Thus my fantasies were not just wistful reveries. They were reactions to my own self-loathing. What's more, I was even a failure in my dreams, for I knew I would run away if I saw a dragon.

Addicts prefer sad, soulful music — what is commonly referred to as crying music. Many have one song they prefer over all others, and it is not unusual for them to sit and listen to it over and over, weeping. Why? Perhaps they are identifying with the story told by the song, or perhaps they are bonding with the sadness of tune and lyric. Maybe their weeping is a manifestation of their own inner sadness, which the song somehow brings to the surface.

Pain

If I had to use one short word to describe the inner beings of addicts, it would be pain. They suffer intensely from the deepest sort of pain. Describing the intensity and severity of this pain to those who have not experienced it is not easy. However, many years ago, I heard it described in an unforgettable way by an alcoholic. Although we had not met before, this man described my inner state of being as if he had lived inside me all my life, and he did so by talking about his own inner condition.

"For the first 15 years of my life," he said, "I felt like I had a big hole right in the middle of me, with the wind blowing through it, and it hurt." After painting this vivid portrait, he went on to say that some people he knew who had the same hole got religion and the hole closed. Others fell in love and it closed. Still others got an education and the hole closed. So he tried these things — all of them — but instead of closing, the hole in the middle of him got bigger and bigger. And the bigger it got, the more it hurt.

Then he told about his first experience with alcohol. And what do you think happened? The hole closed! The pain stopped! This was the effect of alcohol, and right then and there, though he was unaware of it, the effect of alcohol became the most important thing in his life. Why? Because it had done for him what nothing else had been able to do.

When people are in pain, they seek relief, and whatever gives them relief is important to them. The greater the pain, the greater the need for relief, and therefore anything that relieves the greatest pain assumes the greatest value. In order to understand the value of particular drug or euphoria-producing behavior, it is helpful to put yourself in an addict's place. Imagine you have walked around for 5, 10, 15 or 20 years with a big hole in the middle of you, *with* the wind blowing through it, constantly aching inside with the pain of guilt, anger, fear and loneliness. Then imagine one day you take something or do something that instantly, almost magically, closes the hole; stops the pain; changes your outlook; makes the guilt, anger, fear and loneliness go away; slakes your thirst for wholeness and, in addition, makes you feel euphoric. Would the substance or act that produced this miracle be important to you? Of course it would. How important? It would probably become the most important thing in your life.

So it is that the substance or behavior that brings about such changes becomes the most important thing in addicts' lives. Anyone who wants to understand addiction must understand the value of the effect of the drugs and/or behaviors.

Not only do drugs and activities relieve the inner pain of certain vulnerable people, they also bring about some radical changes in their perception, alter their thinking, cause a shift in their values and beliefs, produce a good feeling, and give them a sense of wholeness. In other words, these people feel that their total state of being has been transformed. Such transforming events are called spiritual experiences, and it is this spiritual aspect that hooks people, causing them to seek such experiences again and again.

Contrary to popular belief, addicts are not running away from something when they use; they are seeking something, and that something is a spiritual experience. Unfortunately, the tragedy of their fate is that they will never find it again by using, for chemicals and behaviors only produce one such experience. However, it only takes one experience to hook people who are vulnerable. These vulnerable ones are those who, because of their psychological and/or biological makeup, are the most prone to become addicted.

Side Effects And After Effects

If the drugs and behaviors I have been discussing brought about only these beneficial effects, they could be considered miraculous cures for terrible conditions. I am certain that if alcohol only created these positive effects for me, I would still be drinking. Unfortunately, however, most of what it produced was not in the least pleasant, positive, or beneficial.

The irony is that the very substances and behaviors that seem to relieve the addict's serious and painful condition can, and inevitably do, create new problems. It is sad, but true, that most things that bring about positive effects also have negative side effects and after effects. It seems you can't have one without the other. Side effects and after effects are unavoidable, integral aspects of the illness. Side effects are experienced while the addict is using. After effects occur after using. Both are unpleasant, undesirable, and painful.

I had a friend who used to say, "Drunkenness is a bad side effect of alcoholism." Although his statement seems amusing, it is nonetheless true, for even though it is not sought, drunkenness does inevitably occur, as do others. Almost every alcoholic can tell you about staggering, falling down, and blacking out. Some can tell you about going out to have a couple of drinks and coming to several days later in a hospital or jail.

Drug addicts can tell you about having trouble with the police, about hepatitis, and about AIDS — one of the most deadly side effects. People who are addicted to smoking can tell you about shortness of breath, others about emphysema and lung cancer — two more deadly side effects. There are many more such effects, but these should suffice to illustrate that all side effects are painful, and some are lethal.

After effects usually occur during the period after use, euphemistically called withdrawal. Personally I think it should be called "the sickness unto death." However, no matter what its name, it is a time of misery and suffering. Those who have used drugs, including alcohol, tremble, sweat, hyperventilate, vomit and heave. Some of them may even hallucinate or have convulsions. They can't eat or sleep or rest.

All addicts, I believe, experience intense physical, mental, emotional and spiritual anguish following a period of use. They feel disconnected from people and God; their minds race uncontrollably; they are filled with fear, guilt and self-loathing; and all these generate physical symptoms.

To describe his state of being while experiencing such debilitating after effects, an addict friend of mine once said, "I was afraid I was going to die and scared to death that I wouldn't." After effects sometimes become fixed and permanent mental and emotional conditions and at times lead to death. They are always painful.

The side effects and after effects that are integral to addiction are painful. Isn't it ironic that the drugs and practices that addicts use to relieve pain produce more pain? It is at this point that the "wisdom of addiction" (otherwise known as shallow, twisted, insane, self-destructive thinking) appears.

"I'm in pain," says the addict, "but I know how to relieve it. I'll use some more of 'the dog that bit me.'" And what is the result? Relief, but soon the pain is back. Only this time it is more intense.

The loneliness, fear, guilt and self-loathing are increased; the mental and physical symptoms are more extreme; and the addict feels more disconnected than before. Perhaps at this point, the "wisdom of addiction" is again applied, only this time the addict tries to figure out how to get the effect without getting the side and after effects. And it works — or so it appears. But the results are the same.

The thing that relieves the pain creates more pain. So the addict tries again and again and again, caught up in a vicious cycle called addiction. And unless help is found, it will turn the addict into a babbling idiot or a corpse.

What Is The Core Of Addiction?

Although describing addiction as a vicious cycle paints an adequate picture of the process of the illness, it doesn't help us understand its causes. I say this because the addict's painful state of being, like the drugs or behaviors that alternately relieve or intensify it, are only symptoms of the malady.

Let's face it, nobody is born lonely, guilty, angry or afraid, so these afflictions, despite the prominent role they play in the disease, must be caused by something else. They are not the problem. They are symptoms of the problem. The same is true for defects of character. Although I am well aware of the prominent role they play in addiction, I do not believe that addiction is caused by the flawed character of the addicts.

My reason for this is simple. If character defects come into being when negative feelings and beliefs are internalized, then they, too, must be symptoms, for they are caused by something else. So you see, even though painful states of being, drugs and behaviors that relieve them, and character flaws provide the fuel that keeps the vehicle of addiction running; they are not the engine that makes it go.

What is the core of the illness? What is the engine that powers the vehicle of addiction? Although the main influence on my thinking has been the ideas formulated by the pioneers of Alcoholics Anonymous, I have also been influenced by many others Their thoughts not only have expanded my view, but have also deepened my conviction that the early members of AA were quite correct.

One of those whose thoughts have had an impact on me is the gifted psychiatrist, Scott Peck. He and I became friends as the result of a chain of events that began when I was deeply touched by a book he had written. At some time during the course of our frequent letters and conversations, he shared an insight with me that not only enhanced but also reinforced my own perception of addiction.

What he told me was that the one common characteristic of every unhealthy person he had ever met was that each had an ego that was not submitted to anything or anyone higher than itself. Ever since he shared this insight with me, the unsubmitted ego has been central to my own view of addiction.

Later I was greatly impressed when I read a paper by a psychologist whose thesis was that people become emotionally or spiritually sick, and remain that way, because they assume they have power that they do not have. Ever since reading that paper, the illusion of personal power has been a part of my thinking.

These two ideas, the unsubmitted ego and the illusion of power, came together for me when I read a description of an alcoholic written by Dr. Harry M. Tiebout: "Characteristic of the so-called typical alcoholic, is a narcissistic egocentric core, dominated by feelings of omnipotence, intent on maintaining at all costs its inner integrity . . . Inwardly, the alcoholic brooks no control from man or God."[2]

So there it is. The alcoholic's ego feels it is all-powerful and is not about to submit to any control whatsoever. Not surprisingly, the pioneers of AA presented an almost identical picture, portraying alcoholics as self-centered people who are obsessed with being in control and who are continually attempting to impose their will on others, acting as if they were God. Needless to say, both experience and research have shown this picture to be as accurate for other addicts as it is for alcoholics. To sum up, what we are all saying is that the core of addiction is an ego that believes it is God.

Unrestrained ego is the engine that powers the vehicle of addiction. How does the engine run? Like the one in your car, it runs by internal combustion. Where does the combustion take place? In the mind of the addict.

The Regions Of The Mind

The human mind is the most marvelous creation in existence. It is so complex that, in spite of the substantial amount of knowledge that has accumulated over the centuries, it remains a mystery. Opinions about its nature vary widely. There are those who would reduce mind to those electrochemical processes that occur in the brain, thus confining it to, and identifying it with, that organ. Others perceive mind as a spiritual entity that cannot be confined and that is the boundless, primal energy source from which all matter is created.

Happily, we don't have to take sides in order to illustrate how the mind works in addiction, for there is enough reliable information to enable me to explain what happens in the minds of addicts to perpetuate their illness.

In the interest of clarity and simplicity, it is helpful to view the mind as having two main regions, the conscious and the unconscious. Located in the conscious mind are those values, beliefs, feelings, and memories of which the person is aware, as well as the faculties of perception, intellect, and will. Will is the apparatus the individual employs to make and carry out choices. I call it the "chooser." Intellect is the computerlike mechanism that processes information. I call it the "thinker." Perception is the window through which the person looks out at reality. I call it the "porthole."

The conscious mind is also the residence of the ego. Ego is a two-syllable word that means "I," and it can be defined as a person's awareness of self as a separate, unique entity. Simply put, ego is my conscious awareness that I am not you. Ego is the wall, or boundary, that separates each of us from all other beings and objects. Ego disconnects us from nature, each other, and God.

The ego has a job to do. Its task is to manage the mind in such a way that the individual is taken care of. Your ego takes care of you, and my ego takes care of me. Mine does not even consider your needs, and yours doesn't think about my needs. The ego is self-centered. As manager of the mind, the ego has two basic management objectives: first, to help the individual find pleasure and avoid pain; second, to protect what is valuable to the individual. The ego uses perception, intellect, and will to carry out its tasks. Using these as tools, it helps the individual retain what is pleasurable, dispose of what is painful or threatening, and protect what is valuable.

According to Carl Jung, the spirit-guided, gentle genius of psychiatry, the unconscious is divided into two parts. One part he called the "personal unconscious," and it is clear from the name that this part is unique to each individual. It belongs to that person and nobody else. I call this part of the unconscious mind the Basement because this term clearly illustrates the processes that take place in addiction.

To me, the one word that describes what people store in the basements of their homes is junk. Now what do you think is kept in the Basement of people's minds? That's right — junk! How does it get there? It's simple. Whenever some thought or memory or feeling that the ego perceives as harmful to us or to our values comes into consciousness, it shoves it into the Basement and keeps it there. To do this, the ego uses the intellect and will to formulate and implement processes called ego defense mechanisms, which include rationalization, projection, denial, and euphoric recall. Thus the Basement is a repository for junk that is put in it by the ego.

Jung called the other section of the unconscious mind the "collective unconscious," and, as its name clearly states, it is not the property of the individual. Quite the contrary, it is shared by everyone and contains knowledge that is inborn and inbred in all of us. I call this section the Knower, and I consider it the most amazing and incredible entity in the universe. Why? Because the Knower knows!

Think about it, dear reader. There is a part of your mind that knows things you've never learned, contains information you've not gathered, and holds experiences you've not had! How can this be? All of it has been passed along to you by your ancestors through genetics. Your mind and mine contain the collected wisdom of humankind, even though we may not be consciously aware of that wisdom. At times, however, when needed, it surfaces, and we intuitively know what to say or do.

The Knower knows that all is one — that God is in everything and everyone, and that everything and everyone is in God. "So, waiting," wrote the poet Goethe, "I have won from you the end: God's presence in each element."

Sometimes the Knower knows things in advance, like when you go somewhere you've never been, yet you know where every tree, sign, or building will be. Or perhaps you're talking with someone, and you know what's going to be said before a word is spoken. The Knower sometimes protects you by warning you.

I remember once when, without consciously knowing why, I declined to go out with some friends because I somehow sensed I shouldn't. That night they ran their car off the road and into a lake, and it was only by grace or good fortune that they were not drowned.

The Knower knows exactly where to turn for help in times of trouble, and it does so automatically. For instance, can you remember a time you found yourself in a terrible situation or in imminent danger and you knew you could not handle it? Didn't you cry out, "God help me!" or some similar plea? And didn't you do it without thinking, automatically? Why did you cry out, and how did you know to direct the plea to God? I believe it's because the Knower knows precisely to whom we must turn in times of crisis, and it instinctively does so.

Throughout history, people have recognized the existence of the Knower. Though they have called it by many different names, all have considered it to be an extension of the divine, the offspring of God that lies deep within every person.

To me, the Knower is chairperson of the board for the mind, the internal source of power and intelligence, and one of its functions is to provide us with enough of both to be able to survive, stay sane, and live happy, meaningful lives.

Intelligence is often confused with intellect, but they are not the same. Intelligence is the ability to recognize what is good for you and what is not. When intelligence and power work together, we are sane, for sanity is the ability to recognize what is good for you and do it, and to recognize what is not good for you and avoid it. Thus, if we are cut off from the Knower, we will become insane.

As chairperson of the board, perhaps the main function of the Knower is to supervise the manager of the mind, the ego, controlling, guiding and mediating its actions. Without the restraining influence of the Knower, the ego will run wild. Thus, if the Knower is blocked, the ego will assume the role of chairperson, and the result will be chaos, for the ego has neither the power nor the intelligence necessary for the job.

Psychospiritual Dynamics

Now that we have examined the regions of the mind, as well as the nature and function of each, let us look at the psychospiritual dynamics involved in addiction. As usual, I'll do this by making up a story.

Ray is a drug addict. He is 25 years old and has been using since he was 13. Ray, like all of us, has an ideal image of himself

— that is, the person he wants to be. Since this image is valuable to him, he wants others to see it and believe it, so he "wears" it every day. Although his ideal image of himself is a "macho" man, who is strong, brave and fearless, there are times when he can't live up to the image.

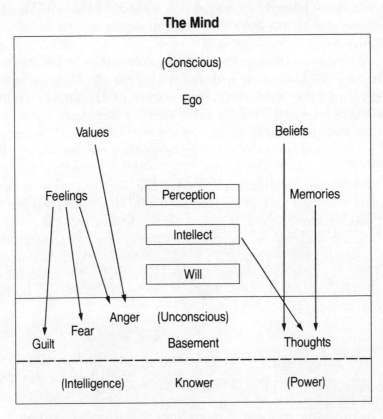

Figure 6.1. How Fear Gets Shoved Into The Basement Of The Mind

Unacceptable feelings, thoughts, memories, values and beliefs, are shoved into Basement by Ray's Ego for more than 20 years.

Inside his Basement is a boiling cauldron of living junk which creates a multitude of problems.

One particular morning, he is out of drugs and money, and he is very frightened. Walking down the street, he meets a friend, to whom his fear is obvious.

"Damn, Ray," says his friend, "what are you so scared about?"

"Me, scared?" replies Ray. "I'm not scared at all."

When Ray denies his fear, what do you think happens inside his mind? The ego, whose job it is to protect his valuable ideal image, shoves the fear into the Basement of his mind. (See Figure 6.1.)

At other times, when Ray has thoughts or feelings or memories that are not consistent with his image, the ego likewise pushes these into the Basement. As a matter of fact, every feeling, thought, memory, value or belief that conflicts with Ray's cherished view of himself, as well as any that cause him discomfort, have been hidden away by the ego ever since his ideal image came into being. (See Figure 6.1.).

What does this mean? It means that Ray has more than 20 years' worth of junk in his Basement, and although it was buried, it was not buried dead, but alive, so inside Ray, there is a boiling, churning cauldron of living junk. Although he is not aware of it, it is there and it creates all kinds of problems. Sometimes he wakes up in a rage or he is depressed and frightened for no apparent reason. At other times, he is literally swamped by feelings of despair or self-loathing.

If asked why he felt these things, his only honest answer would be, "I don't know."

Try as he might, he cannot figure out why he feels as he does. There seems to be no reason for it at all. In truth, he is feeling the way he is because of the cauldron full of junk in his Basement. The thoughts, memories and feelings that have been stored there have now become a part of him. And from the darkness of his Basement, they exercise a powerful influence on his perception, emotions and behavior.

Ray is not a person who feels fear, guilt and anger. He is an angry, fearful, guilty person who is suffering from excruciating inner pain and who cannot control his own behavior.

"So much for his ideal image," you say. "How does this apply to Ray's addiction?" We'll look at that now by continuing his story.

Ray, driven by his painful state of being, enters treatment. He is hurting deeply inside and his physical withdrawal multiplies his misery. For the first week, he is on time for every group, talks openly with his counselor, follows directions, pays attention in recovery meetings and prays daily. Then he begins to change. He is late for group, avoids his counselor, is arrogant and rude, stops praying and creates disturbances in recovery meetings. Finally, after 10 days, he leaves the center, and that very night, he uses.

What happened? Here was a young man who seemed willing to do anything to get well and now he is using again. The answer is simple. When his pain went away, so did his desire to change. First, his physical withdrawal passed, and he felt fine. Second, and most importantly, since the illusive effect of drugs had been so valuable to him for years, his ego had taken action. In just 10 short days, it had pushed all the painful memories, feelings and thoughts into his Basement, so that he could remember only the pleasure associated with drugs. Then having brought about euphoric recall, the ego delivered the coup de grace to Ray, just as it has done to legions of addicts. It convinced him that, since he was indeed a "macho" man, he could use again and get only the good effects without having any side or aftereffects. Convinced, he used.

Having one's Basement full of junk creates, as we have seen, a multitude of problems that bring with them a tremendous amount of pain for the individual. Yet, as terrible as this is, it is not the worst result of the ego's actions. What could be worse? Just this. When the Basement is filled with junk, it blocks us from our inner source of intelligence and power, the Knower (see diagram on page 94). When this happens, we are unable to recognize what is good and embrace it, and equally unable to recognize what is bad and avoid it. In other words, we are insane. (See Figure 6.2, page 94.)

In fact, people like Ray continually do what is not good for them, seemingly bent on self-destruction. They are, indeed, insane, but remember, it is a spiritual rather than a mental form of insanity, for it is based, not on chemical imbalance, but on separation from the power and intelligence within. Even when pain drives them to choose to stop using, they cannot do so, for the needed power is not available. They are powerless.

Finally, when the Knower is blocked out, it cannot control the ego, and the ego, the manager of the mind, begins to act as if it were chairperson of the board. Now unrestrained by the Knower, and thus unsubmitted to anyone or anything higher than itself, it considers itself all-powerful. It believes itself to be God, and thus deluded, it is the engine that powers the vehicle of addiction. By a process of internal combustion in the mind, the ego has become inflated and arrogant, intent on controlling everyone and everything. To reiterate: The core of addiction is an ego that believes it is God.

Before resting my case concerning this matter, I must add that I do not believe this process represents a purely mental problem, for when we deal with such entities as power, intelligence, ego, God, and God's child, the Knower, we are deep into the realm of the spirit. If, as I believe, the illness of addiction cannot be halted because addicts are blocked off from their own internal source of power and intelligence, then addiction is primarily and essentially a spiritual problem. Therefore, I wholeheartedly agree with the AA position that the fundamental dilemma of addicts is lack of power and that addiction can only be arrested by finding and making connection with a Higher Power.[3]

Having said this, I rest my case.

The Mind

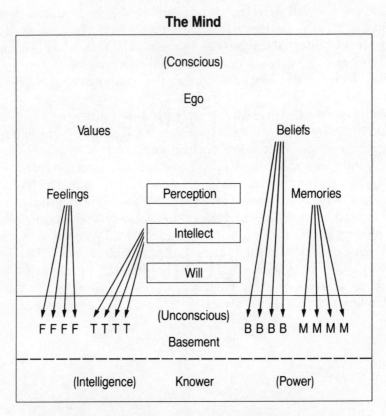

Figure 6.2. How We Become Blocked Off From The Knower

When Basement is full of junk, we are blocked off from the Knower. Without its Power and Intelligence, we become insane.

PART THREE

The Far
Country

7

The Monster Within

Detours

Detours, as I said earlier, are paths that involve using mood-altering chemicals and/or behaviors whose major effect is to change perception in such a way that the addict is deceived into believing that all is well. The drugs and practices are extremely powerful, especially in a spiritual sense, since they seem to transform pain into pleasure, anxiety into serenity and chaos into harmony. Their greatest spiritual power, however, lies in their capacity to create the delusion that the addict is whole — at-one with self, others and God, when in fact there is more separation than ever from all three.

Being on a detour is like looking at the world through a window of illusion. At first, what addicts see appears to be clear, bright and pleasant, and they feel at home. But with the passage of time, what they see becomes increasingly obscure, faded and unpleasant, and at some point they realize they are in a far country, a long way from home. As the detour takes them deeper into this foreign land, the window of illusion cracks, and eventually, it shatters, leaving addicts alone and stranded, far from home.

Detours are always very pleasant in the beginning. However, as time passes, they become progressively more painful, and if their progress is not halted, they may be lethal. As the addict travels along the detour, physical suffering intensifies, mental confusion multiplies, emotional anguish worsens, behavioral consequences increase in number and severity, and spiritual separation broadens. What seemed to enliven the mind, body, emotions and spirit gradually kills them.

Spiritually, the most disastrous effect of any detour is the separation from others, from God, and from one's own deepest self, the Knower — the offspring of God — the wise child within.

Detours are magical, but magic, by definition, is illusion, and illusion is not real. Unfortunately, by the time addicts realize this, they are past the point where they can return on their own power. A friend of mine once said, "The chains of addiction are never felt until they are too strong to be broken."

I believe he was right and his statement highlights the fact that when addicts become aware of their condition, it is too late for them to change it by themselves. Legions of addicts bear witness to the fact that, in spite of tremendous effort, they could not do it alone. Sometimes driven by pain, suffering or circumstance, they stop using for a time, only to start again when they feel better.

Their stories point clearly to the fact that the problem in dealing with the detour is not stopping the drug or behavior; it is staying stopped. In fact, quitting is the easy part, and any addict can tell you this. "Quitting was easy," you'll hear. "I quit a hundred times. Quitting was not the problem. The problem was that I couldn't stay quit."

Why? Why, when they really want to, can addicts not remain clean and sober?

Although answers to this question vary, there are some points of agreement in all of them. For example, stopping the addictive drug or behavior is clearly and invariably related to pain, for when addicts hurt long enough and badly enough, they will quit using. Likewise, starting to use again is apparently related to the disappearance of the pain that caused them to stop in the first place.

How does the pain disappear? As we saw earlier, the ego pushes it into the Basement of the mind, causing addicts to forget about it in a relatively short period of time. With the pain thus gone from consciousness, all they can recall are the pleasant aspects of using.

So courtesy of the ego, painful memories are hidden away and pleasant ones are retained, and now oblivious to the pain caused by using and aware only of the pleasurable aspects produced by the drug of choice, the addict uses again. The process by which the ego deludes the addict is called euphoric recall, and while most everyone, including me, agrees that it is one of the most significant reasons why the addict returns to using, I do not think as some do, that it is the main reason. Based on my experience and that of other addicts, I am convinced there is a deeper reason.

To get to this deeper reason, let's consider a scenario involving one addict. He quits using because of pain and the problems associated with his using. Then, like any addict, he runs around and tries to straighten out the mess his using has caused. He apologizes, pays off and promises. His physical pain passes, his wife is speaking to him again, his boss hires him back, his dog is licking his face again and his little girl is not running from him anymore. To cap it all off, he has returned to church. All is well with him. Things could not be better.

Yet he uses. Why? Euphoric recall? Sorry, that's just not enough to explain why a guy who has everything going for him does the one thing that will destroy it all. Why, then, does he do it? I believe it is because far down in the Basement of his unconscious mind lurks the notion that he does not deserve things to be good. The name of this unconscious notion is self-hate, and it is a monster.

Most addicts are not at all aware that they hate themselves, and most would deny it. Their awareness and denial should not be surprising, however, because their self-hate, which is painful, has been buried in their unconscious minds by the ego. Yet I believe addicts are full of self-hate, and I am convinced that it is the chief reason why they always mess things up when they're doing fine.

Every addict, like the man described in the book *Alcoholic Anonymous*, ". . . uses his gifts to build up a bright outlook for his family and himself, and then pulls the structure down on his head by a senseless series of sprees."[1]

One of the hallmarks of addiction is that addicts apparently can't stand success. When things get good, they mess them up. When one crisis is over, they promptly create another. It has been said that if anything is worse for addicts than bad fortune, it is good fortune. So whether addicts are aware of their self-hate or not, they clearly demonstrate it by their behavior.

It is an unconscious hatred of self that causes addicts to sabotage their recovery, to defeat and damage themselves and others and to undermine their success. If, as I said earlier, character flaws are the fuel that powers the engine in the vehicle of addiction, then self-hate is the octane in that fuel, causing the engine to run smoothly and knock-free. Having said this, I will try to explain the nature of self-hate, its sources, symptoms and effects.

Self-Esteem/Self-Hate

Some people say addicts have no self-esteem, but I do not agree. They have plenty of self-esteem, but it is usually not recognized as such. Usually, we consider self-esteem to be having a proper, positive regard for oneself. If, however, people have too high an opinion of themselves, we look upon them as egotistical, conceited and in love with themselves.

Universally, addicts do not regard themselves in a positive manner. Furthermore, their opinions of themselves are too low, rather than too high. Yet they are just as egotistical and conceited as are the aforementioned people, but in a different way. Whereas those people felt they were better than they were, addicts feel they are worse than they really are. Indeed, they are not in love with themselves, but in hate with themselves.

So addicts have self-esteem, but it is the negative pole of egotism. It is Narcissus frowning at his image in the water. It is not self-love, it is self-hate.

Self-hate consists of a set of unconscious beliefs people have about themselves. Since the beliefs are internalized, they have become a part of their characters and exercise a powerful influence on their thoughts, feelings and behaviors. What are the beliefs that constitute self-hate? There are many, but the most significant are:

1. "I'm unworthy of love;"
2. "I'm no good;"
3. "I'm a failure."

Because of these unconscious beliefs, among others, addicts are their own worst enemy, for these tenets set in motion thoughts and behaviors that make their lives a nightmare.

How? One of my favorite television characters, Flip Wilson's Geraldine, used to say, "What you see is what you get." I think Geraldine was correct, even though "she" wasn't talking about addiction, for if addicts see themselves as no-good failures who are unworthy of love, that's exactly what they will become. It's a self-fulfilling prophecy. What we believe we are, we will be.

The seeds of negative beliefs that are planted deep in addicts' unconscious minds will produce fruits in their lives. In spiritual terms, they reap what they sow. It cannot be otherwise. Addicts are caught up in another vicious cycle. Their beliefs ensure their failures, and their failures reinforce their beliefs, which in turn produce more failures, and on and on. The tragedy is that they really don't know why.

It has been said that addicts are programmed for failure, and I am convinced this is true. But how, when, and why did such programming take place? Where did these beliefs come from? These are difficult questions, and although I'm neither wise enough to know all the answers nor fool enough to claim that I do, I have some ideas on the matter.

Although addiction deepens self-hate, I am certain that it does not cause it, any more than it causes the other flaws in character that perpetuate the illness. My reason?

My personal experience makes it very clear that my self-hate preceded my addiction and has continued during my recovery. You see, in retrospect, I know that I considered myself a failure when I was around five years old, and I had feelings of unworthiness from my earliest memories. In fact, I can remember clearly not liking myself at all.

Since my recovery began, my self-hate has caused me a lot of problems, and even though I have been sober a long while, it still rears its ugly head in various ways almost every day. However let me be quick to add that now it is not nearly so intense, and I have learned to recognize and deal with it in a manner that enhances my growth and makes my self-concept more positive.

Another reason why I don't think self-hate is the result of addiction is that people who are not addicts have it also. Don't think that self-hate and character defects are the sole property of addicts. However, both do exist in relatively pure form in every addict I've ever met, read about, or talked with, and until these unconscious faults are uncovered and dealt with, there is very little chance for a happy sobriety.

The beliefs that constitute self-hate most probably result from the bonding of the guilt, shame, and remorse that have been accumulating in the Basements of addicts' minds over their entire lives. This being the case, if they are to discover the sources of their difficulty, they must look at those life experiences that gave rise to these negative feelings, as well as at the people, groups and institutions involved, looking especially at their formative years, for obviously this is when the problem began. In my case, my examination of my early life enabled me to start to understand where and how my self-hate came into being.

Like you, when I was a child I was innocent and vulnerable and, therefore, open to the influence of those people and groups that were important to me. Thus, I was affected by parents, teachers, friends, family, school and church, just as you were. By far, the two most dominant influences in my early life were my family — especially my mother — and the conservative, fundamentalist church to which we belonged. I'm sure my interaction with both played a large part in creating the guilt, shame, and remorse that later hardened into self-hate. Before telling you how this happened, I want you to know that I do not blame or resent my family or the church. (I once did. However, the principle of forgiveness released both them and me.) Therefore, the comments that follow are observations, not condemnations.

The Effect Of Religion On Early Development

The little church to which we belonged in my early years was both comforting and distressing to me, depending on whether I was in the back, in Sunday school, or in the front, in regular services. Sunday school was nice. Even though there were rules, the atmosphere was informal and warm, and each child was treated with respect, kindness, and concern. We were always given cookies and milk, and each time we attended, we were given a little gold star to stick on our "quarterly" (lesson manual).

All of this was very pleasant, but best of all were the stories they told us about a sweet, kind, wise man who loved little children. As a matter of fact, he loved them so much, he told others they should become like little kids again, and I liked that. He was a carpenter who had lived many years ago, we were told, and he was so good that God brought him back to life after he died. While he was alive, he went around the country taking care of sick people and telling little stories to people. These little stories were called parables, and many of them were about God, whom the carpenter referred to as his father. He said God was our father too, a gentle, loving being who especially cherished little kids.

I really like hearing about the carpenter, knew the stories he told were true, and, though I never met him, I loved him. I thought he was the best man who ever lived, and I believed he told the truth. I still do, for what I accepted as a little child, I accept now.

Regular services, called worship services, were much more formal. Everyone sat on hard wooden benches called pews. The pews were uncomfortable and so was I. Unlike Sunday school, the atmosphere seemed cold and stifling. There were no cookies and milk, and whenever I wiggled or moved, usually because the pew hurt my behind, I was told to keep still, and all the old women glared at me, or so it seemed to me. There was an order of service, printed on the bulletin, and it was strictly adhered to.

No cookies and milk, pews, cold and stifling atmosphere, no wiggling or moving, old ladies staring at me, being still, order of service — all these things made me uncomfortable because they kept me from being and acting like what I was, a child. Though the rigidity made me uncomfortable, it did not disturb me. The disturbance always came when — after the collection was taken — the sermon was delivered.

Our minister was a very nice man, a quiet and gentle person who often visited our home. Although I liked him when he came to our house, I did not always like him when he was in the pulpit.

In fact, sometimes it was hard for me to believe that the man in the pulpit was the same man who visited us, because what he said was often harsh, and it confused and disturbed me. To my young mind, the God he talked about was obviously not the same one the carpenter spoke of, for this God was not loving, but was vengeful and hateful.

According to the preacher, God was out to get sinners, and after he got them he was going to punish them, and the sole punishment was death! Sinners, he told us, were people who didn't live by the rigid set of rules in the Bible, and they were bad, bad people. Furthermore, he said, all people were sinners.

This disturbed me, for even though I did not like what the preacher was saying and did not even know there was a set of rules, if all people were sinners, I must be a sinner — a bad, bad person. I believe that having the idea that I was a bad person continually drummed into my young mind caused me to believe I was a bad person. Furthermore, since God obviously didn't like sinners, I was sure God did not love me.

Many times during my early years, I made up excuses that enabled me to leave or to miss these troubling sermons. Sometimes I just wouldn't show up even though I knew I'd be punished, and as soon as I was able to choose for myself, I left organized religion altogether, taking with me, however, the teachings of the carpenter.

As a youngster, I consciously rejected the notion of a vengeful God. Nevertheless, the idea remained within me for a long time because it had been programmed into my unconscious mind through constant repetition. Certainly, it was with me during the period of my active addiction, and only after some time in recovery was I able to root it out.

As a child, I rejected the concept of a punishing, condemning God who kills people for their wrongs, and embraced the concept of a loving Father who welcomes his children home from their detours. As a sober man, I do the same.

Effects Of Family Expectations

When I was growing up, the dominant member of the family was my mother, and it was from my interactions with her that the web of self-hate grew thicker and stronger. This was, I am absolutely certain, not her intention. Nevertheless, it seemed to me that she had some very definite ideas about our family and some precise expectations of me as a member of it. Though she never actually said so, and may never even have thought it, it was my perception that my mother felt that our family was, or should be, better than other people.

Thus it always seemed that my sister and I were expected to behave better, look neater and achieve more than others, so she and I set out to do just that. My sister did very well, but I became a superachiever, making straight "A's" in school and winning awards in school and church. When I look back, I see myself as a disgustingly perfect little boy.

Yet in spite of my best efforts, it didn't appear to me that mother was satisfied. In fact, a silent message seemed to come from her that said I should do better. Even though I don't think she consciously expected me to be perfect, it looked to me as if she did, so I tried harder and achieved more, to no avail. To the outer world, I appeared to be a very successful little boy, yet in my own deepest heart, I felt like a failure, since the one I wanted to please most was not, I thought, pleased.

Don't get me wrong. She praised me, as did my father, but always and ever came the silent message, "You can do better." At present, I know that all my attempts to excel and all my successes were efforts to win her love, for I believed erroneously that I had to earn her love and that in order to do so, I had to meet her expectations of me fully.

From an early age, I concluded that certain feelings were not acceptable. For example, I got the message that it wasn't nice to be angry, especially with parents, but whether it was nice or not, I sometimes felt anger toward them. Since it was unacceptable, I felt guilty and ashamed whenever it happened, and I never, never expressed the anger. Instead, I suppressed it, along with the guilt and shame that accompanied it. Fear was another feeling that I felt was not allowed, for whenever I expressed it, I was told that there was nothing to be afraid of or that I shouldn't be afraid.

Feelings about sex were, to say the least, discouraged. I never once saw my father pat my mother on the fanny. In fact, I later wondered if they had ever had sex more than twice — once for my sister and once for me. I came to believe that sex was dirty and that sexual feelings were the basest form of lust. These false notions caused an incredible amount of guilt, shame and remorse throughout much of my life.

In thinking back on my early years, I cannot recall seeing any open, demonstrative expressions of love in my family, such as hugging, kissing, or touching. It was not that there was no love in our home, for there was, but even though it was sometimes verbally expressed, it was not demonstrated. This being the case, you can imagine my shock when I joined a recovery group, where love is expressed openly and often. My God, I thought they were all a bunch of sex perverts!

It was even more of a shock when, upon meeting me for the first time, a man who was to become one of my beloved guides in recovery lifted me off the ground in a great, warm bear hug, kissed me on the cheek, set me down, grinned and said, "How're you doing, sugar?" All I could think was, "Oh, shit! I'm in trouble now!" You see, when I was raised, little boys didn't kiss their own fathers after they were a certain age, and here was this sweet bear of a man kissing me! At the time, I was shocked and did not know how to react.

Today, one of the best aspects of my life is my freedom to demonstrate openly my affection to both women and men. And, yes, I hug and kiss men. One of the best parts of my recovery occurred when my father and I began to express our love for one another in this way.

I hope that I have illustrated how I think the guilt, shame and remorse that formed self-hate came into my life. It shouldn't surprise anyone that church and family had such a strong impact on me and, I am certain, on many others for, by their very nature, both deal with the most intimate and important issues of life at a time when we are our most vulnerable and impressionable.

Religion, in particular, has the power to influence our lives positively or negatively, for its function is to provide us with answers to the paramount questions of life, answers that will open to us a pathway leading to the relationships that will make us whole again. It is for this reason that wrongful religious teaching can have a disastrous effect on our lives, especially if it is imposed on us when we are children, for it can push us in the direction of detours that will deepen our isolation, increase our despair, and propel us toward our doom.

Perhaps you can identify with me, or maybe you think you don't have any self-hate at all, and it's possible you don't. Most people however, especially those who have difficulty with life and living, like addicts and those who are involved with them, will find an abundant supply of self-hate deep within themselves if they know how to look for it.

Since self-hate is unconscious, it is also unseen. Like the wind, it is invisible. Yet even as we know the wind exists because we see the leaves move, so do we know that self-hate exists because of its manifestations. Though unseen, it produces symptoms. Thus, if one has these symptoms, one can be certain of its existence. The symptoms of self-hate are numerous, so rather than covering them all, we'll look at a few of the more outstanding ones.

Before we do this, however, let me say that you should not be surprised if these symptoms of reverse, negative self-centeredness closely resemble those that the new mythologists give for co-dependency, for if you remember, it is my conviction that co-dependency is nothing but a new label for an old syndrome. Even though I may be mistaken, it is, nevertheless, my present persuasion and will remain so unless and until I am convinced otherwise. Having said this, let's look at some of the more obvious manifestations of self-hate involved in addiction.

The Symptoms Of Self-Hate

Not long ago, a young woman alcoholic who has been sober for several years phoned me. "Tom," she said, "I guess you're going to think I'm crazy when I ask you, but why do I become afraid when everything is going well?"

I smiled when I heard her question, assured her she was not crazy and went on to share what I had learned from my own experience.

This woman's problem was not unique, for all addicts seem to get worried, or downright afraid, when all is well. Why? I think something deep within them sends the message that it is not okay for things to be so good. It's as if a little voice says, "Uh-oh, things are good, and you know they're not supposed to be because you are really a very bad person." The fear, I believe, comes from the source of that voice and that source is self-hate.

Addicts get scared when things are going well for them, and until they learn to handle it, the fear will impel them to behave in ways that mess things up again. A dear friend of mine, whose name was Manny, used to say of his alcoholism, "When things got good, that was bad." For quite some time, his meaning eluded me, until I reached a point in my recovery where I was forced to examine my life journey more deeply than I had before.

It's funny how, when we're ready, we do understand, isn't it? I must have been ready, for upon examining my life, both drunk and sober, it became very clear to me that Manny's statement fit me perfectly. During my active alcoholism, I seldom drank when there was a problem or crisis. On the contrary, I'd work through the problem or crisis, then, when everything was fine, I'd drink. To my surprise, I found that this was equally true of my recovery for, although I did not drink, when the waters of my life were smooth and calm, I'd sometimes create great tidal waves that carried me and those I loved toward the rocky cliffs of pain and trouble. Fear of success, plus feelings of unworthiness and badness, drive addicts to change harmony into cacophony, hope into despair. Truly, for them, when things get good, that's bad.

All people need acceptance and approval from self and others. This need creates great problems for addicts, for since they neither accept nor approve of themselves, the need to get these from others is magnified. In fact, they will do almost anything to get them. They will agree with opinions they do not agree with, behave in ways that violate their own values, allow others to use and abuse them and remain in unhealthy relationships, to name just a few.

Yet the tragic irony is that even when others do accept and approve of them, tell them they're okay, praise them or express love for them, the self-hate within them prevents them from believing it. Thus, addicts will ask spouses if they love them, and when they say they do, addicts will say, "Really?" When they reaffirm their love, addicts ask, "How much do you love me?" and on and on.

On the other hand, addicts' inability to believe positive feedback is only exceeded by their total inability to handle any kind of negative feedback. In fact, they are completely devastated by it and will do anything to change it. Addicts cannot handle praise or criticism, yet they continue to attempt to pursue the one and avoid the other. Tragically, some things they do deepen their self-hate, which in turn further intensifies their hunger for approval and acceptance. It all gathers momentum like a rolling stone, moving toward self-debasement and finally self-annihilation.

One of the more outstanding symptoms of self-hate can be seen in the way addicts treat themselves. Nobody, in my estimation, treats themselves worse than addicts, yet they are not aware of it. The wind of self-hate moves the leaves and turns the wind-mills of their lives, but they do not know it. On the contrary, they believe their troubles come from people, places and things outside of themselves.

Thus they believe they are victims of outside elements when, in fact, the well from which all their difficulties are drawn lies within them. If they are victims, then they are victimized by their own self-hate and nothing else, and if we observe their actions toward themselves and their reactions to others, this becomes crystal clear, for they put themselves down continually.

For example, if you tell addicts you love them, they will immediately respond with a number of reasons why you shouldn't or say something like "I don't see why you love me" or "How can you love someone like me?" If you tell addicts they have done a good job, they will usually tell you why it should have been done better. It's really an amazing process, as anyone who has ever loved or complimented addicts well knows.

The process is simple and easily observable. You express your positive feelings and addicts turn them down, yet they seem un-aware that they are doing so. The fact is they are unaware, for their responses are unconscious, habitual ones that have been pro-grammed within them over the years. It's like the message on a telephone answering machine — when someone calls, the tape plays its message. When someone tells addicts they love them, a taped message is set off from within which says, "Tell them they should not love me for the following reasons." Anyone who has ever had the guts to love an addict has been rebuffed by such messages.

But this is not all, for if they continue to try, they will be hurt. Indeed, addicts always hurt those who love them most and whom they love most. Why? Because if rebuffs and rebuttals do not work, their self-hate will protect its integrity by bringing harm to those who threaten it. But again, addicts do not know why they have harmed those who are dearest to them. All they know is that they have hurt them, and they are ashamed and remorseful. Thus, their self-loathing deepens and waits for another opportunity to spew forth its venom.

As we have seen, no one needs to put addicts down, for they do it themselves. They are their own worst enemies and they treat themselves as such. Yet they seem unaware of it. Perhaps the prime example of their self-hate is the way they treat themselves when they make a mistake, for they always condemn themselves for it.

One night while walking through the darkness of my living room on my way to the kitchen to get a drink of water, I hit my little toe on the leg of the coffee table.

Boy, did it hurt! Slowly, I became aware of my reaction to the accident. I was jumping up and down, holding my foot in my hand and screaming at myself, "You stupid son-of-a-bitch! You've never done anything right!" To say the least, my reaction was extreme. After all, anyone could hit a toe as I did. Yet rather than reacting in this way, a stream of self-condemnation came rushing forth from within me. So it is with addicts. Minor mistakes are treated as if they are cataclysmic errors worthy of massive punishment.

Self-Hatred And The Higher Power

Before wrapping up my comments on self-hate, there is another symptom that I must include, for, in the final analysis, it may be the most important of all. Addicts, notwithstanding their objections to the contrary, have a very negative concept of the Higher Power. Considering the mass of self-hate they have within them, this is not hard to understand. Indeed, it could not be otherwise, for the kind of Higher Power people believe in is directly related to what sort of people they believe they are.

Simply put, my concept of the Higher Power arises from my concept of self. If I am convinced I am a rotten person, I will believe in a Higher Power who believes I am a rotten person. If I consider myself unworthy of love, I cannot — no matter how I try — believe that the Higher Power loves me. If I think I deserve punishment, I will believe in a Higher Power who will punish me. In the most real way possible, the nature of one's Higher Power is determined by one's concept of one's self.

Addicts, like the Prodigal, feel they have sinned against God and therefore are no longer worthy of being God's children. At best, they feel that the Higher Power wants nothing to do with them; at worst, that God has been keeping a record of their errors, has judged them and is just waiting to execute punishment. Believing thus, they are afraid of a Higher Power, although they will not admit it.

In my opinion, self-hatred, more than anything else, causes addicts to have a negative concept of God. It is the largest single reason why they approach the whole matter indirectly, first using, as I did, the recovery group, then the sponsor, as the Higher Power. Then finally as the recovery program changes their concept of themselves by sufficiently freeing them from self-hate, they approach the living Source.

By this time, I hope you can see what a monster self-hate really is and what a huge role it plays in addiction. We've had a look at some of its major symptoms, and to summarize, I'd like to enumerate those we have covered: feelings of wrongness, fear of success, messing things up when they get good, the illusion of being a victim, an overwhelming need for approval and acceptance, getting into unhealthy relationships, the inability to accept love or compliments or criticism, treating oneself badly and allowing others to do likewise, putting self down, condemning oneself for mistakes, having a negative concept of the Higher Power.

This is quite a list and when its symptoms are carefully considered, it isn't difficult to understand how self-hate keeps addicts locked into the self-destruction detour called addiction. There is grace in all this, however. If they stay on the detour, they will inevitably reach that point where its illusion is totally shattered and the light of truth enters in.

That point is called bottom.

8

The Bottom

Not A Place

Eventually every detour takes addicts to a point called bottom. It may carry them there only once, perhaps twice, maybe more, but it will inevitably carry them there, for it is an integral part of the errant path. Whenever addicts reach bottom, they are at the point of almost complete separation from all of humankind and from their own deepest self, the Knower. Indeed, their souls are stretched to the limit. Like the Prodigal, they are without resources, stranded in a far country, utterly and completely alone. Like a chilling vapor, loneliness surrounds them, and it thickens, becoming even blacker.[1]

In their deepest heart, they know they are totally out of control, and that the drug or behavior they have sought so desperately to control has, in fact, been controlling them. At the bottom, addicts become painfully aware of the perversity of the illusion that the detour has purveyed, for they see clearly that the drug or behavior that seemed to quench their spiritual thirst has instead parched their souls and that the path that seemed to lead home has taken them into a faraway, frightful, forbidding land.

Even though bottom is an agonizing and frightening place, it is not necessarily a bad one for addicts to be in. Why? There are two basic reasons. First, for the time being they are not using their drug of choice. Second, and more importantly, bottom flattens the ego, thereby permitting insights that absolutely shatter the illusion of the detour and allow the light of truth to shine in. Using this light, addicts are able to comprehend their condition and see how it came to be. With the blindness created by ego and its defenses removed for the time being, addicts see clearly that it was not people, places, situations, or circumstances that brought them to this spot, broken and beaten.

On the contrary, in the light of truth, they understand, perhaps for the first time, that they alone are responsible for their own defeat, for their own condition. They now understand that they have been their own worst enemy. Though addicts may not be comforted by these revelations, they are at least, and at last, aware, and they can, if they choose, learn from their errors and change their course.

Many people, including a number of addicts, have erroneous ideas about what bottom is. Therefore, let me clarify what I believe it to be. Due mainly to the false mythology I spoke about earlier, some people think bottom is a concrete place, a geographical location called "Skid Row." Others think it refers to external social, mental, or physical conditions. To them, addicts hit bottom when they are broke, jobless, homeless, brain-damaged, or dying. Others speak of high bottom and low bottom, mental bottom or physical bottom.

Even though these views are held by well-meaning, intelligent people, they are missing the point, for bottom is not a geographical site, a set of external circumstances or an elevation; nor is it mental or physical. Bottom is a spiritual condition that comes into being at a given point in time. Truly, bottom can occur in a gutter or a mansion, and it can happen to a jailbird or a judge, a patient or a doctor, a wage earner or a millionaire, and it occurs in anyone of any description who travels the detour of addiction.

Although mental and physical elements certainly play a part in it, bottom is a spiritual state of being, and hitting it is a spiritual happening. Why do I insist that it is spiritual rather than a physical or mental state of being? My reasons are simple. When people reach the bottom mentally, they are totally insane, their mental processes damaged beyond repair. People who reach mental bottom are kept in institutions.

When people reach physical bottom, they are dead. Their physical processes have ceased to function. People who reach physical bottom are put in graveyards.

So . . . mental bottom is total and complete insanity, and it happens only once and physical bottom is death, which also happens only once. But when people reach spiritual bottom, they are neither insane nor dead (even though they may feel as if they are both). Instead, they are awakened to their true condition.

Hitting bottom is like waking up from a deep sleep and this is exactly what happens to addicts for they are roused from their delusion by the stark light of reality. Moreover, addicts can hit bottom with or without enormous physical or mental damage. They can hit it more than once, and more often than not, they do. Spiritual bottom is when addicts become fully aware of the hopelessness of their situation. More than this, it is a time when they can and must make some correct decisions, for if they don't, the asylum or the graveyard may be their destination.

In my view, bottom is the spiritual state of being that occurs whenever an addict becomes aware of the seriousness and hopelessness of his condition and is desperate enough to seek change. It is the point at which an addict realizes he is licked, looks around and says, "Oh, my God." It is the time when he feels overwhelmed and says, "What's the use anyway?" and thinks about suicide. It is the time when, in the starkly poetic words of Martin Buber, ". . . the incubus over him and the ghost within him whisper to one another the confession of their non-salvation."[2]

Bottom is a truly fearsome place, and when addicts reach it, they experience "the awful awakening to face the hideous Four Horsemen — Terror, Bewilderment, Frustration, Despair."[3] Feelings of hopelessness encompass them, and they feel as if they are at the bottom of a deep hole, unable to escape.

It is important to note that anyone who hits bottom for any reason will experience the same feelings; addicts most definitely are not the only ones who hit bottom. Although it may surprise some, people who are not addicts hit bottom, too. Usually, like addicts, they are spiritually thirsty, seekers of the source of life, ones for whom life must be more than mere existence. Among these, you will find poets, artists, musicians, writers, philosophers and some religious. So it is that just as Bill W. cried out from "the very bottom of the pit,"[4] so did the psalmist cry from "out of the depths."[5]

Many nonaddicts have described the state of being known as bottom, and all of them portray it as fraught with darkness, despair, despondency, disconsolation, and discouragement. Ancient Hebrew prophets called it Sheol, the place of the shadows. St. John of the Cross called it the dark night of the soul. Some philosophers gave it the melancholy label of existential despair. A black gospel song depicts it as feeling like a motherless child who is a long way from home. However it is described, it is the same condition. It is bottom.

A Gift

Even as the bottom is a dark and frightening place, so it can be the point at which light and comfort enter, for bottom, since it is a spiritual condition, is loaded with paradox. It is true, as the old saying goes, that it is always darkest before the dawn. Moreover, it is equally true that birth is contained in death, faith in doubt, and hope in despair, for I am convinced of the soundness of the metaphysical notion that everything includes its opposite.

Paradoxical? Yes, but remember that paradox is the stuff of the spiritual life. So it is that bottom, though it seems like the end, can be the beginning, for its despair includes hope, its darkness, light, its emptiness, fulfillment, and its powerlessness, Power. As I write this, I am reminded of a saying that is part of the oral tradition of some 12-Step groups: "Remember that where your rope ends, God's rope begins." The same principle was stated by the Sufi mystic and poet, Nazir, when he wrote:

When I reached a state of total despair,
hoping that death might rescue me from

this pain, He, my careless Beloved.
Come to me.
Like a mother rushing to her sick child,
He came to me,
sat by my side,
and placed my head upon his lap.[6]

Consider also the words of German mystic Meister Eckhart:

I maintain by God's external truth that God must pour himself,
without reservation, with all His powers, into everyone who
has sunk completely into himself and has touched bottom.[7]

Do you sense from reading the words of Nazir and Eckhart that bottom, though it is a cursed state, can also be a blessed one? Do you feel that its hope is born of its despair, its fulfillment from its emptiness? I do.

Ironic, isn't it, that bottom, which is the point of widest separation from God, is, at the same time, the place where addicts are closest to God? It's as if pain, dejection and powerlessness are a magnet that pulls the Higher Power to heal, assure, and empower addicts. Certainly, all of this is paradoxical, but if you want to understand addiction you must be comfortable with paradox because addiction is a spiritual illness, and that which is spiritual will be, by its nature, paradoxical.

In fact, the illness itself is a paradox, for addicts, who seem to be running away from God, are, in reality, seeking God, but they have chosen a wrong path and have become lost. This path, however, inevitably brings them to the point where they may reconnect with the Source and discover a right path.

As strange as it may seem, bottom may be a gift from a merciful God. To be sure, it is an unusual gift, for it is neither pleasant nor desirable. Quite the contrary, its contents seem to be patently unpleasant and undesirable. In spite of this, however, it can be the most beautiful and useful gift that addicts ever receive, for within it are the seeds of a new life. Whether or not this new life comes into being depends on what is done with these seeds. If addicts scatter them on the rocky ground of the intellect, the wind of ego will blow them away. But if they plant them in the rich soil of the spirit, they will blossom into recovery and a sane, sober life.

What are the seeds in this strange and unusual gift? They are the seeds of total desperation, which comes into being only at the bottom and is the stuff of which radical change is made. Total desperation is born of addicts' awareness of their real condition and their inability to change it. It is, in my opinion, the strongest initial motivation for recovery, for not only does it cause addicts to reach out for help, but it also creates in them the one element recovery requires.

Desire

It creates desire. Desire is born of desperation. The greater the desperation, the greater the desire, and since bottom is the point of complete desperation, it is also the point of complete desire. In short, bottom is the place where addicts want to change more than anything in the world, and this is the type of desire that is necessary for recovery.

Sobriety is not easily attained. In fact, unless and until addicts want it more than anything else, they cannot have it. It must be their top priority, their number-one goal. Why? Because if they do not desire it above all things, they will not do the work that is required to recover. Let's face it, recovery is not a "slide," and any addict who thinks it is, is in for a rude awakening. Recovery is difficult, and it requires hard, often painful and gut-wrenching work, and unless addicts' desire is very strong, they will not be willing to do it.

The first members of AA understood the relationship of desire to recovery, and they used it in their work with others. For example, in Cleveland, due to the publication of the Big Book and some articles in the major newspapers of that city, the early members received a flood of pleas for help. These were handed out to individual members, many of whom had been sober only a short time themselves. Each member had many requests for help to handle alone.

Knowing from their own experience that only a small number of the requests came from people who had the type of desire they knew was necessary in order to recover, they devised a rather ingenious method of identifying these. They "qualified" each prospect on whom they called.

How did they "qualify" them? They used what I call the "desperation-desire" index.

According to my sources, among whom were some early Cleveland members, they did so by asking the question: "What are you willing to do to stay sober forever?" If prospects replied that they would do anything, they "qualified," and they and their sponsors promptly began work on recovery. If, however, the prospects "hedged" on their answers or set limits on what they would do, or obviously wanted something besides sobriety, they were considered not "qualified," or not "ready." You see, these wise early members knew from the answers that these prospects' egos were alive and well and that, therefore, they had not reached the point of desperation necessary to produce the degree of desire required for recovery.

These prospects were encouraged to attend meetings, but little time was spent on them. If this seems harsh, remember there were only a few members, and they were laypeople who had limited time and resources. They were not out to recruit new members. They could not afford to waste time on those who did not have the great desire to recover, for if they did, they might miss some who were ready. They had only one purpose — to give a pearl of great price to those ready to receive it.

Like these early members, I am totally persuaded that a very strong desire to change is a prerequisite for recovery. Most people who know about addiction would agree. Desire is born of desperation. *No desperation, no desire; no desire, no recovery.*

For this reason I am troubled by the use of mood-altering drugs by some individuals and institutions who work with addicts. Since these substances alter perception, they can diminish desperation and thereby reduce the desire to change. Benzodiazepines and other mood-altering drugs may, I know, be helpful to some people when they are in great stress and under certain circumstances, but their use with addicts is extremely dangerous. Why? Because these drugs not only diminish desperation, most of them also produce euphoria, and addicts are addicted to euphoria.

What does all this mean? It means that the use of these drugs with addicts is a double-edged sword. These substances cannot only smother the desire to change, but they can also trigger the desire to use. This is especially true for those who are addicted to drugs or alcohol because such medications can set off the phenomenon of craving. Thus, the unwise and indiscriminate use of mood-altering chemicals not only can prevent recovery, but it can actually prolong addiction!

Why Bottom?

"Why and how," some of you may still be asking, "do addicts hit bottom." The simplest and most correct answer is that addicts hit bottom because of their persistent use of drugs and/or behaviors and the mental, emotional, physical, and spiritual consequences of their use. They are driven by a powerful obsession to control their drug or behavior of choice and are deluded by their own egos into believing they can do so, in spite of evidence to the contrary. Needless to say, their continued use brings in its wake an ever-increasing number of difficulties for themselves, their loved ones, and others who are involved with them.

As their overall health deteriorates, their suffering becomes more and more intense. Guilt, remorse, and shame increase, and there is a continual feeling of anxiety, as well as a sense of impending doom. All of this and more bring them inevitably to the point of defeat and desperation. They have sown the wind and reaped the whirlwind.

Must addicts continue to use for a certain length of time or experience a specific amount of suffering in order to hit bottom? Happily, the answer is no. What is necessary is that the ego be deflated so that addicts can perceive the reality of their condition. Such deflation can sometimes be accomplished by other means.

Years ago, Bill W. wrote about the necessity of raising the bottom for some and suggested that this might be done by sharing one's history of addiction in such a way that other people could see it as a progressive condition that worsened with time and realize that, even though some of the consequences had not yet been experienced, these would inevitably come to pass if they continued to use.[8]

Nowadays, some people attempt to collapse the addicts' egos through a process called intervention, which is an attempt to break down the ego's defenses by the presentation of factual behavioral evidence. If by these means addicts can perceive, admit, and accept the truth about their condition, they have hit bottom just as surely as those who hit it through their own excesses. The saddest part of this is that so many addicts, even when they become aware of the severity and deadlines of their condition, do not act on it in the way that is required if recovery is to commence and endure, and as a result they die.

Let us turn now to a question that has been, and remains, one of the greatest sources of controversy and disagreement concerning addiction: "Does the addict have to hit bottom in order to recover?" My unequivocal answer is yes. Why? Because the shift from addiction to recovery is a spiritual transformation that can only begin, according to some very reliable sources, with deflation of the ego, and it is hitting bottom that produces this deflation.

One of these sources was William James, the philosopher and psychologist, who made an extensive study of spiritual transformations, including the one from addiction to recovery. His study revealed that one of the common elements in every conversion was ego deflation at depth.[9]

Another source was Harry Tiebout, a psychiatrist who was an early supporter of the fledgling fellowship of AA and its notions about addiction and recovery. Dr. Tiebout treated many alcoholics and observed that they all possessed one thing in common: "An unconquerable ego which bitterly opposed any thought of defeat." He believed that, "Until that ego was somehow reduced or rendered ineffective, no likelihood of surrender could be anticipated." Hitting bottom, he continued, "produced a surrender which reduced the ego."[10] To recap, many experts in addiction and/or spiritual transformation agree that addicts must hit bottom in order to recover. But this is not all.

Defeat Deflates Ego

Earlier, when we looked at the dynamics of addiction, we saw how the ego was blocked off from the control of the Knower by the accumulated junk in the Basement and was acting as if it were chairperson of the board. It had become puffed up (inflated), felt all-powerful and was not submitted to anyone higher than itself. Thus, how can this little monster be deflated, reduced to its proper size and role by anything but defeat? Defeat, you see, destroys its illusion of omnipotence and thereby deflates it.

Moreover, when ego is deflated, it cannot use defense mechanisms to block the addict from the truth. What's even more important, however, is that while the ego is reduced to its proper size, a channel is opened to the Knower, and the Knower is able to control the ego. Through information from others and my own experience, I am convinced addicts must be defeated before they will change. Hitting bottom, I am sure, defeats them.

What Happens At Bottom?

It is now time to describe what happens in the minds of addicts when they hit bottom. As we saw earlier, bottom brings about deflation of the ego. When this happens, the internal barriers in the Basement are breached, and channels are cleared through which addicts have access to the Knower, the source of intelligence and power. For the moment, addicts have the intelligence to make a choice and the power to carry it out. They can recognize what is good for them and embrace it and recognize what is bad and avoid it. Therefore, at least for the time being, they are sane.

In addition, when the ego is deflated and its internal barriers are down, addicts' true feelings are released from the Basement, and they become aware of them. Old hidden memories are also freed up and they remember all the disasters connected with their addictions. Soon they become conscious of their deeper, more fundamental values and beliefs. They shudder with the knowledge of how they have violated them during their detour.

As their minds clear, their perception is altered so that they can see with crystal clarity, and as they survey their lives, their loves and their world, they perceive how things really are. With their feelings, memories, values and beliefs now conscious, and their perception unclouded by ego, their intellect has complete and correct information of which to base a decision. Because they now have access to the internal source of power, they not only can choose, but they can carry out the choice.

With all their faculties available and in proper working order, addicts realize the depth and reality of powerlessness and say, "I can't use, and I can't quit using, and I can't do anything about it." At that moment, their restored sanity kicks in, and they recognize the need for help from a Higher Power. Not only this, but somewhere deep inside they know beyond a shadow of any doubt that the Power can and will come to their aid. How do they know this? The Knower knows.

It is, I think, relevant to note here that William James found two elements present in all spiritual conversions. The first, as I mentioned earlier, was ego deflation at depth. The second was the intuitive knowledge that a Higher Power could and would save them. So following the urgings of their innermost self, addicts cry out in desperation from the depths of their being for that Power and surrender to it.

Bottom can be likened to a fork in the road. When addicts reach this fork, they must decide which path to take. One path is the illusive detour and will lead them ever deeper into the far country of separation and illness. The other path is what has been called the straight and narrow way, or the road less traveled, and it will take them home, the place of relation and wellness.

Since their egos are momentarily deflated, a channel has been opened to the Knower, and this wise child of the Source urges them to choose the road that leads home. At the bottom, addicts can heed the Knower and make this choice. In truth, it is the only point at which they can, for, though deflated, the ego is not dead. It will soon revive, and when it does, it will quickly go to work to hide the reality of the addicts' condition far down in the Basement of their minds.

To me, the Prodigal Son and his experiences parallel those of addiction and recovery so closely that his journey seems to be the prototype for the addict's.

In fact, sometimes I wonder if maybe the Prodigal could have been an addict himself. Perhaps he had a problem with wine, hashish, women or gambling. Who knows? At any rate, like an addict, he took the road (detour) that led him into a far country, where he squandered everything he had. He, too, hit bottom, winding up in the pig pen, defeated, hopeless and alone. Then, realizing the truth of his condition and his powerlessness to change it, he knew he had a choice to make, and he chose to take the road that led back to his father's house. Thus, he began his journey home. May it be so for more and more addicts. May more of them choose the road of recovery, which will lead them home.

PART FOUR

The Highway Of Recovery

9

The Turning

The Surrender

Motivated by their spirituality, human beings embark on the journey of life, seeking to quench their thirst for wholeness. As they travel, they soon discover that there are many pathways from which they may choose. Even though the signs on all the routes declare their destination to be the one the travelers want, all of them do not go there. In fact, despite what their signs proclaim, some of them are byways of despair that will take those who choose them into a frightening land, far from home. These byways are not true paths. They are detours.

Those who select true and right paths will experience lives that — though not without problems and suffering — are predominantly full and free, and they will, in time, arrive at their desired destination. Those who pick detours, however, will not really live at all, but will merely exist. Moreover, their existence will be marked by bondage and an ever-increasing neediness, and inevitably, they will end up in locations far, far from home.

There is grace in all this, however, for in every one of these spiritual locations, called bottoms, those who travel the detours of life are, for the moment, off them, and what is more important, they have an excellent opportunity to stay off them. Truly, for them, bottom offers the chance of a lifetime.

There are two basic conditions for a full and lasting recovery. The first is abstinence. If recovery is to commence, addicts must stop using their drug of choice, whether it be sex, gambling, food, religion, alcohol or other substances. Abstinence requires no great amount of intelligence or strength of character, nor does it really require any choice on the addicts' part. It just happens.

Indeed, periodic abstinence is an integral segment of the addictive process. At some point, or points, in time, all addicts will stop using because they simply cannot continue any longer, and when they quit, they have unwittingly and inadvertently met the first condition for recovery. Abstinence gets addicts off the detour. They cannot, however, stay off it for long unless they meet the second condition.

The second condition that is necessary for a full and lasting recovery is spiritual growth. If recovery is to be lasting, addicts must continue to refrain from using their drug of choice, and in order to do so, they must undergo a radical transformation in thought and attitude. Such a metamorphosis is a spiritual process.

You see, although abstinence may launch it, the ship of recovery will not stay afloat for very long unless the addict "can experience an entire psychic change,"[1] as Dr. Silkworth put it. The truth of the matter is that the two basic conditions of recovery are intimately related to one another. In fact, addicts can't have one without the other, for if they do not abstain, they cannot grow spiritually, and if they do not grow spiritually, they cannot remain abstinent.

Unlike abstinence, which just happens because it is part of the disease process, spiritual growth must be chosen. Therefore, it does require intelligence and strength of character (guts). When addicts make a decision to follow the path of spiritual growth, they have begun to meet the second condition for complete and continual recovery. Spiritual growth keeps addicts off the detour.

When addicts hit bottom, they have met the first condition of recovery, for they are not using. More important, however, hitting bottom has temporarily stilled the architect of delusion, the ego, thereby affording addicts an excellent opportunity to meet the second condition by choosing to grow spiritually.

Bottom may be likened to a fork in the road. One path is a continuation of the dreadful detour of addiction. The other, however, is the path of recovery through spiritual growth, and it will eventually lead to home. The choice that addicts make at this fork will have a great impact on their lives. Robert Frost wrote about a choice such as this:

Two roads diverged in a wood, and I —
I took the one less traveled by,
And that has made all the difference.[2]

As with Frost, the choice made by addicts will determine the quality of their lives. It will, indeed, make all the difference. But not only must they decide which road to take, they also must do so quickly, for their egos will soon revive. When this happens, a correct decision will be impossible. Tragically most addicts do not choose the road of recovery. The reason? They wait too long. Thus the road of recovery is, sadly, the one less traveled. Happily a few do choose it, thus changing the direction of their lives.

Recovery is a pilgrimage from illness to wellness that begins when addicts choose to follow its course. It is essentially an inner spiritual process that manifests itself in radical outer change. By it, addicts are transformed; they are reborn into a new and different being. These losers of life become winners — sane, sober persons. Moreover, the major outcome of recovery is that it restores addicts to a childlike state of being — innocent, curious and eager to learn. Recovery moves addicts from the sickness of addiction to the health of sobriety.

Addiction is an illness. People become addicted to many things — games, groups, behaviors, alcohol, other drugs, or people. What a person is addicted to is called the drug of choice. Whatever the drug of choice, those who are most knowledgeable about chemical and other addictions seem to agree that the 12 Steps,* which were originally promulgated by the fellowship of Alcoholics Anonymous, form the finest and most effective path to recovery. Therefore, I will use the initial steps of this path in what follows.

The First Step

Every pilgrimage, no matter what its nature or destination, must always begin with the first step, and the pilgrimage of recovery is no exception. The first of the 12 Steps states: "We admitted we were powerless over [drug of choice] — that our lives had become unmanageable."[3]

What does this mean? Why powerless and unmanageable? This question has been asked and reasked and has been answered in various ways. Sometimes the answers were vague or complicated. However, they need not be, if addiction is properly understood.

To me, the clearest understanding of addiction and recovery is contained in the book that I consider to be the most definitive exposition of the matter ever published, the revered "Big Book," *Alcoholics Anonymous*. Regarding the first of the 12 Steps, the following statement appears in the book: "We learned that we had to fully concede to our innermost selves that we were alcoholics. This is the first step in recovery."[4] The first step, according to this statement, is taken when addicts concede to themselves the truth about their condition. And what is the truth? The very essence of their condition: that they can neither use their drug of choice successfully nor quit using it.

Why can they not use successfully? Both the experience of addicts and scientific research point to the fact that whenever real addicts begin using their drug of choice, they lose control over the amount used. Why? In some addictions, such as alcoholism, the loss of control is due to a physiological condition that is probably inherited. In other addictions, the question remains unanswered. Regardless of what the reasons may be, it is quite obvious that addicts are not capable of controlling their consumption once they begin to use. In fact, they have no control at all. They really are powerless.

---

*See Appendix for the 12 Steps.

Why can't addicts quit using? Again, research and personal experience give us the answer. Addicts become uncontrollably preoccupied — obsessed — with the feeling produced by the drug of choice. They can't get their minds off it, no matter how they try. They think about it constantly, and since thinking always results in behavior, they use again. The truth of the matter is that the drug of choice controls their minds, their behavior, their lives. They are not in control. The drug is. Their lives really are unmanageable.

So the first step suggests that addicts concede. In one sense, to concede means to admit or acknowledge the truth, but there is another meaning that is perhaps more important. To concede also means to surrender. To surrender to what? The truth. What is the truth again? That addicts have an illness, the essence of which lies in the twin facts that they cannot use or quit using and that they have no control over their lives.

Surrender, even when the evidence shows clearly it is the only course to take, is not easy. In fact, it is difficult to accept that one is unable to control or change any situation or condition. Indeed, something in all humans heavily resists it, no matter how great the reason. This something is the ego, and only when it is deflated can addicts take the first step on their pilgrimage.

Moreover, there is grace in surrender, for it pierces a permanent hole in the ego's armor. From this point on, though addicts may use again, their egos will never be able to convince them that it is all right to do so. This is why some say that even though the Steps may not keep you sober, they will ruin your using.

Insanity and delusion are closely related. Every insane person is deluded in some way. Delusion is an interesting word. It means believing in something that is not true. People who are insane, then, believe in something that is false. They believe in a lie. Psychotics who talk to themselves because they believe there is nobody else to talk to are deluded. Paranoids who believe others are out to get them are deluded. Likewise, addicts who believe they can successfully use or quit using on their own are deluded. They, like the others, believe in a lie. So, like them, they are insane.

What is the lie that addicts believe? Basically, it is that someday, somehow, they will be able to control their drug of choice in such a way that they will be able to enjoy its effects without experiencing any negative consequences. Time and again, they try. Time and again, they fail. Yet, they persist. Why? Because they are obsessed with the feeling produced by the drug. This feeling is extremely valuable to them, thus their obsession is extremely powerful. In fact, it is so powerful, they may follow it, as the rats followed the Pied Piper, to their death.

Friends and family watch in disbelief as addicts who nearly died from an overdose nonchalantly use again. Aghast, they wonder how they can do this. Are they crazy? Yes. They are locked in a world of delusion, held captive by an obsession that makes them unable to distinguish the true from the false where the drug of choice is concerned. Can this be? Yes. What is obviously a lie to others seems to be truth to addicts. They are asleep to the obvious, out of control, and killing themselves in increments. They are unable to stop using. Such is the power of their obsession.

Unlike others, the addictive obsession does not respond to traditional or routine therapeutic procedures. Medication does not eliminate or alleviate it. On the contrary, medication seems to make it worse. Aversion therapy fails because the kind of defense that keeps one from putting one's hand on a hot stove after being burned does not exist.

Concerning aversion therapy, a friend of mine once told me a story, supposedly true, about a friend of his who had undergone aversion therapy. The procedure was simple. They gave the man Antabuse (a drug that makes one violently ill if one drinks alcohol while taking it) and then forced him to drink lots of liquor. Of course, he got terribly sick and felt as if he would die. Later, my friend asked him if the treatment had worked. "Oh, yes," he said. "It worked very well. I still drink booze but I have never taken any more Antabuse."

The Next Step

So it is that medication and other therapies, including aversion, simply do not work on the addict's obsession. Why? According to the 12-Step groups, none of these methods is powerful enough. Based on their collective experience, these groups believe that, once the addictive obsession has a grip, addicts are beyond the reach of human aid. Neither they nor any other human being, nor any group of human beings, nor any methods or medications created by human beings, can remove the obsession. Therefore, help must come from a power that is greater than human. Thus, Step 2 states: "Came to believe that a Power greater than ourselves could restore us to sanity."[5]

Sanity and delusion are not closely related. No sane person is deluded. A sane person can distinguish between the true and the false. Addicts who perceive that they cannot use without dire consequences and that their insanity cannot be corrected by human resources are on their way to becoming sane, for this insight releases their basic intelligence (common sense). Their basic intelligence has a homing instinct. It knows what they must do.

And what are addicts moved to do? The natural thing — the thing that makes good sense. And what is that? To reach out to a Higher Power for help. That's right! It is perfectly natural for people to reach out for someone or something greater than themselves when they see that things are out of control.

All children, when any situation is beyond their control, turn to someone bigger for help, usually a parent. Addicts who realize their situation is out of control turn for help to a Power greater than themselves, usually their Parent.

It is important to understand that, when addicts turn to a Higher Power for help, they do not have to think about any concept, any theological construct, or any religious version of that Power. Why? Because it is totally and completely unnecessary — turning to a Higher Power for help is a spiritual act, not a religious one.

The only necessary ingredients are the realization of powerlessness and the intuition that there is a greater power that can and will help. So 12-Step groups believe that an understanding of the Higher Power is not necessary. All that is needed, they say, is the willingness to believe. When addicts do believe or are willing to believe that a Higher Power can restore their sanity, they have taken another step on their pilgrimage.

Changing Guides

For addicts who recover, the journey of life is divided into two parts. These parts are, of course, addiction and recovery. Although both parts involve paths that are full of paradox, all similarity ends there, for each path takes addicts in different directions to different destinations under the guidance of different powers. Step 3 offers addicts an opportunity to change direction and destination by changing guides.

The path of addiction is well known. When addicts travel it, they move inexorably in the direction of ever more serious illness, and their final destination will be total insanity and/or death. The guide on their trip will be ego. It is the nature of the human ego to want to be in control. The desire to control is called selfishness, and it is the root of all human difficulties, including addiction.

One of the main reasons why addicts like their drug of choice is that it gives them the illusion of control. Then, the inevitable happens. They begin to lose control over their use. Alarmed, desire becomes an obsession, and they increase their efforts, but the more they try, the less control they have, until, finally, they have no control at all.

What has happened? The inevitable paradox has come to pass. This paradox is a spiritual axiom. Anyone who tries to gain control will lose it, and if one is obsessed with control, one will lose it totally.

The path to recovery is well known. When addicts travel this route, they move in the direction of wellness, and their destination will be wholeness. Their guide will be a Higher Power, which will carry out its guidance both directly and through humans who serve as channels for it.

However, there is a condition for this. In order to be guided by this power, addicts must give up the need to control. When they do this, they find themselves able to say no to their drug of choice. This is the paradox of recovery, and it, too, is a spiritual axiom, which could be stated as follows: Anyone who gives up control will gain it, and if one eliminates the need for it entirely, one will be free.

Free? How? When addicts attempt to control their lives, their drug of choice, and the people and circumstances around them, they have taken on a full-time job. In fact, it demands all their time, energy and attention. In short, they become prisoners of their need to control. On the other hand, when they give up, or give over, the need to control, they become free.

As an analogy, think about the driver of a bus and a passenger on it. Who has time to relax and enjoy the ride? Certainly not the driver, for this job requires vigilance. The driver is a prisoner of the task. The passenger, however, can sit back, relax and enjoy the ride. So it is with addiction and recovery. Addiction says to addicts, "You must and should drive the bus of life." Recovery, however, says, "Go back into the passenger section, kick back and enjoy the ride!" When addicts decide, in Step 3, to place themselves in the care of God, they become passengers on the bus of life and leave the driving up to the Higher Power. Once prisoners, now they are free.

The first three steps on the road to recovery are not philosophical abstractions. Quite the opposite, they make up a natural, down-to-earth, common sense process that is routinely carried out by little children. As I said before, when small children are faced with problems they cannot handle, they get someone larger than themselves to take care of it. They may turn to a parent or a friend, but they will always turn to someone bigger and more powerful than they are. You did this, when you were a child. So did I. Let me give you an example from my life.

For a period of time during my childhood, I had a friend whom I shall call Randy. Randy was, without a doubt, the filthiest kid I've ever known. He smelled so bad you could smell him coming. His nose always seemed to be runny, and he had the habit of picking it, rubbing what he picked in his hair, then twisting his hair. Because of this, he had little spikes of hair sticking out all over his head.

Those of you who are familiar with the "Peanuts" comic strip may remember a character named Pigpen, a dirty little boy who had flies circling around his head. Well, Randy was the Pigpen of my neighborhood.

Randy was a good baseball player. We'd always put him at shortstop and tell him to play deep. That way, we didn't have to be close to him. Randy couldn't help being dirty and stinking because he had no one to take care of him. His mother and father were hopeless alcoholics who, because of their illness, were incapable of doing so.

I liked Randy and he liked me. We were good friends and often played together, yet I was afraid of him. One of the games we played was marbles. When I was growing up, shooting marbles was a very popular pastime, and all us kids carried an assortment of marbles in our pockets. We carried "steelies," "roley-poleys" and "black beauties," and so on. When we shot marbles, we played for keeps — whoever won got to keep all the other person's marbles.

I was good at marbles. It was one of the few games at which I was better than Randy. In fact, I beat him consistently. But there was a problem. Even though I won, and was supposed to keep all the marbles, Randy would take them. Since I was afraid of him, this put me in a bad position, but I always knew what to do. I'd go home, tell my father what had happened, and he would get my marbles back.

What had I done? Instinctively, I had done exactly what the first three steps suggest should be done.

When we were children, we knew what to do when we were powerless. Moreover, even after we're no longer children, this kind of knowledge remains deep within us, and although it is obscured by the ego over time, it automatically moves us to act in a specific way in times of crisis.

And so it is with addicts. When their egos are reduced, they have access to the child within them who knows what they must do. Realizing they have lost their marbles and can't get them back, they turn to a power greater than themselves to do so. The beautiful thing about recovery is that if they persevere along its path, they will get their marbles back — and much, much more.

An AA old-timer once told me that steps were numbered because any "rummy" (which was what he called alcoholics) can count. Like him, I believe the 12 Steps are in the correct order, each flowing into the next like branches flow into the main stream of a river that courses its way into the presence of the one Source of all being.

So, I am fully convinced that the first three steps should be the first three. Why? Because when addicts concede the hopelessness of their condition, believe a Higher Power can correct it and decide to turn themselves and their situation over to its care and direction, they have deflated the ego, removed themselves from its control and restored it to its proper role as servant, not master.

Rebirth

In short, the first three steps deal with the source of the difficulties, the ego, and for the best of reasons. If the ego is not dealt with at the outset, addicts will be unwilling to do the work required to uncover and eliminate the root causes of their illness and to clean up the mess that it, the ego, has created. So these three simple propositions put the ego back into its proper role as manager, not chairperson of the board, and, by so doing, free addicts from their obsessive need to drive the bus of life. Also, the steps place addicts, of their own volition, under the care of a Higher Power, just as any child should be.

When addicts follow the directions of their child within, they take the road less traveled. They turn in the direction of home and wholeness and begin to grow down. Truly, they are reborn and are embarking on the pilgrimage of regeneration.

A note of caution. Although addicts are reborn, they must remember that the rebirth is only the beginning of the recovery process. As significant and indispensable as it may be, it is not enough, and addicts who assume that it is will not be sober very long. Truly, if they want to achieve and maintain sobriety, they must realize that this second birth, like the first one, is only the barest start.

More importantly, however, addicts must be aware that, though birth and rebirth are similar, they are radically different. How? When they were born, addicts began life with a clean slate. When they were reborn, they didn't. As a matter of fact, their slate is full to overflowing with those beliefs, ideas and habits that form the framework of their addiction.

The addicts' families also should realize that rebirth is only the barest beginning of the process that will change them into a new person. Truly, it is very important for families to be aware that sobriety is not an event, but a process that takes time. Moreover, they must understand that at this point addicts are not capable of behaving in a mature fashion, for literally, not figuratively, they are newly born spiritual infants.

Therefore, families should not be surprised if addicts behave like babies. Further, they should not be shocked if addicts' behavior is erratic or if they seem anxious and depressed, for they are without their medicine — their drug of choice — and because of this they will seem at times to be not only erratic, anxious and depressed, but also totally insane.

I remember my ex-wife once saying, "I always thought I wanted him to be sober, and all of a sudden there he was, stark, raving sober!" Simply put, in the beginning stages of recovery, addicts' families should not expect more of them than they do of infants, and furthermore, they must treat addicts the way they would a tiny baby. Why? Because that's what they are. This is a huge job for the families, a job they will need help with. Happily, this help is readily available through Al-Anon and other support groups, and families should fully participate in them.

Then there is the ego. The ego is tough and determined, and although it is temporarily submitted, it would be extremely dangerous for newly sober addicts to assume it will remain so. As a matter of fact, it won't. Truly, it will soon begin to hide the pain and despair that drove addicts to take the new road in the first place. When it does, it will just be protecting what has been most valuable up until now — the addicts' drug or behavior of choice and the beliefs, ideas, and habits that form the framework of addiction.

What's more, the ego will continue to act this way until a shift in values has taken place, and sobriety becomes the number-one priority. Until then, it is absolutely vital for addicts to be with those who do value sobriety above all else as often as possible. Now, more than at any other time, addicts need community. This is why they are advised to go to a recovery meeting every single day for a certain period of time.

There is great wisdom in the dictum, "Don't use, and go to meetings," because for a time it is all that newly recovered addicts are capable of doing. But the old dictum has a deeper, more significant meaning, for when addicts don't use and go to meetings, they are living out the first three steps.

That's right! Each time they walk into a meeting clean and sober, they are not only reaffirming their acceptance of powerlessness and their belief that a Higher Power can help them, but they are, by their presence, submitting themselves to the care and direction of that Power. You see, the initial steps are not just a matter of one-time assent. No, indeed. They must be practiced, just like all the rest.

To conclude, although turning onto the road to recovery is a singularly significant act, it is only a beginning. If their recovery is to continue, addicts must take other steps, and they will need help. Truly, since the path they have chosen is a new one, they will need guidance, companionship and more information.

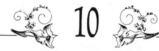

10

The Path

Quite a number of very fine paths are available to those who wish to quench their spiritual thirst for wholeness and return home. Each path is a system that includes such common elements as directions for the journey, a guide to accompany and aid the traveler and a group of fellow travelers. If the pilgrims fulfill the conditions of the system, they will reap the benefits of it.

Some of the pathways (systems) are philosophical, psychological or religious. Others are spiritual. Some, such as Christianity or Judaism, are well known. Others, however, such as Sufism, Stoicism, Taoism, the 12 Steps, or humanistic psychology, are unfamiliar.

The Directions

Whether they are familiar or not, these paths have more in common than their destination. Yet, in spite of all their similarities, each is also different from the others, for, though all are good systems, each was designed to meet a special need. If people have a special need, choose the correct path and follow its course, the need will be met. If they choose the wrong path, however, it will not be. It is important to remember as we go on that all good paths, though similar, are also different. Though they have much in common, each is aimed at solving a particular problem.

The first thing that all good paths have in common is that they are built on the same principles. No matter which you choose, you will find such precepts as honesty, acceptance, unselfishness and love, to name just a few. Furthermore, all require their pilgrims to surrender.

In fact, people who want to tread any one of these avenues to freedom must get off (surrender) the road they have been traveling and give up (surrender) their old way of doing things. Surrender is the gateway. We cannot travel any good path until we have met the first condition of all of them. That first condition is surrender.

In addition to sharing common principles and requiring surrender, these paths provide directions. Some give directions that are simple, clear and concise, while others do not. Nevertheless, each furnishes some kind of road map to those who want to proceed along its route. Having such a map is helpful; however, it will not bring travelers to their desired destination. In fact, the map can be understood perfectly and even committed to memory, but it will be of no use until the travelers act and follow its directions.

You see, the key to a successful journey on any good path is not only knowing where you want to go and how to get there — it is actually taking the prescribed route. Action is the key requirement on all good paths. Without action, nobody goes anywhere.

I remember hearing a story once that illustrates the need for action very well. It seems a rabbi and a Catholic priest went to a boxing match together. Before the bout began, one of the boxers knelt in his corner and crossed himself.

"That's one of your boys, isn't it?" the rabbi asked the priest.

"Yes," the priest replied.

"Tell me," the rabbi queried. "What does it mean when he makes the sign of the cross?"

The priest replied, "It doesn't mean a damned thing if he can't fight."

So it is. People do not become winners by belief alone, but by action. Too many people mistake the road map of faith for the journey of action. When the losers of life become winners, their character has been changed, and character cannot be changed by thought or belief. Character is changed only by action. As one of my teachers, a crusty old curmudgeon I called Grumpy, used to say, "Boy, you can't think your way into good living. You have to live your way into good thinking."

Both the priest and Grumpy were right. Without action, thought or belief is like smoke in the wind, floating aimlessly, going nowhere in particular, then disappearing.

Another interesting thing common to all good paths is that each of them came into being at a time when they were needed for a specific reason by a particular group of people. The path of Moses came into being to meet the needs of the Hebrews in the wilderness, the path of Lao Tzu (Tao) to help those who were being spiritually stifled by Confucianism in China, the path of Jesus to aid those under the domination of a foreign nation and a cold, legalistic religious bureaucracy in Palestine, the good psychological paths to free those under the yoke of Freudianism, and the 12-Step path to provide a way for those who were dying of alcohol addiction in America.

Even though each of these excellent paths, and others, came into being in this limited way, each has become universal because the principles on which it is based are universal.

The many fine paths to wholeness have much in common. However, if we conclude the matter at this point, I think we will miss the most amazing thing of all. You see, my own experience has convinced me that all good paths — every one of them — converge at a certain point and become one path. This, in turn, has persuaded me that really there is only one path that leads home.

"How can this be?" you ask. "If there is only one path, why do we have so many? Why can't we all take the same one?"

The truth of the matter, I believe, is that each of the good paths is, in reality, only an entryway to the one path, and we can't take the same entryway simply because we are not entering at the same place. To illustrate, imagine a main highway that may be entered at many different ramps along its course. I am at ramp #192, and if I want to get on the highway, that is where I must enter. You are at ramp #190, and no matter how much you may want to, you cannot get on the road at the same point as I because you are not where I am. We must enter where we are. Yet, though we enter at different places, we both end up on the same main road. Get it?

All good and true paths enter the main highway, and which one we take is based on our own specific needs. For example, a schizophrenic obviously needs to get on the road via a psychological route, whereas the sinner needs a religious one. Not only is the path we take based on our particular need, it is also based on common sense. For example, common sense tells us not to take a psychological path when having appendicitis, nor a religious route when experiencing epileptic seizures, nor the 12-Step road when undergoing a psychotic break, for these routes would not be appropriate to meet our primary needs.

This brings us to a very important point concerning addiction. Addicts' primary need is not to be freed from sin or relieved of a neurosis; it is to recover from an illness. Therefore, addicts must enter the main highway by a path specifically designed to meet their particular needs. Because neither the religious nor the psychological paths were devised to deal with recovery from addiction, they are inappropriate. Thus, addicts' condition and common sense dictate that they take the path that came into being to help people recover from addiction. This path is the 12 Steps.

Religious and psychological avenues almost invariably fail to lead to recovery from addiction. Why? Because they are bad pathways? No! Most emphatically, no! In fact, the good psychological and religious routes are wonderful, graceful boulevards that bring about miraculous changes in the people whom they are designed to help.

So the problem is not that these paths are not good; it is that they were not designed to meet addicts' primary needs or correct their condition. In short, they are ineffective simply because they do not start where addicts are. Moreover, the 12-Step road is so effective not because it is better than other routes, but because it starts precisely where addicts are.

Right now, I want to say that both religion and psychology have been quite helpful to many addicts — after a sufficient time in recovery. Early in recovery, addicts must deal with staying clean and sober, and until they have accomplished this, little or nothing can be done for them in a religious or psychological sense. It's a simple matter of priorities.

You see, there really is a time and a place for everything under the sun, and addicts must deal with each matter in its proper order, giving what is most important top priority. *"First things first"* goes the slogan, and it is correct. Truly, for addicts, sobriety is, and must be, first. Those who give it top priority stay sober. Those who don't usually return to the detour of addiction.

Each time I consider how the 12-Step program came into being, I become more convinced that God is a poet. Why? There are three reasons. First, God sent the specific path for recovery from addiction through people who were addicted to alcohol, and in my opinion, nothing could be more poetic than this! Indeed, only a poet could, or would, have met the need in such a way.

Second, the program was designed so that it would meet the needs not only of alcoholics, but of those who were addicted to any substance or behavior. Like any fine poem, the program is timeless, designed by its author to be just as meaningful to sex addicts in the 1990s as it was to alcoholics in the 1930s, and so it endures to save and enrich the lives of all who travel its course.

Third, the manner in which the program evolved flowed as smoothly as the most beautiful sonnet.

If you want to understand what I mean you must study how the premier path of recovery came into being. Despite what some may think, it was not invented by one person or group. Quite the contrary, it evolved through a graceful process by which ideas and people came together in a way no one could have planned. Some call this process coincidence. Others, including myself say that it goes far beyond the realm of the coincidental and enters the realm of the miraculous. Why? Because from the merging of these ideas and people came the 12 Steps, the poem of recovery, the only path that is tailor-made for addicts who want to get well. Let others think what they will. As for me, I am convinced that only a Poet could have written such an inspired poem.

Like the paths of buddha, Lao Tzu and Jesus, the 12-Step path is a design for living that is marked by love, respect and tolerance for other people, as well as reverence and concern for all things, living and nonliving. Like them, it is a way of life that emphasizes personal responsibility and the importance of acting and reacting positively to the people and problems encountered on the journey. Like them, too, it is a system that is designed to meet a specific need for a particular group of people.

As with any system, the 12 Steps contain certain key elements and conditions that must be fulfilled if the desired result is to be achieved. Addicts who utilize the key elements and meet the conditions of the 12-Step program will recover from their illness. The elements are:

1. Directions for the journey
2. A guide
3. Fellow travelers.

Since the 12 Steps are obviously the directions, let us turn to the second element — the guide.

The Guide

I once had a friend who pretended to know everything about everything even though it was obvious to all but the most gullible that he knew little about anything. You know the type, the classic "know-it-all." My nickname for this guy was World Book, after the encyclopedia of that title.

He invited me to go fishing with him at one of the most renowned fishing spots in this country. I had heard and read about this place, and I knew the waters were full of fish just waiting to be caught. So off we went. When we arrived, I got into the waders I had bought just for this trip. You see, World Book told me he had been to this place before and that the way to catch fish was to get out of the boat, wade into the coves and cast toward the banks.

We got into the boat and went to the other side of the lake, where we stopped and anchored. Following his directions, I climbed out of the boat and went into the water. When my feet touched bottom, I could feel myself being sucked down in the muck and mud that lay there. Then, my waders became flooded with icy cold water, and there I stood, freezing and stuck.

I called to World Book for help and discovered that he was in the same situation. Finally, after what seemed an eternity, I freed my feet, managed to get back into the boat and helped my friend do likewise. Shivering, we headed for camp, where we changed our clothes and built a fire.

While we were drying out, I noticed other fishermen coming in. None of them was wet or freezing, none wore waders, and all had caught a number of fish. I talked with some of them, asking them how they caught so many fish. Their answer was simple. They had hired a guide who knew where the fish were and how to catch them, and following his directions, they had caught a lot of fish.

Here I was at the same lake as these people, and I wanted to catch fish as much as they did, yet I didn't. Why? Because I didn't have a guide. World Book was a good guy, but he didn't know where the fish were or how to catch them. Right then and there, I made up my mind that whenever I went fishing in a strange lake, I would get an experienced guide.

The same is true of recovery. No matter how much addicts may want to travel its path, they have a much better chance of reaching their desired destination if someone guides them — some experienced traveler who knows where the fish are and how to catch them. It is interesting that all good paths stress the need for the novice to be guided by a veteran journeyman, and the 12-Step path is no exception.

In fact, the need for guidance was emphasized at its beginning. Although in the early days the experienced guide was called the spiritual adviser, this term soon gave way to the one most commonly used today — sponsor.

Sponsorship is one of the most vital parts of the recovery process, for it is through sponsorship that the most essential elements of the program are passed from one generation of addicts to another. Truly, sponsorship is the needle that contains the healing thread of principles by which the garment of sobriety is stitched together.

Sponsorship

Sponsors are not personal bankers, financial advisers, or employment agencies, neither do they solve addicts' problems or serve only as an emergency (911) resource. In addition, as many addicts have ruefully discovered, they are not fools. What is not so well known is that they are not counselors either. A counselor will ask a person to do something, then ask how they feel about doing it. The sponsor, on the other hand, will direct an addict to do something and doesn't seem to care how the person feels about it.

For example, in the very early days of his recovery, a close friend of mine was told by his sponsor to carry out a certain task that he really didn't want to do, so he asked his sponsor why he had to do it.

"Boy," said the sponsor, "you don't ask me why. You do what I tell you to do."

Apparently, the sponsor didn't care how my friend felt about carrying out his directions. Obviously action was more important to him than feelings. He simply knew what my friend should do, and he told him to do it. Moreover, he knew what to do because he had done it. From his own experience, he knew where the fish were and how to catch them. Was he harsh? My friend thought so at the time.

Later on, however, he came to know that nobody cared more about how he felt than his sponsor. Yet when this incident happened, this experienced guide knew that feelings had to take a back seat, that action, not emotion, was more important. Now my friend understands that his sponsor was just doing his job. He did it well, by the way.

Don't be misled, however, for, ironically, many sponsors do serve as emergency resources for those they are guiding, and they may help newcomers find jobs or unscramble finances. And, yes, they may even do a little individual or family counseling. However, they will only do these things if they feel it is appropriate. If they find that new people are more interested in these matters than they are in recovery, they will not waste time on them for very long.

To sponsors, money, jobs and other concerns are peripheral to the main task of sponsorship, which is to guide the novice along the road of recovery. To accomplish this, sponsors will walk side by side with newcomers through the steps, make sure they follow directions, teach them about the principles of the program, help them to avoid the many detours, keep them going in a steady manner by speeding them up or slowing them down, and do the many other things that must be done for a spiritually growing baby. In short, sponsors make sure new people fish or cut bait.

Sponsors may or may not be well-educated and may not seem to be the sort of people one would expect as guides for a spiritual journey. As a matter of fact, many who have guided addicts to sobriety and an abundant life would seem, at first glance, to be unsuited to the task, yet they carry it out with masterful grace. They are, indeed, an unusual mixture, made up of lawyers, accountants, plumbers, construction workers, brokers, ministers and doctors, to name a few. A diverse crew, right? One friend of mine says that they are a bunch of what he lovingly calls "spiritual mongrels." Who would choose them for a guide?

On the face of it, this seems like a reasonable question, at least until we consider the guides chosen by God over the years. In nearly every case, God has chosen unlikely people. Moses stuttered, Siddhartha Gautama (Buddha) was a disillusioned prince, Muhammad was illiterate, and Jesus was a carpenter.

A strange crew, right? Yet each was chosen by God as a spiritual guide for his people. Some people didn't take them seriously when they were alive because they didn't have the proper background or credentials, and as a result of such nit-picking, many people missed their chance to go home by way of the paths these men laid out, and this is still true today. Sadly, and tragically, many addicts miss their chance at sobriety for the same reason.

In fact, it is not vocation, education, social status, or the like that determines whether a person can guide you or not, for in the life of the spirit such things are irrelevant. What really matters is a person's ability to lead you where you want to go. Experienced people who guide addicts to sobriety have this ability because they have trodden the road of recovery themselves and have been reunited with their own deepest self — the wise child of God within.

Thus, they are able to guide the novice down the same road they have traveled and lead addicts to their own internal source of intelligence and power. In addition, since guides have been reconnected with their deepest selves, they become companions who are sane, sensible, and wise, fellow travelers who can make addicts' most difficult problems seem small. And because they have learned to laugh — mainly at themselves — they can add the wonderful element of humor to the pilgrimage. Above all, however, they have become like children again — loving, spontaneous, joyful and full of wonder.

How do addicts get a sponsor? In my opinion, the first thing they should do is pray. Being as clear and concise as possible, they should state their need to the Higher Power in a simple way, such as this: "I need a guide to help me, and it must be the right person because my life is at stake. I don't know who it is, but you do, and if you will guide me to that person, I'd appreciate it."

Having asked for help, addicts go to recovery meetings in search of that person. They watch everyone there, observing how they act. They listen, paying close attention to what people say. Soon, by watching and listening, they know those whose words and actions match, and they become sure that any of them can be a guide. Then, before too long, they know exactly which one is the right guide. So they ask, and if the person agrees to take on the task — as is usually the case — the correct guide has been located.

So, you see, getting a sponsor is simple. Addicts request God's help, go where guides gather, observe and listen, then ask. Getting a sponsor begins as a cooperative effort between two beings — the addict and the Higher Power. Through their cooperation, a guide is found, and now three are on the journey of recovery. As they travel, they meet others who are on the same pilgrimage and join with them, becoming companions moving toward a common destination. So it is on the journey of spiritual growth. First, there is one, then there are two, then three, and then there is a community.

The Community

Recovery is a process of spiritual growth. Spiritual growth is a journey that moves the individual from addiction to wholeness. Addiction is marked by separation and disconnection, wholeness by relation and connection.

Addicts are isolated and powerless. If they want to recover, they must grow spiritually, and to do this, they must accept their powerlessness and move into relationship, for spiritual growth is impossible in isolation. Alone, addicts are a powerless "I," an incomplete being. If they join with other "I's" who share the same needs and goals, however, they are no longer alone, but are part of a community, a "we." They are thereby empowered, for "we" can do what "I" cannot.

In such a group, addicts will find all the elements that are most conducive to spiritual growth. Indeed, they will find equality, unity of purpose, a sense of belonging, a feeling of worthiness and the kind of sharing that has no price tag on it.

But this is not all, for sooner or later they will understand that the group considers them as important to its survival as they consider the group to be to theirs. Addicts will realize they have become an integral and vital part of the living, breathing body called community. They will know that, even as they are given power by the group, they give the group its power. In a spiritual way of life, individual and community are intimately interdependent. The well-being of each depends on the other. So it is.

The absolute necessity of community has been fully appreciated by 12-Step groups from their beginning and has been stressed in their writings and in their recovery program. Thus, it is no accident that "we" is the first word in the foreword to the first edition of the book *Alcoholics Anonymous*, as well as the first word in the Steps, nor that AA is called a fellowship.

Let's face it, 12-Step groups are "we" groups who use "we" books and have a "we" program. Truly, the foundation stone of their success is their emphasis on the primary importance of community in recovery through spiritual growth. The 12 Traditions of AA provide the strongest evidence that this is the case, for they came into being to ensure the survival and the integrity of the group. If we study these traditions closely, we can easily see that the principles they contain preclude reification. Therefore, if they are followed, not only are the integrity and survival of AA ensured, but the fellowship will never become a bureaucracy. Whether AA and its sister groups endure is up to their members, for as in all spiritual groups the well-being of the community is the responsibility of its individual members.

The 12-Step fellowships are spiritual communities, and as in all such groups, the members are bound together, not by rules and regulations, but by having shared a common problem and a common solution. Also, like other such groups, they have only one purpose — to share the solution with others who have the same problem, or as they put it, "to carry its message to those who still suffer."[2] And how do they carry the message? By telling stories. You see, carrying the message means no more and no less than telling one's story.

As I said earlier, story-telling has always been the chief means of transmitting spiritual truth as well as being a powerful tool for teaching and learning. People in all times and in all places have used stories to convey messages that could be of great help to others, and the members of 12-Step groups are certainly no exception.

In fact, they tell their stories to help new prospects identify as addicts and realize that they, too, can recover. If they respond positively, they join the community, solve their problem and go on to help others by sharing their story. And so it goes, an unbroken circle of people caring for one another through sharing their stories.

No other groups with which I am familiar believe more in the power and effectiveness of story-telling than do the 12-Step fellowships. This is why they have meetings where one member shares his story with the group. It is also why so much of their basic textbook is devoted to stories. For example, more than half of the pages in the big book of AA are used for personal stories. For these groups, story-telling is one of the foundation stones of recovery, not only for those who hear the tales, but also for those who tell them.

These groups believe that recovered addicts who share their stories strengthen their recovery. To them, story-telling benefits both listener and teller.

I agree with them, because even if the listeners cannot hear the message, the story-tellers will benefit; they will be reminded of what they were like, what happened and what they are like now. In short, they will remember the horror of addiction and the miracle of recovery.

As Barry Lopez writes in his beautiful little book, *Crow and Weasel*:

> The stories people tell have a way of taking care of them. If
> stories come to you, care for them and learn to give them

away where they are needed. Sometimes a person needs a story more than food to stay alive. That is why we put these stories in each other's memory. This is how people care for each other.[3]

The Signs

As I have said, a number of excellent paths exist for those who wish to quench their spiritual thirst and return home. Each is a system that includes direction, guides and companions for the traveler, and each is designed for particular people who have a specific need. In order to get on the right road, travelers must choose the one that meets their special need.

If travelers choose correctly, adhere to the directions, carry out the instructions of the guide, and stick closely to their peers, they will reach their desired destination. But since so many roads go where travelers want to go, how can addicts be certain they have chosen the right one?

They will know by the signs. To explain, let me tell you a true story.

I have a very close friend, so much like me that we are mirror images of one another. This friend is an alcoholic, and though he has now been sober for more than 26 years, it looked for a time as if he would die of his addiction, for, try as he might, he could not find a way to recover. At one point, he tried religion, but in spite of heroic efforts on his part, he continued to drink and his condition worsened.

Through it all, he perceived that his need was different from the others in the religious community, and he found himself unable to bond with them, even though he tried. Then, too, he sensed that they did not understand his condition, although a few of them tried. He felt like an outsider — alone and different.

At another time, he tried to find a solution through psychiatry, but again his efforts failed. He realized that once more his need was not the same as that of his fellow patients, and although he was friends with them, he was totally unable to bond with them.

Again, he felt like an outsider — alone and different. Depressives got better, schizophrenics improved but, in spite of his efforts and those of a good doctor, he got worse. In fact, his condition became so bad that he slipped out one night, got very drunk and created such a disturbance on the psych ward that his frustrated doctor discharged him from the hospital. He knew by the signs that he was not on the right path.

Despairing of any relief, my friend began attending AA. For a long time even this program did not work for him. Now, he realizes why. He had three big barriers blocking him: (1) denial of his alcoholism; (2) intellectual pride; and (3) religious arrogance.

Just his denial would have been enough, for it made it impossible for him to bond with the other members. However, my friend was much sicker than this. He was a person whose academic success had caused him to believe his intellect was superior, and his religious background and training had brought him to the conclusion that he knew a great deal more about spiritual matters than anyone else. Thus his denial made him feel alone and different, and his intellectual and religious hubris prevented him from following directions from anyone in the group.

The worst thing about all this, however, was that he was not aware of his denial, his pride or his arrogance, for all were unconscious. Yet although unconscious, they were there, and they blocked him from listening to the house painter who had never read Plato and the housewife who had never read Paul Tillich, even though what they said was sane, sound, and wise. In other words, his unconscious denial, pride, and arrogance kept him from receiving the message that would save his life. With all the seriousness I can muster, let me tell you that nobody is more difficult to deal with than a pseudo-intellectual, religion-warped drunk.

Finally, mercifully, alcohol totally and completely defeated my friend, demolishing both his belligerent denial and his overwhelming arrogance and replacing them with raw desperation. For the first time, he was willing to follow the directions and do what he was instructed to do. In fact, he was most anxious to do so. At last, his feet were planted firmly on the 12-Step path and he has been growing ever since. And he knows by the signs that he is on the right path.

What are these signs? First, and most obvious, he has been sober for a long time. Second, he is bonded to his peers in the recovery community and no longer feels alone and different. Third, a really good sign, the surest evidence that he is on the right road, are the warm showers. That's right, ever since my friend has been on the 12-Step path, he has experienced the warm showers of spiritual experience many times, and each time he has felt peacefully whole and at-one with all of creation. He has been blessed, if you will, by the presence of the Creator. Moreover, he has discovered how and why such experiences come to pass. He has learned the great secret. He has become aware of the power of love.

In spite of what most people think, love is not a feeling. Feelings come and go. Love remains. Love is a combination of unconditional acceptance, positive attitude, and responsible action. Therefore, when we really love our sisters and brothers, our world and ourselves, we accept them just as they are; look on them with respect, concern and compassion; and behave responsibly toward them.

In the final analysis, I am convinced that love is our responsibility to, and for, our fellows, our world, and ourselves. Love is the purest form of spiritual action, the one creative force in the universe. By love were all things made, and by love do all things come to pass. So it is.

My friend and I, and many others, have learned the great secret concerning love. What is it? One receives love through giving love. You see, it is a spiritual law that whatever one gives, one will receive. Indeed, this law has been stated by every spiritual teacher. Whether they said that we reap what we sow or that what we do for others, we do for ourselves, or that what we put on the karmic wheel will return to us, all stated the same law. If these most spiritually wise ones were right, and I believe they were, then the secret of love is obvious. When we give love, we receive love. It's that simple.

Whenever we relate to others in love, the chances are good that we will have a spiritual — warm shower — experience. In others words, when you and I love another person, animal, or thing that God created, or when we relate with love to a poem, song, or work of art which one of God's children has created, our chances of having a spiritual experience are increased.

All of us do, in fact, have such experiences, for they are not uncommon. Think about it, and remember. Have you ever been listening to a piece of music and all of a sudden chill bumps spread over you or tears come to your eyes? Have you ever embraced a person you love and felt that the two of you had become one? And when this happened, did you not feel warm and fuzzy all over? Of course you did.

I once had such an experience with a dog, and it was one of the most memorable events that has ever happened to me. One day, not too many years ago, I was very depressed. Deciding, for some reason, to go for a walk, I was plodding along, head down, on a road that circled through my neighborhood. Soon I became aware of something behind me. I turned and saw I was being followed by an ugly hound puppy, so skinny his ribs showed.

Taking my glance as an invitation, he pawed at my heels as I continued to walk, and he panted the message that he wanted me to stop and play. Since I was in no mood to play, or to be bothered by this ugly creature, I tried to chase him away, to no avail. He stayed right on my heels, panting and pawing.

Finally I gave up, sat down, and opened my arms to him. He ran to me, jumped in my lap, and began licking my face. He had the worst breath I have ever smelled! Suddenly, as this ugly mongrel loved me, I felt tears flow down my face and the fuzzy feelings of chill bumps spread over my shoulders. Then the rest of the world disappeared and all that remained was me and the puppy, loving one another.

I have no idea how much time passed, but when I got up, I was no longer depressed and the puppy and I walked happily home, side by side, down the road. He is still with me today. The memory of this experience and the lesson learned have remained with me. The lesson? When I relate in love to another being, or allow that being to love me, the chances are good that I will have a noetic — warm shower — experience.

But why do such events occur? Because love begets love. In short, when I am loving you, and you are loving me, God sometimes joins us, and when that happens, you or I, or both of us, experience God's presence as what I call a warm shower. Sometimes, it feels so good that you or I or both of us weep for joy. When one person embraces another person, being or thing in love, both embrace God, and sometimes God embraces them also. At such times, we are literally wrapped in the arms of unconditional love! Mind you, this does not happen every time. I don't know why, but I have a hunch that God chooses the times to join us. My guess is that God is smart enough to know that if He joined us every time, we would soon become bored and stop loving each other. So, God keeps us loving by wisely rationing that warm shower.

Perhaps I can further clarify by using the simple graph below:

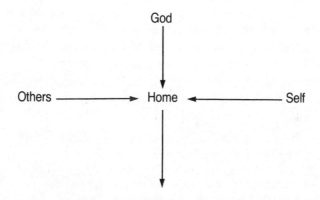

To me this graph, consisting of two intersecting lines, one vertical and one horizontal, represents the totality of the spiritual way of life, for it includes relationships among self, others, and God. Some of you will immediately think of the cross, which is the central symbol of Christianity. Yet, two intersecting lines have been a central symbol of many other spiritual paths also.

The vertical line, even though it denotes the individual's relationship with God, is not the one which takes the person into the presence of the Creator. On the contrary, every spiritual path teaches the primary importance of the horizontal plane. In other words, these paths are designed to help the individual move in the direction of others, and their basic teachings have to do with treating one's fellows with respect, concern and compassion. In short, the roads emphasize the need to love one another. If you doubt this, look at the Buddhist, Christian, 12-Step and other paths and you will see that they all emphasize relationships with others.

The beauty of each of the great highways home is that, as we move along the horizontal line and learn to love others, the Creator descends along the vertical to join us. When the vertical and horizontal lines intersect, we have a spiritual experience — a warm shower falls on us and bathes us with love. What's more — and this is important — the point at which the lines intersect is home. You see, home, like bottom, is not a geographical location, but a state of being. Warm-shower experiences are visits home. And such visits are sure signs that the traveler is on the right path.

The journey of life is a search for home and God, but in order to find either, we must follow a good path, which may for a time seem to be an indirect route. Yet even though the route may seem indirect, it is the most direct. Confusing? Perhaps I can clarify by sharing something I once read or heard:

I sought my soul, my soul eluded me.
I sought my God, my God I could not see.
I sought my brother, and I found all three.

And so it is. When we seek each other, we find God. Seeking and loving others bring us into the presence of the Almighty. This is why all good highways home deliberately move us in the direction of our fellows.

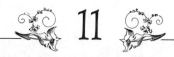

11

The Awakening

Life is a quest for wholeness and home. It is a journey on which one must choose from many different paths. All too often, travelers choose a path that leads them into the bondage of addiction, and they find themselves alone in a foreign land a long way from home. There, they have an opportunity to choose a road that will lead them home — the road of recovery. If they choose this road, they will reach their desired destination, for even as addiction is a detour leading into a far country, so recovery is the path that leads home.

Recovery is a process of spiritual growth that takes addicts in the direction of home. Spiritual growth is essentially an inner journey that moves addicts back toward their innermost self — the wise child within. Recovery from addiction is the spiritual process that transforms addicts into brand-new people. Since it is a spiritual process, it contains those elements that are universally present in all such processes — the death of the old self and the birth of a new one. Through recovery, addicts are reborn. They become children once more.

Throughout all time, in most cultures, such transformational processes have been symbolized by the ritual of immersing people in water and raising them up again. Called baptism, this ritual symbolically illustrates the process of spiritual growth. When they are immersed, the old selves are buried, and they are cleansed of sins — that is, those things that have separated them from others and God. When they are raised from the water, they are new beings. They are reborn. They are children again.

It is important to remember that although the ritual of baptism symbolizes what happens in the process of spiritual growth, it is only a symbol. All too often, people confuse the symbol with the process and assume that since they have been baptized they have grown spiritually. Such an assumption is, of course, in error; until they walk the path of spiritual growth, their baptism will be only a ceremonial dunking in some water. Baptism, although it may be important and its effects powerful, only symbolizes what will occur if one follows a path of spiritual growth by acting on its principles.

The same applies to addicts who act out the ritual of joining a recovery group. Though their decision to join is important and the effects may be powerful, there will be no lasting effect until they follow the course of action laid out in the program of the group. If, however, they realize that joining is symbolic and they then follow the program's path to the best of their ability, they will be transformed. Indeed, the precepts of the program will turn off the engine that has powered their addiction — their unrestrained and unsubmitted egos; help them gather and drain off the high octane fuel that has made that engine run — their character flaws, including self-hate, and change them into new people.

In spiritual terms, the precepts of the recovery program will bring about the death and burial of their self-centeredness, cleanse them of their shortcomings, and make them like children again. Through the process of spiritual growth, their egos will no longer be master, but will become servant. They will find they no longer need to be in control or to be right all the time or to be better than others or to be dishonest. Fear and anger will subside and they will experience peace. They will become content to be just another passenger on the bus of life. They will be free.

How does such a transformation occur? According to spiritual teachers, it comes about through the renewing of the mind. It is significant to note that 12-Step groups agree with them. This is why the single result of their program is such a renewal, which they call a spiritual awakening.

To renew means to make new. How does a person obtain a new mind? By following a path of spiritual growth. The transformation that results makes the mind new. When the mind is made new, there is a radical shift in thinking and feeling, a deep alteration in values and beliefs, a significant modification of behavior.

Perception

It will be helpful to look more closely at what transpires within the mind to bring about the changes I have just described. To do this, I will turn again to that part of the mind which is called perception, for, to me, renewal of the mind is essentially a matter of perceptual change.

You may recall that earlier I likened the faculty of the mind called perception to a window through which one looks out at reality. Looking out of this window, we form opinions about what we see and put labels on people, places and things. Perception exerts a powerful influence on behavior, for how we behave depends largely on how we perceive others, ourselves and our surroundings.

For example, if I perceive you to be a friend, my behavior toward you would be different than if I perceived you as an enemy. By the same token, if I see this world as a dark, forbidding place, I would act differently than if I saw it as a friendly, good place. From these examples you can see how perception impacts behavior. Clearly, then, if we wish to change our behavior, we must change our perception — our outlook on life.

Changing our perception is not simply a matter of choosing to do so, for our outlook on life is not changed so easily. Why? Because our view of reality is influenced by our feelings, memories, values, and beliefs. This being the case, perception can be changed only if these are changed.

Moreover, since we are what we are largely due to the life experiences we have had and the feelings, values, and beliefs we have formulated as a result of our experiences, it is easy to see that if we wish to change our outlook, we must change ourselves. Thus, if addicts want to change the behavior that is killing them, they have to change themselves and in order to do so, they must change those things that make them what they are. Clearly, this is not easy. Yet although it is not easy, it can be accomplished if one has the proper tools.

If the key to recovery is a renewal of the mind through perceptual change, perhaps it would be good to look a little more closely at perception. Just what is it anyway? To simplify the matter, it will be helpful to view perception as a window having four panes in it. When we are born, the four panes are clear and for a while they remain so. The baby in the crib has no opinions and has yet to label anyone or anything. Thus, we have no particular outlook on life.

Soon, however, we begin to have experiences with people and objects, and as a result, we develop a storehouse of remembered experiences (memories), a pattern of feelings and certain beliefs about ourselves and the world. In addition, we begin to consider some things and people as more important than others. Thus, as a result of our own experiences, we begin to have values, beliefs, feelings and memories, and each of these takes its place in one of the four panes in the window of perception.

Now the panes are no longer clear. They are colored, or tinted, by these influences (see diagram below). Now we have opinions and labels. Now we have a definite outlook on life. Thus is our perception of reality formed, and it will exert a powerful influence on our behavior.

The Window Of Perception

Values	Beliefs
Feelings	Memories

If our perception of reality is healthy, our behavior will be healthy also. If our perception is not healthy, however, we will behave in unhealthy ways. Since addiction is marked by behavior that is destructive to others and self, it is safe to assume that addicts have an unhealthy perception of life.

Moreover, if they would change their behavior, they must change their perception. To do this, they must change their values and beliefs and be rid of those negative feelings and unhealed life experiences that make the world seem to be a dark, forbidding place. Therefore they need a program that is designed to help them accomplish this formidable task.

The 12 Steps

The 12 Steps constitute such a program. By applying them, addicts can discover and examine their feelings, values and beliefs through looking closely at their life experiences. The program provides the means for them to express those feelings that have been hidden in the dark recesses of the Basement of their minds, to heal their painful memories, to discard or modify the values that have been a part of their illness and replace them with healthy ones, and to be rid of those negative beliefs that have led them to do so much harm to themselves and others.

By following the precepts of the program, addicts can clear away the things that have colored the panes in their window of perception, and having done so, they will have a new and clear view of the world, others and themselves. In other words, the program will renew their minds.

By using the portions of the program that deal specifically with discovering who and what they really are, addicts are able to uncover those negative feelings that have hardened into flaws of character, discern those things that have motivated them, and see how their life experiences have influenced their view of reality and, thus, their behavior. In short, by utilizing these portions as directed, they can now answer the question that has been continually on their mind: "What in the world has been the matter with me?"

Then, by utilizing the precepts of sharing, releasing and forgiveness, they can express and be rid of their flaws and heal the painful memories that have had such a great impact on their thinking and behavior. Having thus dealt with their life experiences, they can now use their past as a guide for their present and future. Moreover, when they have uncovered and let go of their unhealthy feelings and memories, they have wiped clean the panes of their perceptual window which have been colored by these things.

Unfortunately many addicts use the program to deal only with their negative feelings and unhealed memories, while overlooking those values and beliefs that have played such a large role in their illness. When they make this mistake, they are often dismayed when their behavior and point of view are not significantly changed, and they are at a loss to understand why.

Why don't they use the process of self-examination to uncover their true beliefs and values? I think part of the reason is that they, like most people, are oblivious to the importance of values and beliefs in their lives. How important are they? They are the foundation on which I stand, and they form the framework from which I live my life.

In a real way, my left foot rests firmly on my values, my right foot on my beliefs and I live in accordance with what I believe and what is important to me. I am not alone in this for all people, whether they are conscious of it or not, do likewise. In truth, I am convinced that beliefs and values are the dominant influences on any person's life and that they play a key role in addiction.

Another reason why values and beliefs are often overlooked is that most people are not aware of them or their impact on their lives. Some people tell us that all of us have a system of values and beliefs and that they are arranged in order of their priority somewhere in our psyches. Yet if asked to list our top five values or our top five beliefs, most of us could not do so. Oh, we might make a list of what we think they are. Unfortunately what we think we believe and value may not be what we *really* believe and value.

Watching

How then do we know what we really do believe and value? It's simple. We look at our behavior.

That's right! Since we behave according to our real beliefs and values, our behavior will reveal what they are. We use the same procedure of self-examination that identified our negative feelings and bad memories. It may shock us to discover what our beliefs and values really are, but once we do know, we can begin to make some changes, to modify or discard some of them. Now we can begin to build a firm foundation to stand on and construct a healthy framework from which to live our lives.

Caution! Beliefs and values are not easily changed, for they have been with us for a long time — so long, in fact, that they have become a real though unconscious part of our being. Even though we may not be conscious of them, they cause us to behave in ways that are often destructive to self and others. Addicts who are in the process of recovery should be aware that discovering their values and beliefs and deciding to change them is one thing, but changing them is quite another. Change requires diligence and effort.

Take beliefs, for example. In an earlier chapter, I showed how addicts' negative beliefs about themselves caused them to behave in ways that were detrimental to themselves and others, and I outlined the role these unhealthy beliefs played in their illness. You may remember that I mentioned three beliefs that form the core of the self-hate which plays such a large part in addiction.

To refresh your memory, these three beliefs were: (1) I'm not worthy of love, (2) I'm no good and (3) I'm a failure. I pointed out that addicts, or any person for that matter, will live out their beliefs about themselves. In other words, they will be the kind of people they believe in their deepest hearts they are. It's a self-fulfilling prophecy.

So how do addicts change their beliefs? Is there a way? Yes. They can use the ancient spiritual practice of watching. Watching is a combination of self-observation and immediate self-correction. To practice it, addicts observe themselves as they go through each day, carefully noting their responses to expressions of love, compliments about them or their work and affirmative statements about their worthiness as people. Whenever they become aware that they are responding to positive statements in a negative way, they stop themselves immediately and correct their response so as to accept the affirmation.

You see, self-hate and the beliefs that constitute it cause addicts to respond to any positive statement by immediately putting themselves down. These put-downs are not consciously thought out.

On the contrary, they are automatic, instant, habitual reactions that are based on those beliefs about themselves of which addicts are not conscious. This is why the process is so difficult to correct. However, if addicts will diligently apply the practice of watching, the task can be accomplished, although progress is often slow and painful. Let's face it, self-hate is ingrained very deeply into addicts, and getting rid of it is a large task.

The good news is that it can be done.

To illustrate how watching can change beliefs, I will use the addicts' belief that they are unworthy of love. Because of this belief, they continually hurt those who attempt to love them, and any time anyone professes love, they give them reasons why they shouldn't.

For instance, if the wife of an addict tells him she loves him, he may say, "How can you love me? Can't you see what I am? Don't you know I'm no damned good?"

When addicts respond this way, they are really saying that they are not worth loving, and when they hurt others, they are trying to prove it. Yet all the while, they are unaware of the process. It's as if their unconscious belief sets off a taped message to anyone who expresses love for them. And what is the message? "I'm unworthy of love."

It would be nice, and easy, if we could just erase such tapes and the messages they contain. Unfortunately this is not possible. The only way such messages can be changed is to put new ones over them until the new messages are the only ones on the tapes. How? Enter the practice of watching.

Once addicts know that they believe they are unworthy of love and are aware of the verbal and behavioral responses it produces (the tapes it plays), they watch for such responses. When someone expresses love, or is loving, and an old tape begins to play, they stop it and give a new, positive, accepting response. In so doing, they put a new message over the old one on the tape. When they have done this for some time, they will begin to notice that the new message plays more and more often. They will realize that they are putting themselves down less often and are hurting those who love them less frequently. Then one magic day they may become aware that the new message is now the only one that plays.

So it is that through utilizing the practice of watching, addicts who habitually gave reasons why they were not worthy of love to all who tried to love them now respond, in both words and actions, "I know you love me. I love you, too."

In all seriousness, when addicts can accept and give love, they have made a quantum leap in recovery.

By taking the actions prescribed in the 12-Step program, addicts can rid themselves of unhealed memories and hurtful feelings, and they can discover and change their values and beliefs. Having thus cleaned their inner house, they can repair the damage their outer behavior has done to others. Through the auspices of the program, they can become new people, living in a different world.

Needless to say, this will not be an overnight matter. However, if they persist, they cannot fail to grow spiritually, and as they do so, they move farther and farther away from the detour of addiction and come closer and closer to home. As they grow, the panes of their perceptual windows become cleaner and clearer. So clear that they realize they don't see things as they did before.

What has happened? The addicts have undergone a massive change in perception that has transformed their attitude, outlook, and behavior. The panes in their windows of perception are clear. Their minds have been renewed. In short, they have had a spiritual awakening.

Once more, they see the world and all it contains as they did when they were little children, and they are awed by it. Their actions are more spontaneous and loving, they exhibit common sense, and they are more content to be themselves. It's as if they had become little children again. In a very real way, they have. You see, they have grown down.

Through spiritual growth, addicts recover, return to their Father's house, assume their role as children of God, and resume the dance of life. And from now on, their chief purpose in life will be to help others to recover so that they, too, can dance once again.

So it is.

 # POSTSCRIPT

Sometimes, the children of addicts are not aware of the important role they play in their parents' recovery. Yet their love, understanding and support can be absolutely indispensable. In my own case, I will never be able to express fully to my three children how grateful I am for the hugs, kisses, smiles, counsel, and admonitions they gave me. They seemed to understand and appreciate my struggles in recovery, and they were, and are, an integral part of my sobriety. Their gifts to me have been the most precious of all, and though they may not know it, there have been times when those gifts kept me sane.

This being the case, I would be remiss if I did not express my gratitude to Crystal, Jason, and Frances, who, when she first learned to write, sent me a heart-shaped card that she had cut out which contained the following words: "Dear Dad, I love you more than my Teddy bear. Love, Frances."

Thanks, kids! I love you!

 A P P E N D I X

The 12 Steps

1. We admitted we were powerless over alcohol [or drug or behavior of choice] — that our lives had become unmanageable.
2. Came to believe that a Power greater than ourselves could restore us to sanity.
3. Made a decision to turn our will and our lives over to the care of God *as we understood Him.*
4. Made a searching and fearless moral inventory of ourselves.
5. Admitted to God, to ourselves and to another human being the exact nature of our wrongs.
6. Were entirely ready to have God remove all these defects of character.
7. Humbly asked Him to remove our shortcomings.
8. Made a list of all persons we had harmed, and became willing to make amends to them all.
9. Made direct amends to such people wherever possible, except when to do so would injure them or others.
10. Continued to take personal inventory and when we were wrong promptly admitted it.
11. Sought through prayer and meditation to improve our conscious contact with God, *as we understood Him,* praying only for knowledge of His will for us and the power to carry that out.
12. Having had a spiritual awakening as the result of these steps, we tried to carry this message to alcoholics, and to practice these principles in all our affairs.

CHAPTER NOTES

Chapter 1

1. "The Bill W. — Carl Jung letter," *AA Grapevine*, January 1963.

2. William James, **The Varieties of Religious Experience** (New York: Macmillan Publishing Co., 1961), pp. 393-94.

3. Matthew Fox, **Meditations with Meister Eckhart** (Santa Fe, NM: Bear & Company, 1983), p. 28.

4. Robert Subby, **Lost In The Shuffle** (Deerfield Beach, FL: Health Communications, Inc., 1987), p. 63.

5. "Letter to the Hebrews," chap. 11, ver. 1, **Today's English Version of the New Testament** (New York: Macmillan Publishing Co., 1968), p. 501.

6. "Proverbs," chap. 23, ver. 7, **The Holy Bible,** King James Version.

7. Chuck C., audio tape, Blue Ridge Retreat, 1970.

8. Fox, **Meditations,** p. 20.

9. "Gospel of Matthew," chap. 18, ver. 3, **The Holy Bible.**

10. Fox, **Meditations,** p. 7.

Chapter 2

1. Carl G. Jung, "Archetypes of the Collective Unconscious," in Collected Works, vol. 9, pt. 1 (Princeton, NJ: Princeton University Press, 1959).

2. **Alcoholics Anonymous,** 3rd ed. (New York: Alcoholics Anonymous World Services, Inc., 1976), p. 62.

=== Chapter 3

1. Joseph Campbell, **The Power of Myth** (New York: Doubleday, 1988), p. xix.

2. Jung, "Archetypes."

3. **Confessions,** St. Augustine.

4. Alcoholics Anonymous, p. xxvi.

5. Mel Tillis, "Detroit City," (MCA).

=== Chapter 4

1. Kris Kristofferson, "Jesus Was a Capricorn," (Miami, FL: CPP/ BELWIN, Inc.).

=== Chapter 5

1. Richard R. Peabody, **The Common Sense of Drinking** (Boston: Little Brown and Company, 1935).

2. **Alcoholics Anonymous,** p. 44.

3. "Psalms," chap. 139, ver. 14, **The Holy Bible.**

4. **Alcoholics Anonymous,** pp. xxvi-xxviii.

5. Ibid., p. xxviii.

6. Ibid., p. 38.

=== Chapter 6

1. **Alcoholics Anonymous,** p. xxvi.

2. Harry M. Tiebout, **Alcoholics Anonymous Comes of Age,** (New York: Alcoholics Anonymous World Services, Inc., 1957), p. 311.

3. **Alcoholics Anonymous,** p. 45.

=== Chapter 7

1. **Alcoholics Anonymous,** p. 21.

Chapter 8

1. **Alcoholics Anonymous,** p. 151.

2. Martin Buber, **I and Thou** (New York: Charles Scribner's Sons, 1958), p. 46.

3. **Alcoholics Anonymous,** p. 151.

4. Tiebout, **Alcoholics Anonymous Comes of Age,** p. 63.

5. "Psalms," chap. 130, ver. 1, **The Holy Bible.**

6. Jonathan Star, **Two Suns Rising: A Collection of Sacred Writings** (New York: Barton Books, 1991), p. 134.

7. Ibid., p. 157.

8. **Twelve Steps and Twelve Traditions** (New York: Alcoholics Anonymous World Services, Inc., 1953), p. 23.

9. Tiebout, **Alcoholics Anonymous Comes of Age,** p. 64.

10. Ibid., pp. 248-49.

Chapter 9

1. **Alcoholics Anonymous,** p. xxvii.

2. Robert Frost, **The Poems of Robert Frost** (New York: Random House, 1946).

3. **Alcoholics Anonymous,** p. 59.

4. Ibid., p. 30.

5. Ibid., p. 59.

Chapter 10

1. **Alcoholics Anonymous,** p. xiii.

2. Ibid., p. 564.

3. Barry Lopez, **Crow and Weasel** (San Francisco: North Point Press, 1990), p. 48.

Other Books By . . .
Health Communications

ADULT CHILDREN OF ALCOHOLICS (Expanded)
Janet Woititz
Over a year on *The New York Times* Best-Seller list, this book is the primer on Adult Children of Alcoholics.
ISBN 1-55874-112-7   **$8.95**

STRUGGLE FOR INTIMACY
Janet Woititz
Another best-seller, this book gives insightful advice on learning to love more fully.
ISBN 0-932194-25-7   **$6.95**

BRADSHAW ON: THE FAMILY: A Revolutionary Way of Self-Discovery
John Bradshaw
The host of the nationally televised series of the same name shows us how families can be healed and individuals can realize full potential.
ISBN 0-932194-54-0   **$9.95**

HEALING THE SHAME THAT BINDS YOU
John Bradshaw
This important book shows how toxic shame is the core problem in our compulsions and offers new techniques of recovery vital to all of us.
ISBN 0-932194-86-9   **$9.95**

HEALING THE CHILD WITHIN: Discovery and Recovery for
Adult Children of Dysfunctional Families — Charles Whitfield, M.D.
Dr. Whitfield defines, describes and discovers how we can reach our Child Within to heal and nurture our woundedness.
ISBN 0-932194-40-0   **$8.95**

A GIFT TO MYSELF: A Personal Guide To Healing My Child Within
Charles L. Whitfield, M.D.
Dr. Whitfield provides practical guidelines and methods to work through the pain and confusion of being an Adult Child of a dysfunctional family.
ISBN 1-55874-042-2   **$11.95**

HEALING TOGETHER: A Guide To Intimacy And Recovery For
Co-dependent Couples — Wayne Kritsberg, M.A.
This is a practical book that tells the reader why he or she gets into dysfunctional and painful relationships, and then gives a concrete course of action on how to move the relationship toward health.
ISBN 1-55784-053-8   **$8.95**

3201 S.W. 15th Street,
Deerfield Beach, FL 33442-8190
1-800-441-5569

Health
Communications, Inc.®

Subscribe to America's
Leading Recovery Magazine

Changes
MAGAZINE

$18* per year for 6 bi-monthly issues!

Discover **Changes** today and receive the vital tools you need to inspire your own personal growth.

Every issue of **Changes** brings you valuable information on personal recovery concerns like self-esteem, intimacy, and spirituality.

Subscribe today!

Just return the coupon below, or call toll-free (800) 851-9100. And give the operator this code: HB212

☐ **YES!**

Please enter my subscription to *Changes* Magazine at the special introductory rate of just $18*.

Name: _____

Address: _____

City: _____

State: _____ Zip: _____

Payment method:

☐ Payment enclosed   ☐ Bill me

☐ Charge my   ☐ VISA   ☐ MC

Acct. #: _____

Exp. Date: _____ Sig: _____

Mail to: CHANGES MAGAZINE   HB212
        Subscription Services
        3201 S.W. 15th Street
        Deerfield Beach, FL 33442-8190

*Florida residents add 6% sales tax. Canadian orders add $20; foreign orders add $31. Please allow 4-6 weeks for delivery.